SRA Open Court Reading

Program Overview

McGraw Hill Education

Credits for Program Overview

Text

13 THE KISSING HAND by Audrey Penn, Illustrated by Ruth E. Harper and Nancy M. Leak. Copyright ©1993 by Audrey Penn. Permission arranged with Tanglewood Publishing, Inc., Terre Haute, IN 47083. All rights not specifically granted herein are reserved.
25 Hungry Little Hare by Howard Goldsmith, illustrations by Denny Bond. Copyright ©1998 by McGraw-Hill Education. All rights reserved.
77 Adapted from *Is this Panama?* By Jan Thornhill, illustrated by Soyeon Kim. Used with permission of Owlkids Books Inc.

Photos

9 ©PhotoAlto/SuperStock, Photo by Ron Nichols, USDA Natural Resources Conservation Service, Radius/SuperStock; **19** Global_Pics/Getty Images;
24 Bianka Wolf/EyeEm/Getty Images; **59** Cylonphoto/iStock/Getty Images, ©iStockphoto.com/Goddard_Photography; **67** shene/Moment Open/Getty Images, arlindo71/E+/Getty Images, Ingram Publishing/SuperStock; **76** Artyom Rudenko/Getty Images, michaklootwijk/Getty Images, PBNJ Productions/Getty Images;
82 Elena Kalistratova/Getty Images, Mint Images/Art Wolfe/Getty Images, Ablestock.com, Oxford Scientific/Getty Images, ©Daniel Dempster Photography/Alamy, micut/Getty Images, U.S. Fish & Wildlife Service/John & Karen Hollingsworth, Partha Pal/Getty Images.

MHEonline.com

Send all inquiries to:
McGraw-Hill Education
8787 Orion Place
Columbus, OH 43240

ISBN: 978-0-02-145682-6
MHID: 0-02-145682-8

Printed in the United States of America.

1 2 3 4 5 6 7 8 9 QLM 20 19 18 17 16 15

Table of Contents

Program Overview

Introduction

Welcome to **SRA Open Court Reading,** the comprehensive K–3 reading and language arts program with over 50 years of proven results helping students learn to read. Building on the foundation of phonological and phonemic awareness skills introduced in Grade K, teachers help students assign spoken sounds to written language through phonics skills in Grade I as students learn to read. In Grades 2–3, students transition from reading smaller units—such as sound-by-sound to word-by-word or sentence-by-sentence—so that students become fluent readers, applying comprehension, vocabulary, and word analysis skills along the way. The more students comprehend and read fluently, the more likely they are to becoming lifelong learners.

The primary focus of **SRA Open Court Reading** is having students become confident readers. Each grade level builds upon the foundation taught in the previous grade level and uses a daily lesson format that is easy to follow. The daily lesson employs a three-part lesson cycle:

- Part I Foundational Skills
- Part 2 Reading and Responding
- Part 3 Language Arts

At the beginning of Grades K–I, students will spend much of the year in Part I learning about letters and sounds, attaching sounds to certain spellings, and learning to decode with a certain amount of fluency. After learning the prerequisite phonemic awareness and phonics skills, they will move onto Part 2 comprehension and vocabulary development as well as Inquiry before moving onto Part 3 language arts skills.

In Grades 2–3, students will spend some time on foundational skills such as phonics and word analysis, but a substantial amount of the reading block will be spent on developing vocabulary, fluency, comprehension, and inquiry skills in Part 2 as well as writing, spelling, and grammar skills in Part 3. Within and among grade levels, skills are taught and reinforced within a spiraling curriculum. The overlapping pattern of skill-building allows teachers the opportunity to introduce new skills while simultaneously reinforcing those previously learned.

An in-depth explanation of the core elements of the program can be found beginning on page 28.

Literacy

3	Phonics / Word Analysis	Fluency	Vocabulary and Comprehension	Inquiry	Language Arts, Writing, Spelling, and Grammar
2	Phonics / Word Analysis	Fluency	Vocabulary and Comprehension	Inquiry	Language Arts, Writing, Spelling, and Grammar

1	Letter / Book / Print Awareness	Phonemic Awareness	Phonics and Fluency	Vocabulary and Comprehension	Inquiry	Language Arts, Writing, Spelling, and Grammar

K	Letter Recognition	Print / Book Awareness	Phonological and Phonemic Awareness	Phonics and Fluency	Vocabulary and Comprehension	Inquiry	Writing and Grammar

Themes

Through the engaging themes that stretch across grade levels in *SRA Open Court Reading,* students learn about universal truths such as kindness and friendship as well as about cross-curricular subject areas such as life science and government. Genres vary among grade levels but include informational articles, songs, plays, persuasive essays, poems, and so on. The literature and nonfiction selections in the program can be found in the following components:

- Unit Big Books/Little Books
- Cross-Curricular Big Books for Science and Social Studies
- First Readers
- Student Anthologies
- Teacher Read Alouds

Each unit of each grade level begins with a Teacher Read Aloud to introduce the unit theme. All selections within the unit tie to the theme, giving students a slightly different perspective as they progress through the selections in their Big Books, Cross-Curricular Big Books for Science and Social Studies, First Readers, or Student Anthologies.

In the latter half of Grade I as well as in Grades 2–3, the culminating selection in each unit is often significantly longer and is used to give students one last look at how selections tie together and to the theme.

Six overarching topics or motifs carry across the grade levels in *SRA Open Court Reading.* These include Character, Changes, Communities, Life Science, Government, and Creativity. All themes within a grade level relate to one of these six topics. This allows for different grade levels within a school to be linked together at any given point in time. Note that in Grades K–I, students will progress through 12 units that are each three weeks in length. Two subthemes in these grade levels relate to the overarching topic or theme. In Grades 2–3, students have six units that relate to the overarching theme and are each six weeks in length.

	Character		Changes		Communities		Life Science		Government		Creativity	
K	Off to School	Let's Be Kind	What's the Weather?	Pushes and Pulls	Home, Sweet Home	Our Country, Our Cultures	Ready to Grow	Animals Homes	Rules We Follow	Great Americans	Color Our World	Stripes, Spots, and Dots
1	Back to School	Be My Friend	Science Cycles	Light and Sound	Around Our Town	Around Our World	Roots, Seeds, Leaves	Animals From Head to Toe	Red, White, and Blue	Stars and Stripes	Art for All	Art in Motion
2	Teamwork		Earth in Action		My Country at Work		Plants and Animals		Citizenship		Story Time	
3	Respect		Extreme Weather		A Changing Nation		Animals and Their Habitats		Government at Work		Art on the Move	

Differentiated Instruction

SRA Open Court Reading uses a Teach/Practice/Apply model of teaching:

- **Teach** Teachers teach the lesson, modeling the skill or strategy used in that part of the lesson.
- **Practice** Teachers give students the opportunity to have some guided practice with the skill or strategy. That is, teachers guide students as a class through the skill.
- **Apply** Students now get the chance to apply the skill independently. They may still, of course, ask questions of the teacher.

Whether students are learning phonemic awareness activities, comprehension strategies, or writing process skills, they will go through the Teach/Practice/Apply process. This will give students multiple opportunities to watch a teacher model different strategies and then to practice these strategies with the teacher and the rest of the class. Finally, students can apply what they are learning in an independent manner.

As students go through this process, teachers may notice that not all students are progressing at the same pace. *SRA Open Court Reading* offers multiple ways for teachers to differentiate instruction and provide additional support for English Learners and for students Approaching Level, On Level, and Beyond Level, including:

- *Intervention Guide*—this online teacher's guide in each grade level provides scaffolding for below-level students.
- *Intervention Support Blackline Masters*—the activities in this grade-level component give students more practice at a lower level in features such as phonics or word analysis, comprehension, vocabulary, and grammar.
- *English Learner Support Guide*—this online teacher's guide in each grade level provides support for four levels of English proficiency for Parts I-3 of each lesson.
- *English Learner Photo Library Cards*—available for Parts I and 2, these cards include a photograph of a word on one side with the definition as well as the English phonetic spelling of the word in 10 different languages.
- *English Learner Glossary*—this online glossary gives additional ideas for teachers to explain unfamiliar words and phrases to English Learners.
- *English Learner Tips*—these tips, at point of use in each lesson in each grade level, provide extra support for cognates, vocabulary, grammar, usage, and so on.
- *Differentiated Instruction Tips*—at point of use in each lesson in each grade level, these tips give teachers concise activities to do with students who would benefit from extra support or extended practice.

Example tips from the printed Teacher Editions appear below; more intensive Intervention and English Learner instruction can be found at point of use in the online Teacher's Editions.

 English Learner • Grade 3 EL Tip

COGNATES If students' native language is a Romance language, they might recognize several cognates that appear on pages I59-I6I of *Student Anthology I,* such as: ***technology, risks, observe, dramatic, capture, tornadoes, operate, conditions, continue, severe, study, hurricanes, transmit,*** and ***form*** (Spanish: *tecnología, riesgos, observar, dramático, capturar, tornados, operar, condiciones, continuar, severo, estudiar, huracanes, transmitir, formarse*).

 Differentiated Instruction: Predicting

AL **APPROACHING LEVEL** Review with students that any predictions they make must be supported by information from the text. Help them identify any supporting evidence whenever they make a prediction.

OL **ON LEVEL** Remind students that not all of their predictions will be confirmed. Encourage them to note whether or not each prediction is eventually confirmed.

BL **BEYOND LEVEL** Challenge students to explain how making predictions is similar to making inferences.

Assessment Overview

Assessment in **SRA Open Court Reading** happens continuously. Whether teachers use informal assessments such as Skills Practice pages or Comprehension Rubrics, or whether they use formal assessment such as the Lesson and Unit Assessments or Benchmark Assessment, they will be able to monitor the progress of students in their classrooms and differentiate instruction based on the needs of their students. Because assessment is an ongoing cycle, teachers will constantly assess, diagnose, differentiate, and measure student outcomes.

Assessment is an ongoing cycle.

1 Screen
Administer the Diagnostic Assessment to students entering class after the school year has begun to identify those who are at risk for reading failure.

2 Diagnose and Differentiate
Diagnose students' strengths and weaknesses, and differentiate instruction according to their abilities.

3 Monitor Progress
Monitor progress weekly, monthly, or anytime as needed with formative assessments. Group students based on these formative assessment results.

F FORMAL ASSESSMENT
- Lesson and Unit Assessments
- Benchmark Assessments
- Writing Rubrics

I INFORMAL ASSESSMENT
- Skills Practice
- Comprehension Rubrics
- Listening and Speaking Rubrics
- Inquiry Rubrics

4 Measure Outcomes
Assess student understanding and measure outcomes by using results from the Lesson and Unit Assessments or Benchmark Assessments.

For more information about Assessment, see page 108.

Workshop Overview

The best way to differentiate instruction is during Workshop. Workshop is a built-in time within the *SRA Open Court Reading* lesson that allows for small-group instruction. Teachers can spend time with students who need extra support with parts of the lesson. This may be done individually with students or in small groups.

During this time, teachers may want to concentrate on the following:

- Preteaching skills, including phonics, comprehension, and vocabulary
- Reteaching content, including reading and writing instruction
- Providing enrichment activities for Beyond Level students
- Supporting English Learners for portions of the lesson that may pose the biggest hurdles for students whose primary language is not English
- Reinforcing Approaching Level students with extra scaffolding

Workshop can be implemented during the reading/language arts timeframe in a flexible manner. This can come before the core instruction begins, sometime in the middle of the reading/language arts block, or at the end of that time period. Workshop may last 15–30 minutes, depending upon the needs of the classroom.

During this time, other students may be working in small groups or independently on a variety of things, including the following:

- Read a Decodable
- Complete homework
- Work on inquiry
- Fill in Skills Practice pages
- Complete writing assignments
- Reread the selection
- Practice skills with eGames

For more information regarding Workshop, see page 112.

Seven Pals

by Greg Frazier
illustrated by Jennifer Emery

McGraw Hill Education

Name _____ Date _____

Prefix *dis-*

> **FOCUS**
> - A **prefix** is added to the beginning of a word and changes the meaning of that word.
> - The prefix *dis-* means "the opposite of" or "not."
>   **Example:** dis + comfort = discomfort (the lack or opposite of comfort)

PRACTICE Add the prefix *dis-* to the base words below. Write the new word on the first line. Then write the meaning of the new word.

Base Word	New Word	New Meaning
1. advantage		
2. appear		
3. order		
4. respect		

APPLY Write two sentences using the new words from above.

5. _____

_____

6. _____

_____

Skills Practice 2 • Word Analysis   UNIT 4 • Lesson 3 **31**

Inquiry

Inquiry is the time during the **SRA Open Court Reading** lesson where students learn more about the unit by investigating something related to the theme. Students are introduced to the theme in the Unit Opener, and they learn different facets of the overarching unit theme by reading each selection. Over the course of six weeks, students also conduct an investigation into something that interests them related to the theme. Whether the investigation is done individually, in small groups, or as a whole class, students learn valuable research skills, such as

- Searching Internet Web sites for information
- Determining what information is reliable and what is not
- Interviewing subject-matter experts
- Collecting information
- Taking notes
- Working collaboratively

- Presenting information in a variety of ways, including the following:

  - Research report
  - Slide show
  - Play
  - Oral presentation

In each grade level, Inquiry is done in the first couple of units as a whole-class endeavor. After students start to get a feel for what Inquiry entails, then they may be allowed to work in small groups or individually on investigations of interest to them. At the beginning of the year, the teacher will model the steps of the investigation for students, who will then learn to use these for subsequent investigations. Below is an example from Grade 2 regarding an investigation into the theme *Teamwork*.

	STEPS	EXAMPLES
LESSON 1	Develop Questions	*Why do people and certain animals work well together as a team?*
LESSON 2	Create Conjectures	*People and dogs work well together because people know how to train dogs. People and dogs work well together because dogs are very smart animals.*
LESSON 3	Collect Information	*I need to learn more about dogs and how they are trained. I will look in books and online and also ask a dog trainer to find out more information.*
LESSON 4	Revise Conjectures	*People and certain breeds of dogs work well together because certain breeds are easier to train.*
LESSON 5	Develop Presentations	*My group will create a slideshow that shows the different breeds of dogs that work well with people. The slideshow will display photos along with lists of qualities for each breed.*
LESSON 6	Deliver Presentations	Student groups will present their research findings. The class should then discuss the presentation and ask any new questions they have about the information presented.

For more information about Inquiry, see page 84.

Professional Development

Professional development is one of the cornerstones of **SRA Open Court Reading,** and along with the teacher can help create successful classroom environments where learning is not only expected but is a joy.

In **SRA Open Court Reading,** professional development comes in many forms:

- in-person training
- within the Program Overview
- at point of use within the program
- on the digital Professional Learning Environment

In-person training usually occurs before the beginning of school and may include refreshers during the school year. The Program Overview gives explanations of each portion of the program and the rationale behind each section. At point of use within the program, teachers may click on "Show Me How" videos that

- offer quick video tips supporting the lesson instruction,
- relate information specific to the grade level,
- include support for English Learners, and
- are part of a digital library of over 500 coaching videos.

New to **SRA Open Court Reading** is the Professional Learning Environment, which offers a variety of resources, including the following:

- Implementation Course
  - features model videos, interactive tutorials, and PDFs that offer just-in-time resources and highlight instructional routines for teachers
  - supports teachers with access to the Online Teacher Community so that teachers can share ideas, discuss best practices, and connect with colleagues, coaches, and curriculum specialists nationwide
  - gives targeted training and support for specific grade levels
  - offers professional development hours to teachers who complete the course requirements
- eLearning modules such as
  - Getting Started
  - Foundations of Phonics Instruction
  - Teaching with Instructional Routines
  - Exploring your Foundational Skills Kit
- Online support 24/7/365 and instruction on program implementation and best practice to extend knowledge and understanding of the program

Technology

Technology in *SRA Open Court Reading* is engaging and easy-to-use, for both students and teachers. All components in this K–3 core reading program are available digitally and can be used on multiple devices, including desktop computers, laptops, and tablets. Electronic components include the following:

For the Teacher

- **Interactive Teacher's Guides** help teachers plan, teach, or annotate lessons as well as to assign homework to students.
- **Big Books** allow for a more hands-free way to teach students print and book awareness and listening comprehension.
- **ePresentation** can be used during the lesson as a motivating and engaging presentation tool of the elements within the lesson.
- **Professional Development** offers short videos at point of use with models of lesson elements as well as more involved modules.

For the Student

- **Student Anthologies** allow students the opportunity to read or listen to a fluent reading of the selection as well as offering additional vocabulary support.
- **Pre-Decodables and Decodables** give students practice reading at their own pace as well as listen to a fluent model of reading.
- **eGames** provide students a fun way to practice skills learned in class.
- **Alphabet Sound Cards** introduce the letters of the alphabet to kindergartners.
- **Sound/Spelling Cards** develop students' understanding of how sounds and spellings are linked together and are used to form words.
- **eInquiry** help students with the Inquiry process with activities for students to follow.
- **eActivities** give students additional practice with high-frequency words, spelling, and writing.
- **eAssessments** deliver tests digitally for students and offer grouping ideas for teachers.

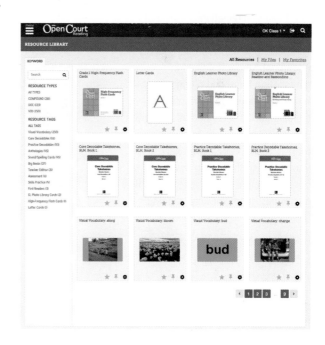

Phonemic Awareness

Phonemic awareness is the awareness of the sounds that make spoken words. In English, letters represent sounds, or phonemes. The ability to distinguish individual sounds within words is an essential prerequisite to associating sounds with letters. Students need a strong phonemic awareness in order for phonics instruction to be successful. The basic purpose of providing structured practice in phonemic awareness is to help students hear and understand the sounds from which words are made.

Phonemic awareness activities, found primarily in Grades K and I, provide students with practice in discriminating the sounds that make words. These are brief, teacher-directed exercises that involve taking words apart and putting them back together. With the support of a puppet, students delight in manipulating the sound of language and playing language games. At the beginning of the year, students are given a great deal of support. As students progress, the support is gradually removed. As students gain awareness of how sounds combine to make words, they can progress to phonics and reading.

Oral Blending and Segmentation

Oral blending and segmentation are used for teaching phonemic awareness. Oral blending helps students understand that words contain parts—syllables and single sounds—and that these parts can be put together to make words. Oral blending encourages students to combine sounds to make words. Segmentation, conversely, requires them to isolate sounds in words. Segmentation and oral blending complement each other.

LESSON 1 · DAY 5 · Foundational Skills

Resources:
- *Lion Puppet*
- *Alphabet Sound Cards*
- *Letter Cards*
- Routines 3, 4, 5
- *Magnetic Dry Erase Boards* or writing paper
- Supply Icons

- *Skills Practice I,* pp. 67–68
- *Core Decodable 2*
- *High-Frequency Flash Cards at, to*
- *Practice Decodable 2*
- *Lesson and Unit Assessment I,* p. T97

Objectives: Students will
- produce and expand spoken sentences.
- blend final phonemes to make words.
- review sound correspondences for letters *Hh* and *Tt*.
- practice building and reading words.
- practice printing capital and lowercase letters *Hh* and *Tt*.
- read and review common high-frequency words.
- read and respond to a *Decodable*.
- identify the title of a *Decodable*.

Warm Up

Oral Language

(EL) MAKE and extend silly sentences with students that involve words beginning with /h/. For example:

Harry hikes on the hilltop.
Harry and Hannah hike on the hilltop.
Harry and Hannah hike on the high hilltop.
Harry and Hannah hurriedly hike on the high hilltop.

Play the I'm Thinking of Something that Starts with _____ game to review words beginning with /t/. Look around the room until you see something that starts with /t/. Say, "I'm thinking of something that starts with /t/."

Give a clue, such as the object's size or color, or direct students' attention to the correct part of the room. Objects you might name include *table, tape, telescope, telephone, television,* or *toy.* Help students to form complete sentences when identifying the object you reference.

Phonological Awareness

Phoneme Blending: Final Sounds

BRING OUT the *Lion Puppet* to help students concentrate on blending the first part of words with the final consonant sound /t/.

Use the following words:

ha.../t/ *hat*	righ.../t/ *right*	heigh.../t/ *height*	abou.../t/ *about*	classma.../t/ *classmate*
ar.../t/ *art*	bes.../t/ *best*	coun.../t/ *count*	ho.../t/ *hot*	amoun.../t/ *amount*
gif.../t/ *gift*	hear.../t/ *heart*	hur.../t/ *hurt*	ben.../t/ *bent*	differen.../t/ *different*
hin.../t/ *hint*	swee.../t/ *sweet*	whi.../t/ *white*	wri.../t/ *write*	presiden.../t/ *president*

(EL) English Learner

SILLY SENTENCES Help students come up with words beginning with /h/ by displaying *EL Photo Library Cards* 95, 96, 97, 98, and 99. If necessary, say the name of the card, and then have students repeat the word after you.

T268 Unit 4 · Lesson I · Day 5

Alphabetic Principle

Reviewing the Sounds of *Hh* and *Tt*

REVIEW *Alphabet Sound Card Hh.* Display the card and play the sound and the story. Have students say the words along with the story. Tell them to imitate Harry hurrying.

Display *Alphabet Sound Card Tt.* Have students describe the picture. Then play the sound and the story. Have students join in making the sound of the ticking timer.

Listening for Initial /h/ and /t/

○ **GIVE** each student one *Hh* and one *Tt* **Letter Card.**

Tell students you will say a word and they should repeat it. Explain that if the word starts with /h/, on your signal, they should hold up their *Hh* **Letter Cards.** If the word starts with /t/, they should hold up their *Tt* **Letter Cards.** Use the following words:

table	home	top	target	teacher	hint
help	taste	hungry	tiptoe	hem	hope

Building and Reading Words 🔵5

○ **GIVE** each student the *a, m,* and *t* **Letter Cards.** Have them place all the cards in a row at the top of their desk or table. Follow Routine 5, the <u>Word Building Routine</u>, to complete the activity.

Say *at,* use it in a sentence, and then repeat the word. Say, "I am *at* school today. The word is *at.*" Have students say the word.

EL Ask students what is the first sound they hear in the word *at.* /a/ Have them check the *Alphabet Sound Cards* and tell which letter says /a/. Aa Point to the *Alphabet Sound Card* Short *Aa.* Have students pull down **Letter Card** *a.*

Ask students what sound they hear next in *at.* /t/ Tell them to check the *Alphabet Sound Cards* and say which letter says /t/. Tt Point to *Alphabet Sound Card Tt.* Have students pull down **Letter Card** *t.*

Display *at* and have students proofread their word. If necessary, they should correct their spelling of the word.

Have students put their letter cards back on their desk or table, and repeat the process with the word *mat.*

Remind students that when they are writing words on their own, they should say the word to themselves, think about the sounds in words, and then write the letters. They should always check the *Alphabet Sound Cards* if they are unsure of the letter for a sound.

🍎 Teacher Tip

Hh **AS A FINAL CONSONANT** If a curious student questions why they are not working with words with the letter *h* at the end, explain that the sound /h/ does not appear at the end of words.

🍎 Teacher Tip

WORD BUILDING Beginning with this lesson, students will take another important step toward becoming independent readers and writers. Up to this point, students have been blending words using their knowledge of sounds and letters. In Building and Reading Words, students will combine their ability to segment words into individual sounds and then connect those sounds to letters to spell words.

ePresentation

🐕 Hh	⏱ Tt
🐑 Aa / a	⏱ Tt

Building and Reading Words

Words
1. at
2. mat

EL English Learner

BUILDING WORDS Preview the sound for each letter, particularly if you have students who have been struggling with /a/, /m/, and /t/. If students have difficulty hearing the sounds, say the words sound by sound.

Alphabetic Principle

How the Alphabet Works

Students not only focus on phonemic awareness in Grade K, but also on the alphabetic principle. The alphabetic principle states simply that there is a fairly predictable association between sounds and the letters that represent them. An understanding of the alphabetic principle extends students awareness that words are made of sounds to include the notion of how those sounds relate to letters and writing.

Alphabetic principle lessons in Grade K introduce students to the relationships between sounds and letters through collaborative classroom activities. The activities present a limited set of letters and their corresponding sounds and focus solely on the concept of those relationships. Students begin to explore and understand the alphabetic principle in a straightforward and thorough manner. This lays the foundation for explicit, systematic phonics instruction.

The alphabetic principle is reinforced throughout kindergarten. By the end of Grade K, most students should have established an understanding of the alphabetic principle. Strategies and scaffolding appear throughout the lessons for students who have not yet fully developed an understanding of the alphabetic principle.

To help students with the alphabetic principle but also to remind students of the sounds of the English language and their letter correspondences, *SRA Open Court Reading* uses the *Alphabet Book* and the *Alphabet Sound Cards* to introduce sounds. Students learn a sound, reinforce it with the visual cues on the cards, practice writing the letter, and apply their knowledge as they read *Pre-Decodable* and *Decodable Books.*

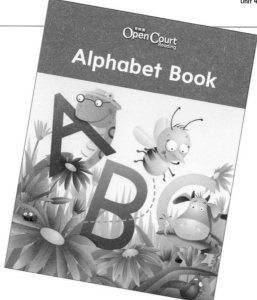

Alphabet Book

Reading and Responding

In Part 2, kindergartners learn about print and book awareness, reading comprehension strategies, the importance of vocabulary, what writers do to make their selections more interesting, and how to access complex text. Here in this section lies the heart of **SRA Open Court Reading:** making sense of the text.

Print and Book Awareness

As students get used to the alphabetic principle as practiced in Part I, they learn how the alphabetic principle is put into practice. For example, students learn that when reading English, they will read from left to right, and from top to bottom. So, for example, as the teacher will read aloud the left-hand page first, beginning at the top left corner. As the teacher comes to the end of a line of print, he or she then go to the next line, beginning on the left. This process continues onto the next pages. At the end of a right-hand page, the teacher turns the page, and then the process repeats itself.

Teachers use **Big Books** in this program to make students aware that letters can be put together to form words, words can make up a sentence, and sentences can be added together to create paragraphs. Spaces appear between words to separate them from one another. In addition, students find out that sentences have some distinguishing characteristics: capital letters appear at the beginning of each separate sentence, and each sentence ends with some sort of punctuation, depending upon the type of question it is. And students learn that paragraphs are usually indented, which is how they know a new paragraph begins.

Print and Book Awareness

○ REVIEW the story with students. Use the following suggestions to reinforce students' understanding of print directionality and picture-text relationships.

Print Directionality

HAVE volunteers come to the **Off to School Big Book** and point to the first and last words on different pages. Have each volunteer run his or her hand under each line of print from left to right as you read the words aloud.

Picture-Text Relationships

TELL students that you are going to reread page 22, and they will tell you which illustration or part of the illustration describes each sentence or sentence part. Read the first sentence on the page. Have a volunteer come to the **Big Book**. Ask, *Which part of the illustration shows Chester scampering across a tree limb? volunteer should point to Chester scampering across a tree limb* Read the next sentence. Ask, *What words that I just read tell us what Mrs. Raccoon presses to her cheek? her left hand*

Discuss the Selection

Discussion Starters

HAVE students discuss their favorite parts of the story. Remind students that you asked them to think about what the raccoon is feeling and thinking in the story.

Continue the conversation about the selection by asking them the questions that follow. Tell students to speak loudly enough so that everyone can understand and to answer using complete sentences.

- Did you feel like Chester Raccoon before you started school? Why or why not?
- How is the way Chester Raccoon feels about school similar to Alex's feelings in "The One with the Freckle"?
- Think about how "The Kissing Hand" adds to what you know about school and feelings about going to school. Check whether questions on the **Concept/Question Board** have been answered, and post any new questions that have come up.

Essential Question

REVISIT the Essential Question for this selection and have students discuss their answers.

What are some ways you are brave? Possible Answer: *I try new things, even when I'm scared.*

○ Teacher Tip

PRINT AND BOOK AWARENESS As you review print and book awareness, take time to connect to the alphabetic knowledge students learned earlier. For example, allow students to search for and identify the letters *Ee* and *Ff* on pages 22–23, as in the words *Chester, enter, pressed, left, filled.*

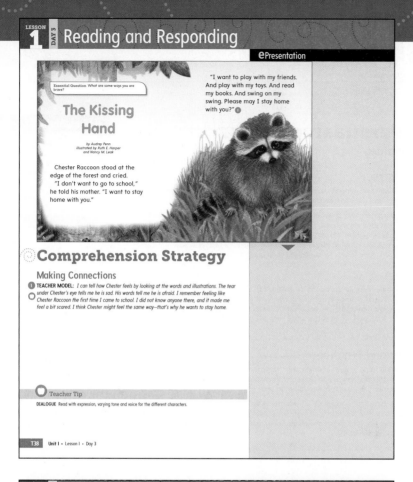

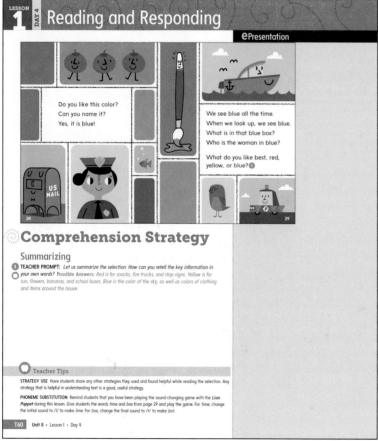

Reading Comprehension Strategies

In Kindergarten, students first learn the comprehension strategies used throughout this K–3 reading program. Teachers will use these strategies on the first read of a selection. The strategies can be found below:

- Asking/Answering Questions
- Clarifying
- Making Connections
- Predicting/Confirming Predictions
- Summarizing
- Visualizing

Teachers use the **Big Books** from the various units to model how to figure out what the text is about. The teacher may model how to clarify the meaning of an unfamiliar word, visualize a scene or a process in order to understand it better, or summarize the page(s) read in order to make sense of it. Students will take over some of the responsibility of coming up with their own clarifications or visualizations, after teachers go through the process of modeling and prompting over the course of the school year.

First Reader

In Units 10-12, in addition to using **Big Books,** students transition to using a **First Reader.** The **First Reader** lets students read selections on their own. Each student has a **First Reader,** so it is not a shared reading experience with the teacher in charge of reading a selection from a single **Big Book.** Now students have the opportunity to practice all of their comprehension strategies and skills in a book of their own.

Language Arts

Kindergartners learn about the writing process as well as about grammar, usage, and mechanics in the Language Arts portion of *SRA Open Court Reading.*

Writing

During the course of the program, students learn to physically form the letters of the alphabet, both capital and lowercase letters. In addition, over the course of the year students learn the steps of the writing process in Kindergarten. Teachers will guide students to

- **Prewrite** Students learn to plan what they will write or draw.
- **Draft** In this stage students learn to get their thoughts down on paper as a starting point. They may write or draw anything that comes to mind that is about their topic.
- **Revise** During this stage students may rearrange the order of words or they may decide to change their drawing altogether.
- **Edit/Proofread** Students settle on the words or phrases or final drawing that best reflect their thoughts.
- **Publish or Present** Students may present their final work to the class or they could publish the final result.

Objectives: Students will
- discuss reasons that support an opinion and choose the best reasons for persuading others.
- begin creating persuasive posters.
- learn to identify connections between information in a selection.

Persuasive Poster
Drafting

Instruct

○ **REMIND** students they will be creating persuasive posters to convince others to care for their school home and keep it clean and safe.

Display an Idea Web. In the center, write *taking care of our school.* Lead a discussion with students about why it is important to help take care of the school. Remind students that the purpose of the poster is to persuade others to agree that this idea is important, so their reasons should be convincing and relevant. Record students' ideas in the web. Possible Answers: *could trip over trash; distracting to be in a dirty place; bugs; fun to work as a group when cleaning; helping care for the school shows you like the school; teachers can focus on teaching instead of cleaning*

Ask students who the audience for the poster will be. *other students* Discuss which reasons in the Idea Web are most or least suited for convincing a student to help take care of the school. Guide students in choosing the three best reasons, and write them on the board as complete sentences. Possible Answers: *A clean school is safe. Let's show our school love. We can work together. We can have fun.*

Guided Practice

DISTRIBUTE large sheets of drawing paper to students, and make available art supplies. Model writing the three sentences on chart paper. Leave space at the bottom of the poster, and explain to students that you will add a concluding sentence later.

ⓘ Have students follow your model to begin creating their posters. Circulate around the room, and help students as needed with forming letters, including spaces between words, and using proper sentence mechanics. Be sure students are leaving room at the bottom of the poster to add a concluding statement.

Ask students to sign their names to their posters. Collect students' posters, and store them for the next day's lesson.

○ **Teacher Tip**

PLAN AHEAD In preparation for the activity, have drawing paper and art supplies on hand.

ⓘ **Differentiated Instruction**

AL **ADDITIONAL WORK TIME** If students need additional time to create their posters, work with them in small groups during Workshop.

T42 Unit 5 • Lesson I • Day 3

Idea Web

Story Crafting

Story Frames

REMIND students that some stories give information. Point out that the selection "Homes Around the World" gives information about different kinds of homes.

Display the Story Frames for "Homes Around the World." Point out to students that each frame shows an important detail that is discussed in the selection. Explain that these frames do not show every detail from the selection. As you point to each frame, ask students to recall the information depicted. Have students explain what the illustration shows and identify any important vocabulary. Have students use the frames to help them answer the following questions about the selection:

- What are some different shapes and sizes of houses? Possible Answers: *Houses can be tall. Houses can be round.*

- What are some places where houses can be built? Possible Answers: *Houses can be built on cliffs. Houses can be built in trees. Houses can be built over water.*

- What types of parts can houses have? Possible Answers: *Houses can have a porch. Houses have doors. Houses have windows.*

Encourage students to ask any questions they may have about the illustrations in the frames or about the types of homes presented in the selection "Homes Around the World."

Guide students to understand how all the frames connect to each other. You might ask: "How are all these pictures connected, or related?" Possible Answer: *They all tell us something about homes.* Tell students they will spend more time connecting the information in the frames the next day.

Differentiated Instruction

AL **ANSWERING QUESTIONS** If students are having difficulty answering the questions, connect the frames to the text by rereading the sections of text that align with each frame.

Homes Around the World | DAY 3 | LESSON 1

ePresentation

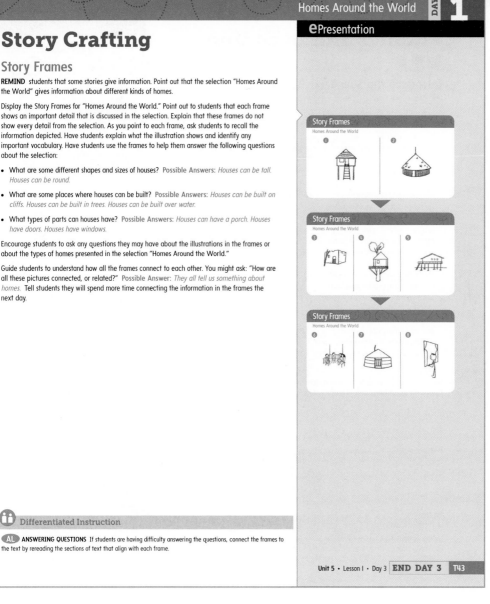

Unit 5 · Lesson 1 · Day 3 | **END DAY 3** | **T43**

Story Crafting

Kindergartners learn that not all stories have words, and pictures often help to tell stories as well as to convey emotions. Students see how illustrations help to build a story. Within this section, the teacher draws or projects story frames that develop sequencing skills for students, which helps them to understand that all stories have a beginning, a middle, and an end. This important skill transfers to other parts of the program, helping students understand the sequence within selections they are listening to, as well as to their writing, where they must put things in a logical order.

Language Arts ePresentation

Additional information regarding the skills being taught in this section of the program can be found in the Language Arts portion of ePresentation. The ePresentation appears in the right-hand column of the print Teacher's Editions. In the digital version, this component is easily launched at the touch of a finger to show examples, definitions, and instruction crucial to students' understanding of elements such as the following:

- Steps in the writing process
- Graphic organizers
- Ideas for writing
- Excerpts from the Big Books or First Reader
- Story frames for story crafting
- Revising and editing checklists

Grade 1

In Grade I students review the letters of the alphabet during the first few weeks of school and have intensive phonemic awareness instruction and activities. These activities continue throughout the year but also lay the groundwork for the main focus in Grade I: phonics instruction.

Phonics

Phonics is a way to teach decoding and spelling that stresses sound/symbol relationships. Explicit, systematic phonics is a system of teaching that introduces the spelling of each sound to students, teaches blending directly, and follows up with **Decodable Takehome Books** for practice so that the reason for learning the sound/symbol relationships is reinforced. In **SRA Open Court Reading,** students learn to relate sounds to letters in a systematic and explicit manner.

Beginning in Kindergarten, students learn the sounds and letters of the alphabet plus the five short vowels. This knowledge forms the foundations for first grade, which incorporate the use of 44 Sound/Spelling Cards. These cards contain the uppercase and lowercase letters, spellings that represent those sounds and a picture that contains the target sound at the beginning of the word for the consonants and in the middle for short vowels. In addition, the picture associates a sound with an action. This action-sound association is introduced through a short, interactive poem found in the Appendix as well as at point of use in the lessons. In these poems the pictured object or character "makes" the sound of the letter. These cards are a resource for students to use to remember sound-letter associations for both reading and spelling.

ePresentation

Phonics and Decoding
/g/ spelled g

○ Introduce the Sound/Spelling 🔲

USE Routine I, the <u>Introducing Sounds and Spellings Routine</u>, to introduce /g/ spelled g.

Point to the back of **Sound/Spelling Card** 7—Gopher, and ask students what they already know about the card. *G is a consonant.* Have them identify the capital G and lowercase g on the card.

Turn the card. Point to the picture and tell students that the animal it shows is a gopher, and it is the Gopher card. Point to and name the g spelling for /g/. Tells tudents that this is the spelling for the sound they hear at the beginning of the word *gopher.*

Play or read the Gopher story:

Gary's a gopher.
He loves to gulp down food.
/g/ /g/ /g/ /g/ /g/, gulps the gopher.
Gary the Gopher gulps down grass
because it tastes so good.
/g/ /g/ /g/ /g/ /g/, gulps the gopher.
Gary the Gopher gulps down grapes.
Gobs and gobs of grapes.
/g/ /g/ /g/ /g/ /g/, gulps the gopher.
Gary the Gopher gobbles green beans
and says once more, /g/ /g/ /g/ /g/ /g/.
He's such a hungry gopher!
Gary the Gopher gobbles in the garden
until everything is gone.
What sound does Gary the Gopher make?
(Have students join in:) /g/ /g/ /g/ /g/ /g/.

Review the name of the card, the sound /g/, and the spelling g.

Write the spelling g on the board. Have students use their fingers to write the spelling several times in the air, on their palms, or on the surface in front of them as they say the sound.

○ Teacher Tip

ADDING ACTIONS Some teachers find it helpful to have students use actions as an aid in remembering the sounds. For example, for /g/, you might have students put their hands to their mouths as if eating as they say the sound.

Unit 2 • Lesson 2 • Day 3   T3

Foundational Skills

LESSON 2 · DAY 3

Generating Words

ASK students to think of words that begin with /g/. Write their suggestions on the board. Circle the spelling *g* in each word, and tell students to say the sound as each *g* is circled.

Repeat the activity with words that end in /g/.

End the activity by reviewing *Sound/Spelling Card 7*—Gopher. Have students give the name of the card, the sound, and the spelling. Ask them how they can use this card to help them remember the sound and spelling. *We can look at the card and think about the sound Gary the Gopher makes: /g/ /g/ /g/ /g/ /g/.*

Blending **ROUTINE 2** **ROUTINE 4**

USE Routine 2, the <u>Sound-by-Sound Blending Routine</u>, and Routine 4, the <u>Blending Sentences Routine</u>, to have students blend the words and sentences.

Before blending the sentences, introduce the high-frequency words *big* and *got*. Encourage students to read each word without sounding it out. If they have difficulty, tell them they can blend the words sound by sound. Read each word, repeat it, and have students read it. Then spell each word with students. Write the words on index cards and add them to the High-Frequency Word Bank.

About the Words

1. Have students identify the spelling that is different in each word. *The final spelling is different in each word– s, b, g, p.*

2. Point out the word *tag*. Ask students what the word means. Listen for different definitions, including "a game," "to touch someone," and "a small card." Explain that all of these definitions are correct, because *tag* is multiple-meaning word. Have students use *tag* in a sentence. **Possible Answer:** *I put my name on a tag so Sally would know the present was from me.*

3. Point out the initial consonant blends in the words. Tell students to remove the first sound in each blend and say the new word. *rip, rid, lad, lass* Have them identify the spelling differences in the words *grip* and *grid*. *p and d* Have them do the same for *glad* and *glass*. *d and ss* Remind them that a change of one sound/spelling changes the meaning of a word. Ask students what each word means. If they are unfamiliar with *grid*, explain that it is a pattern of lines used to divide a map or chart into squares.

4. Use the words to review the final /s/ sound spelled *ss*. Ask a volunteer to explain the sound for the spelling. *A double consonant spelling makes one sound.*

About the Sentences

1-2 Remind students that every sentence must have end punctuation. Have students identify the end punctuation for the sentences. *question mark, period*

Differentiated Instruction

AL APPROACHING LEVEL Work with small groups of students who need additional practice with /g/. Explain that you are going to say some words and they should give a thumbs-up signal when they hear /g/ at the beginning of a word. Use words such as the following: **goat**, house, **grapes**, **girl**, ball, brick, **gate**.

EL English Learner

COGNATES *Gas* is a cognate in Romance languages (Spanish: *gas*).

92 Unit 2 · Lesson 2 · Day 3

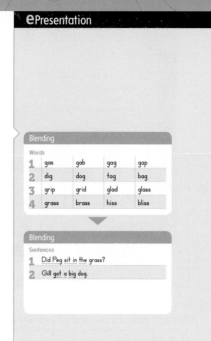

ePresentation

Blending

Words

1	gas	gab	gag	gap
2	dig	dog	tag	bag
3	grip	grid	glad	glass
4	grass	brass	hiss	bliss

Blending

Sentences

1. Did Peg sit in the grass?
2. Gill got a big dog.

Blending

Blending—learning to put separate spelling sounds together smoothly to read words—is the heart of phonics instruction. Blending involves combining the sounds represented by letters to pronounce a word. It is the key strategy that students learn in order to apply the alphabetic principle and open up the world of written text.

The purpose of blending is to teach students a strategy for figuring out unfamiliar words. Learning the sounds and their spellings is only the first step in learning to read and write. The second step is learning to blend the sounds into words. Initially, students blend sound by sound, and then word by word. By blending words sound by sound, students learn the blending process, which allows them to work out for themselves the words they encounter in their reading. The connection between the blended words and the word meaning is constantly reinforced so that students recognize that the sounds they have blended are indeed the word they know from spoken language.

Fluency

Students use the blending strategy when they read *Decodable Takehome Books* and other materials. Ultimately, students will blend only those words that they cannot read. The systematic introduction of sounds and spellings, coupled with blending, develops independent readers in first grade. As students learn the sounds and spellings, they review, reinforce, and apply their expanding knowledge of these sound/spelling correspondences with *Decodable Takehome Books.* Each story supports instruction in new phonics elements and incorporates elements and high-frequency words that have been previously taught.

Reading and Responding

In this section, first graders undergo a series of transitions—from listeners to readers, from **Big Books** to **First Readers** to **Student Anthologies,** and from unsure, hesitant readers to confident and fluent ones.

Big Books

Teachers use the **Big Books** in Units 1–6 to model how to confirm and expand students' knowledge of both print and reading. Beginning with the **Big Books,** the teacher models how to

- Use comprehension strategies in the first read of a selection in order to understand what is happening.
- Access complex text in the second read of a selection by examining how the author structures the text.
- Expand students' vocabulary with various oral development activities before, during, and after reading.
- Learn about different methods authors use to craft a particular selection, including techniques such as the use of captions and headings, dialogue, sentence variety, and so on.

First Reader

In Units 5–6, in addition to using the **Big Books,** students undertake their first transition by using a **First Reader.** Just as in kindergarten, the **First Reader** in Grade 1 allows students to read selections on their own. The collection of stories, poems, and informational texts in the **First Reader** is a precursor to the **Student Anthologies** that first graders will use starting in Unit 7. All students have a **First Reader,** which provides them with the opportunity to apply the comprehension skills and strategies they have previously learned to use with the **Big Books.**

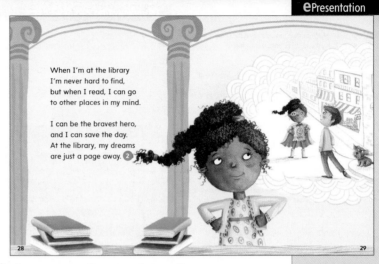

When I'm at the library
I'm never hard to find,
but when I read, I can go
to other places in my mind.

I can be the bravest hero,
and I can save the day.
At the library, my dreams
are just a page away. ②

Comprehension Strategy

Clarifying

② **TEACHER MODEL:** *I am not sure what "just a page away" in the last line means. I will reread the stanza to clarify it. After rereading, I realize that the poet is saying that dreams can be found on the page of any book.*

○ **Teacher Tip**

FLUENCY At this early stage of reading, accuracy is important. But reading poetry with rhythm and expression will add interest for readers and listeners alike.

ℹ **Differentiated Instruction**

AL CLARIFYING To help students clarify any words, lines, or ideas in the poem, reread the poem with them. When they seem confused, ask guiding questions to help them identify the problems.

Unit 5 • Lesson 3 • Day 5   T207

ePresentation

LESSON 2 **DAY 2** **Reading and Responding**

What do the different parts of plants do?

Most pond plants have roots that grow in the water. Roots can also hold plants in place.

LEAVES

STEMS

ROOTS

Writer's Craft

Text Features: Illustrations

○ **HAVE** students read pages 44 and 45. Remind them that "Pond Plants" is an informational text.

⊕ Ask, *Why do informational texts often use photographs?* Possible Answer: *Informational texts are about real things. Photographs of real things would help support the words in the text.* Then point out that the picture on page 44 is the only illustration in this selection. Ask, *Why would an author put one illustration in the middle of a selection that contains photographs?* Possible Answer: *It would be hard to take a photograph of pond plants that shows the top of the water and the bottom.* Explain that authors might choose to add an illustration to a text that is filled with photographs for a couple of reasons. In this case, taking a photograph of pond plants that includes a view above and below the water is difficult. Sometimes a photograph might not exist. In selections about history, if the topic is about something that happened before photography was invented, then there are no photographs, so illustrations would have to be used.

○ **Teacher Tips**

VOCABULARY Call attention to the selection vocabulary word *place* on page 45 and have students give its meaning.

EXTEND KNOWLEDGE Point out that there are no photographs of the early presidents, such George Washington, because there were no cameras when they were alive. Whenever they see a picture of George Washington, it will always be a drawing.

⊕ **Differentiated Instruction: Text Features**

AL For additional support, read pages 44 and 45 with students and discuss with them how the illustration helps support the words on the page.

OL For additional practice, have students browse the selection, identifying how the photograph or illustration helps support the words on the page.

BL For a challenge, have students choose another book about plants and identify the information on the page that relates to the pictures.

Student Anthologies

Beginning in Unit 7, students now read all of their main reading selections from their *Student Anthologies.* Students have fully "graduated" from *Big Books* and the *First Reader* to the *Student Anthologies,* which are also used in the upper elementary levels. The *Student Anthologies* include new features for students:

- The lesson opener includes the genre type and essential question for the selection.
- Comprehension questions allow students to make text connections and to look closer at how writers craft their selections to develop concepts.
- An Apply Vocabulary section gives students another context to review and extend their vocabulary development, including concept vocabulary.
- A Science or Social Studies Connection offers a cross-curricular connection to each of the main selections.

Language Arts

First graders continue to learn about the writing process in addition to spelling and grammar, usage, and mechanics in the Language Arts portion of *SRA Open Court Reading.*

Writing

Teachers follow the same instructional pattern that has been used throughout the program by first instructing students with models of good writing, guiding their practice, and then allowing them to apply the skills they have learned to their own writing.

The writing strand in Grade I makes use of one main graphic organizer—**POW**—for the planning and drafting stage.

POW is the mnemonic device for a strategy to plan and draft informative text or persuasive text or narrative writing. The initials in **POW** stand for the following:

- **Pick my idea** Students choose something to write about.
- **Organize my notes** Students create notes to put down their ideas quickly on paper. They then organize those notes to create a piece of writing.
- **Write and say more** Students use their notes to say more about their reason, topic, or story.

Resources:
- Writer's Notebooks
- *Lesson and Unit Assessment 2,* p. T63

Objectives: Students will
- draft their summaries.
- take the spelling assessment.
- form the letters *T* and *H* correctly.
- use present-tense and past-tense verbs.

Writing an Informative Summary
Drafting

Instruct

REMIND students that a informative summary retells important details about a book or a selection. The main topic should be included in the first sentence of the summary.

Guided Practice

DISPLAY your story map and the draft you wrote the previous day. Ask students to review both and tell you if you left out any important information in your draft. Then ask them to write their own drafts using the information in their story map and their Writer's Workbooks.

Have students indent their paragraphs and skip a space between each line for editing. They need to make sure they write the information in their drafts in the same order it appeared in the selection or book. The sentences that contain the important details should always stay on topic. For example, if the story is an informational text like "Patriotism," the summary should not include information about going on vacation to Florida. That has nothing to do with the selection.

Remind students that you write more interesting sentences when you answer *what, how, when,* or *where* questions in your writing. Use your draft to illustrate an example. **Teacher Modeling:** *Say, if I wrote "The flag flies in our communities" that would be a correctly written sentence. However, if I added words to explain "where" the flag is flown, the sentence would be more interesting and give the reader more information. "The flag is flown at schools, libraries, fire stations, police stations, town halls, and in front of businesses" is a much better sentence.*

Display the **POW Planning Strategy for Writing** using the ePresentation visual and review each step with students. Remind them that the second step is **O**rganizing their notes.

POW Planning Strategy

The POW Planning Strategy for Writing will help students with everything they write. It will give them the POWer to become good writers.

▶ P = Pick an idea
▶ O = Organize your notes
▶ W = Write your draft

T78 Unit 9 · Lesson I · Day 5

Review **DAY 5** **LESSON 1**

Penmanship
Capital Letters *T* and *H*

Guided Practice

REVIEW with students how to form capital, or uppercase, *T* and *H*. Have students come to the board to model the capital letter formations. Remind students that they should use capital letters for the pronoun *I*, at the beginning of a sentence, and for proper nouns such as names of days and months. Distribute handwriting paper.

Apply

○ **WRITE** one word that begins with each letter on the board to model proper spacing between a capital and a lowercase letter; for example, use the words *Toy* and *Help*. Have students write each of the words twice to practice letter formation. Ask them to underline their best words.

Help students brainstorm a list of proper nouns that begin with uppercase *T* and *H*, such as *Tom* and *Helen*. Write them on chart paper or on the board. Have students compose short sentences that begin with capital *T* or *H* and include a proper noun from the list; for example, *His ball rolled into Tamara's yard*. Then have students proofread their sentences. They should circle any incorrect words and underline their best *T* and *H*.

Grammar, Usage, and Mechanics
Present-Tense and Past-Tense Verbs

Instruct

REVIEW with students that verbs show action. Ask students to tell what is added to most verbs to show action that happened in the past. *-ed* Remind them that sometimes the spelling of a verb changes to show that something has already happened. Those verbs do not use an *-ed* ending.

Guided Practice

DISPLAY these sentences on the board and read them aloud. Then have students choose the word that makes each sentence correct.

Apply

HAVE students browse their compositions for places where they might add different present-tense verbs. Also have them look for places to add sentences with past-tense verbs. Remind students that using sentences that tell about the past as well as the present can make their writing more interesting. Circulate and answer any questions as students work. When they finish, have them share their new sentences with partners.

○ **Teacher Tip**

WRITING LINK As students work on writing assignments throughout the year, remind them to make sure that they are forming their letters correctly and using proper spacing between letters, words, and sentences.

ePresentation

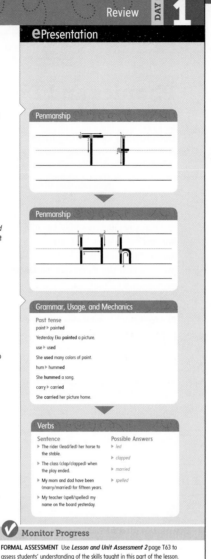

Penmanship

Penmanship

Grammar, Usage, and Mechanics

Past tense
paint ▸ painted
Yesterday Eko **painted** a picture.
use ▸ used
She **used** many colors of paint.
hum ▸ hummed
She **hummed** a song.
carry ▸ carried
She **carried** her picture home.

Verbs

Sentence	Possible Answers
▸ The rider (lead/led) her horse to the stable.	▸ led
▸ The class (clap/clapped) when the play ended.	▸ clapped
▸ My mom and dad have been (marry/married) for fifteen years.	▸ married
▸ My teacher (spell/spelled) my name on the board yesterday.	▸ spelled

✓ **Monitor Progress**

FORMAL ASSESSMENT Use *Lesson and Unit Assessment 2* page T63 to assess students' understanding of the skills taught in this part of the lesson.

Unit 9 · Lesson I · Day 5 **END DAY 5** **T8I**

Penmanship

Students practice forming letters of the alphabet—both capital or uppercase as well as lowercase letters. In addition, students learn to form numerals. This practice is critical in helping students understand the relationship between sounds and letters or numbers.

Grammar, Usage, and Mechanics

Students learn that grammar, usage, and mechanics are critical for comprehension and are important to both readers and writers. If the writer's intended audience cannot understand what the writer is trying to communicate because the text is full of grammatical errors, then the writer has not accomplished his or her intended purpose. Among other things, first graders learn to

- Capitalize the beginning of sentences, a person's name, a place, and the letter *I*.
- End a sentence with the appropriate punctuation mark.
- Make sure that a sentence has a complete thought, with a subject and a verb.
- Write from left to right, and from the top of the page to the bottom of the page.
- Insert a space between words.
- Understand the difference between a letter and a word.

Foundational Skills

In Grades K–I, students practiced oral language development daily through a variety of phonemic awareness activities, singing songs and joining in the *Alphabet Card Sound* stories or the *Sound/Spelling Card* stories, blending the word lines in phonics instruction, and reading aloud the *Pre-Decodable Takehome Books* and the *Decodable Takehome Books.* In Grades 2–3, daily oral language development is available to students through

- blending multisyllabic words on the word lines in Phonics or Word Analysis,
- participating in oral language activities,
- reading aloud the *Decodable Takehome Books,* and
- reading aloud the fluency passages in *Skills Practice.*

Fluency

By second and third grade, most students have had much practice and application of phonics instruction but need more practice with fluency and comprehension.

Fluency develops naturally for some students while others experience more difficulty and need more explicit instruction. Some students may be able to decode and read words, but lack the critical phrasing, intonation, and expression that support meaning. *SRA Open Court Reading* provides the text characteristics that support fluency, allows for models of fluent reading for students through the use of the *eDecodables,* and gives students regular opportunities to practice fluency.

Resource:
Decodable Stories, Book 6, Story 44

Objectives: Students will
- build oral language skills.
- read a *Decodable Story.*
- build fluency.

Phonics and Decoding

/oo/ spelled *oo*

Developing Oral Language

EL HAVE students create sentences using the words in Line I as verbs. Then have them create sentences using the words in Line I as nouns.

Have students identify the part of speech for each word in Line 2. *nouns: hood, wood; verb: stood; adjective: good* Ask students to identify the tense of the verb. *past tense*

Fluency: Reading a Decodable Story

Book 6, Story 44: Look How Pets Adapt

New High-Frequency Words: *warm, wash*

Reviewed High-Frequency Words: *are, how, now, put, their, your*

HAVE students read "Look How Pets Adapt." Tell them to focus on reading the story accurately.

▸ Checking Comprehension

Have students respond to the following instructions and questions to check their understanding of the story. Tell students to point to their answers in the story.

I. Name one way pets adapt to warm weather. Possible Answers: *Pets adapt to warm weather by shedding more fur, by eating less food, and by looking for a cool place away from heat.*

2. Name one way pets adapt to cool weather. Possible Answers: *Pets adapt to cool weather by shedding less fur, by eating more, and by curling up tightly to stay warm.*

3. How do people provide for their pets in winter? Possible Answers: *People provide warm homes for their pets. People also might provide clothing for their pets.*

▸ Building Fluency

Build students' fluency by having them read "Look How Pets Adapt" with a partner. Have the partners reread the story aloud several times. Check students' reading for accuracy.

EL English Learner

PHONICS AND DECODING The *English Learner Teacher's Guide* provides more reinforcement for students during Workshop who need additional help with Foundational Skills.

Differentiated Instruction

AL For additional practice with the target sound/spelling in this lesson, during Workshop have students read Story 44: "The Rookie Firefighter" from *Practice Decodable Stories.*

ePresentation

Developing Oral Language

Words				
1	look	book	cook	hook
2	hood	good	stood	wood
3	shook	crook	woof	soot
4	overlook	cookbook	footloose	parenthood

Decodable Stories, Book 6

Look How Pets Adapt

Comprehension

The primary aim of reading is comprehension. Reading is about problem-solving. As students move from decoding words to reading sentences fluently, they must be able to understand what they read. Instruction accompanying the *Decodables* highlight that students are expected to understand what they are reading by pointing out in the text where they find answers to comprehension questions.

Foundational Skills

Resources:
· Routines 7, 8, and 10
· *Skills Practice 2*, pp. 95–96

Objectives: Students will
· understand words with the prefixes *dis-* and *auto-*
· spell dictated words with the prefixes *dis-* and *auto-* correctly.
· build oral language skills.

Word Analysis
Prefixes *dis-* and *auto-*

Decoding **ROUTINE 10**

REVIEW with students that a prefix is a word part added to the beginning of a base word or root that changes the word's meaning. A prefix will not change the spelling of a base word. Remind students that knowing the meanings of prefixes will help them understand unfamiliar words.

Use Routine 10, the Words with Prefixes and Suffixes Routine, to review using prefixes to understand words.

Display the word lines and sentences, then have students read each word and sentence. Have students discuss the capitalization and punctuation of each sentence.

About the Words

1-3 **The Prefix *dis-*** Have students reread the words on Lines 1-3. Have them identify the base words and use academic language to explain the difference between a base word and a prefix. Then have them identify the prefix *dis-*. Explain that *dis-* means "not" or "the opposite of." Have students use the meanings of the prefix and base word to explain the meaning of each word.

4 **The Prefix *auto-*** Have students identify the prefix and the base words. Explain that the prefix *auto-* is derived from Greek and means "self." Ask students which word on the line contains another Greek root they have studied. *graph in autobiography means "write"* Have students explain the meaning of each word. Point out that adding the prefix *auto-* also adds two more syllables to a base word.

About the Sentences

1-2 **The Prefixes *dis-* and *auto-*** Have students identify the words with the prefixes *dis-* and *auto-* in the sentences. *disregard, disconnect; automobile, autopilot* Review the meanings of the prefixes and the words.

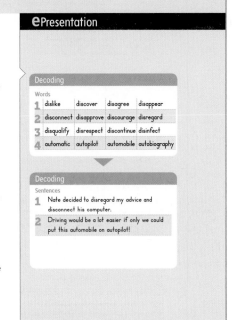

ePresentation

Decoding

Words

1 dislike · discover · disagree · disappear

2 disconnect · disapprove · discourage · disregard

3 disqualify · disrespect · discontinue · disinfect

4 automatic · autopilot · automobile · autobiography

Decoding

Sentences

1 Nate decided to disregard my advice and disconnect his computer.

2 Driving would be a lot easier if only we could put this automobile on autopilot!

Teacher Tip

SYLLABICATION Help students apply what they've learned about open and closed syllables to identify the syllable breaks. Remind students that affixes are separate syllables as well.

dis/like	dis/cov/er
dis/a/gree	dis/ap/pear
dis/con/nect	dis/ap/prove
dis/cour/age	dis/re/gard
dis/qual/i/fy	dis/re/spect
dis/con/tin/ue	dis/in/fect
au/to/mat/ic	au/to/pi/lot
au/to/mo/bile	au/to/bi/o/gra/phy

Differentiated Instruction: Word Lines

AL Reinforce the meanings of the words on the lines for students by using them in sentences. Have students identify the word with the prefix and explain the meaning.

OL Have student pairs use a dictionary to find other words with the prefixes *dis-* and *auto-*. Tell students to note the dictionary definitions and discuss with their partners how these compare with the meanings they constructed using their knowledge of the affixes and roots.

BL Challenge students to use some of the words on the lines in a short autobiographical paragraph. Students may write about themselves in general or about a particular event in their lives.

Word Analysis

As students move into the upper grades, the emphasis shifts from phonics to morphology, or the study of word structure. In ***SRA Open Court Reading***, this is called Word Analysis. Word Analysis activities in Grades 2–3 support the development of fluency as students learn to identify and read meaningful chunks of words rather than individual spellings.

Word Analysis also supports the development of vocabulary as students learn how inflectional endings change a word's tense, number, and so on and how affixes can be added to a root or base word to create or derive a new but related meaning. Being able to identify key-word parts not only helps with the pronunciation of longer, unfamiliar words, but it also helps with understanding the meaning of words. Students learn how to deconstruct words—to identify the root or base of a word as well as the affixes. They also learn how to construct new words by adding affixes to base words and roots, and to enhance their vocabulary.

Reading and Responding

Students read each selection twice—once to practice comprehension strategies, and the second to understand not only the kinds of techniques writers use but also how to access complex text by searching for specific types of information. Before, during, and after both reads of the selection, vocabulary development and application is stressed.

Vocabulary

Teaching vocabulary is one of the strong foundations of *SRA Open Court Reading.* Getting students to understand what a selection is about involves not only the reading process, but also the process of expanding students' vocabulary so that they comprehend both simple stories and more complex informational selections. In this program, some initial vocabulary is pre-taught, but most of the selection vocabulary words are encountered for the first time within the selection. Students have multiple opportunities after reading the selection to work with the vocabulary daily through the use of a Selection Vocabulary Routine to develop, practice, apply, extend, and review the words.

Social Studies and Science Connections

Students have the chance to connect what they have read to a short, cross-curricular selection. This allows students to have multiple opportunities with different text features and with social studies and science content. It also offers some additional vocabulary review with selection words used in context.

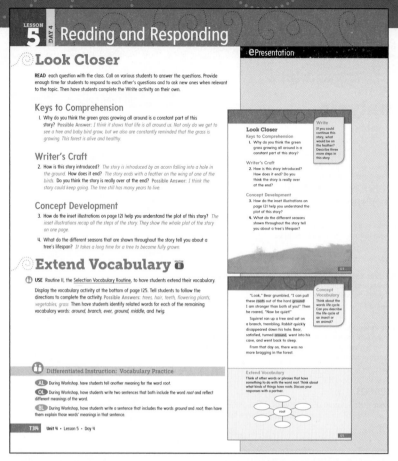

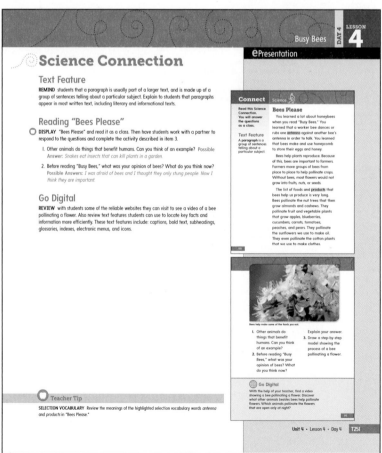

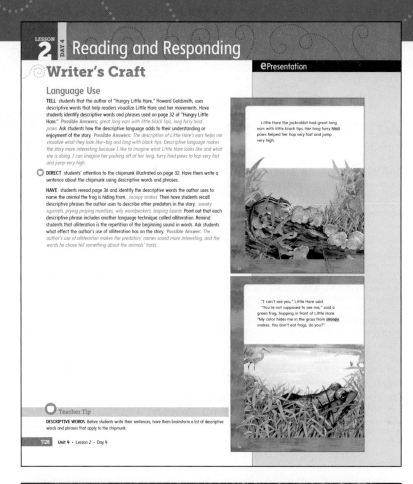

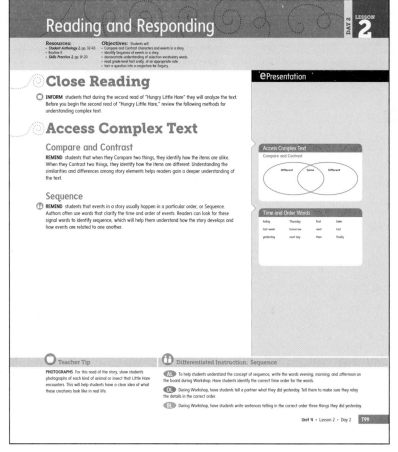

Writer's Craft

During the second read of a selection, students learn about some of the ways writers create or craft a piece of writing. Whether it is through the use of alliteration in a poem, characterization in a narrative, or text features such as headings in an informational selection, students learn that writers can use many different techniques to write a selection. The techniques used often depend upon the genre of the selection. Attention to these types of details make the writing interesting and more enjoyable to read. The point of Writer's Craft is to expose students to these different techniques so that they can perhaps transfer some of these to their own writing.

Accessing Complex Text

Learning vocabulary and understanding the ways authors use certain techniques to craft a selection helps students to understand what they are reading. So, too, does looking for specific information in a text by analyzing it closely during the second read of a selection. Skills involved in accessing complex text include the following:

- Cause and Effect
- Classify and Categorize
- Compare and Contrast
- Fact and Opinion
- Main Idea and Details
- Making Inferences
- Sequence

By learning these skills, students learn how writers organize or structure a particular text. They come to understand that looking for specific information may mean skimming over some text but reading other sentences or paragraphs very closely. Students learn to make sense of what is written, which lies at the heart of the *SRA Open Court Reading* program.

Language Arts

Writing

The teacher oversees and models each step of the writing process for students. The teacher starts the process by offering the model provided in the *Teacher's Edition.* Then the class works together to go through the process on a class assignment before students work individually to create their final products. In addition to learning the steps of the writing process, students also learn about audience, purpose, genre, main idea, and details.

The writing strand makes use of one main graphic organizer—**TREE**—for the planning and drafting phase of writing. This graphic organizer is a simple mnemonic device that students will learn to internalize and use to help them write both informational and persuasive pieces. The initials in **TREE** stand for the following:

- **Topic Sentence** Tell what you believe
- **Reasons**
  - Three or more reasons
  - Why do I believe this?
  - Will my readers believe this?
- **Explain Reasons** Say more about each reason
- **Ending** Wrap it up

Resource:
• Routine 16

Objectives: Students will
• learn about informative/explanatory texts.
• review the writing process.
• brainstorm topics for an informative/explanatory text.
• learn about /ē/ spelling patterns, contractions, and possessives.

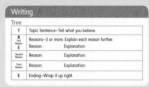

Writing to Inform
Prewriting

Instruct—Introduce/Model Planning Strategy 16

EL **EXPLAIN** to students that their next writing assignments will be writing informative/explanatory texts. Tell students that this type of writing informs the reader about a topic or explains how to do something. Locate examples of informative/explanatory texts in the classroom, and describe each in terms of its purpose to inform or explain. Possible Answers: *This is a book about weather. Its purpose is to inform the reader about different types of weather events and what causes them. This is a book about paper airplanes. Its purpose is to explain how to fold paper to create different kinds of paper airplanes.*

Tell students that an author's main purpose when writing to inform is to provide facts, not opinions, about the topic. Informative writing should be accurate and impartial.

Inform students that they will work together as a class to write the first informative/explanatory text. Remind them of the five steps in the writing process: Prewriting, Drafting, Revising, Editing, Publishing. Display a blank TREE graphic organizer, and use Routine 16, the Graphic Organizer Routine, to explain how it is used for informative/explanatory writing.

Remind students that they used the TREE diagram to plan and organize their opinion writing in the previous unit. Explain that it can be used similarly when writing to inform.

- **T** is for Topic Sentence. The text should begin with a topic sentence that tells clearly what you are writing about.
- **R** is for Reasons. Use the three spaces for reasons to list three facts about your topic.
- **E** is for Explanation. Each fact should have at least one sentence that explains it further.
- **E** is for Ending. The text should have a good ending that sums up the information about the topic.

Remind students that using a TREE diagram to plan their writing will ensure that it is well-organized and they have provided sufficient details to inform their readers about the topic

Writing

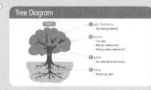

Tree	
T	Topic Sentence—Tell what you believe.
R First Reason / E	Reasons—3 or more. Explain each reason further. Reason: Explanation:
Second Reason	Reason: Explanation:
Third Reason	Reason: Explanation:
E	Ending—Wrap it up right.

Tree Diagram

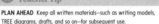

Teacher Tip

PLAN AHEAD Keep all written materials—such as writing models, TREE diagrams, drafts, and so on—for subsequent use.

EL **English Learner**

GRAMMAR AND WRITING The *English Learner Teacher's Guide* provides grammar, usage, and mechanics lessons on Days 3 and 5 of each week. These lessons reteach the strand or strands being taught during the week and highlight linguistic hurdles English learners might face in their speaking and writing. A more structured and streamlined writing assignment is provided for students who are not able to complete the core writing assignment.

T18 Unit 2 • Lesson 1 • Day 1

Spelling

/ī/ spelled _igh, _ie, and _y; Irregular Verbs and
Abstract Nouns

Pretest

GIVE students the pretest by reading aloud the words and sentences below. Have student write each spelling word on a sheet of paper, and then have them proofread and correct any misspelled words. Give the challenge words and sentences to students as well.

Pretest Sentences

1.	lie	I didn't feel well, so I went to lie down.
2.	ties	My dad had two ties to choose from.
3.	went	The Nelsons went to the opera last night.
4.	faith	I have faith that all my students will do their best.
5.	gave	Louisa gave her aunt a birthday card.
6.	reply	He did not reply to my question.
7.	sank	The fish sank slowly to the bottom of the aquarium.
8.	lit	The campers lit their fire using the last match.
9.	sigh	I heard her sigh, so I knew she was tired.
10.	bravery	The firefighter's bravery was honored by the mayor.
11.	cycles	There are three cycles of the washing machine.
12.	flies	The goldfinch flies straight to the birdfeeder each morning.
13.	fight	The hero will fight the villain in the movie.
14.	paid	Nellie paid for a new notebook with money she had saved.
15.	truth	It is important to tell the truth.

Challenge Pretest Sentences

1.	brought	Ms. Ling brought her daughter to dancing lessons.
2.	power	The car's engine had more power after the tune-up.
3.	brighter	The moon seems brighter than usual this evening.

Diagnose

Diagnose any misspellings by determining whether students misspelled /ī/ or some other part of the word. Then have students use the pretest as a take-home list to study the spelling of words with /ī/, irregular verbs, and abstract nouns.

Spelling

Students have spelling as part of their Language Arts lesson in the last half in Grade 1. Spelling is then a critical part of the Language Arts lesson in both Grades 2 and 3. The spelling words are taken from the skills taught in the Foundational Skills portion of the lesson, thereby allowing students more opportunities to practice these skills.

Grammar, Usage, and Mechanics

Grammar, usage, and mechanics remains a crucial part of the Language Arts portion of the lesson. Among other things, second and third graders learn to do the following:

- Distinguish among different types of sentences.
- Use different parts of speech correctly.
- Write and extend sentences to include compound and complex sentences.
- Learn that the beginnings of sentences as well as proper nouns and titles need to be capitalized.
- Understand that all sentences need to include end punctuation such as a period, a question mark, or an exclamation point.
- Know that sentences also have internal punctuation such as commas, colons, apostrophes, and so on, and be able to use these types of punctuation correctly.

Foundational Skills: Phonological and Phonemic Awareness

The key to learning to read is the ability to identify different sounds and to connect those sounds to the letters of the alphabet. The basic purpose of providing structured practice in phonemic awareness is to help students hear and understand the sounds from which words are made. Before students can be expected to understand the sound/symbol correspondence that forms the basis of written English, they need to have a strong working knowledge of the sound relationships that make up the spoken language. This understanding of spoken language lays the foundation for the transition to written language.

Phonological awareness is an umbrella term. It incorporates a range of oral language skills that involve the ability to notice, think about, and manipulate individual sounds in words. Phonological awareness involves working with sentences, words, rhymes, syllables, and sounds. The objective is for students to be able to manipulate words, word parts, and sounds without regard to meaning.

Phonological and phonemic awareness activities initially provide students with the opportunity to think about sentences and to break them into words and then to play with words and to break them into parts. It involves easy and fun activities that engage students in playing with and exploring the parts and sounds of language. The goal of these gamelike activities is to help students understand that speech is made of distinct, identifiable sounds. The playful nature of the activities makes them appealing and engaging, while giving students practice and support for learning about language. When students begin reading and writing, this experience with manipulating sounds will help them use what they know about sounds and letters to sound out and spell unfamiliar words when they read and write.

Developing phonological awareness engages students in activities that move from working with words and syllables—the larger units of language—to individual sounds (phonemes). Students progress by

- identifying sentences
- identifying words
- working with rhymes
- exploring compound words
- listening for syllables
- blending syllables
- oral blending
- deleting and substituting sounds
- segmenting phonemes

As students engage in various phonemic awareness activities, they will become proficient at listening for and reproducing the sounds they hear. It is essential for their progression to phonics and reading that they are able to hear the sounds and the patterns used to make up recognizable words. The phonemic awareness activities support the phonics instruction. Initially, students are not expected to read the words they are exploring and manipulating, so any consonant and vowel sounds may be used, even if students have not been formally taught the sounds and their spellings.

> *As students progress through various phonemic awareness activities, they will become proficient at listening for and reproducing the sounds they hear.*

After students have an awareness of phonemes, they can begin to connect sounds to letters and to engage in a variety of activities in which sounds and letters are substituted to make new words. Students begin to understand that if a sound changes, a letter must change, and a new word is created. As students move into phonics, research suggests that connecting sounds to spellings actually heightens their awareness of language. Phonological and phonemic awareness is both a prerequisite for and a consequence of learning to read.

Research suggests that the instructional focus should be on two critical phonemic awareness tasks:

- phoneme or oral blending and
- phoneme segmentation.

These activities are supported by discrimination and elision activities (deleting and substituting sounds) and general wordplay. Oral blending encourages students to combine sounds to make words and lays the foundation for decoding and reading. Segmentation, conversely, requires students to break words into discrete sounds and lays the foundation for spelling. Other activities support discrimination, or recognition, of particular sounds. Sometimes simple songs, rhymes, or games engage students in wordplay. In these, students manipulate words in a variety of ways. From these playful activities, students develop serious knowledge about their language.

Oral Blending

Purpose

In oral blending, students are led through a progression of activities designed to help them hear how sounds are put together to make words.

Until students develop an awareness of the component parts of words, they have no tools with which to decode words or to put letters together to form words. Oral blending helps students understand these component parts of words, from syllables down to single sounds, or phonemes. Oral blending is not to be confused with the formal blending of specific sounds whose spellings students will be taught through phonics instruction. Oral blending does not depend on the recognition of written words; it focuses instead on hearing and blending the sounds.

Oral blending focuses on hearing sounds through a sequence that introduces the most easily distinguished word parts and then systematically moves to oral blending of individual sounds that contains all the challenges of phonic decoding (except letter recognition). This sequence provides support for the least-prepared student—one who comes to school with no concept of words or sounds within words. At the same time, the lively pace and playful nature of oral blending activities hold the interest of students who already have some familiarity with words and letters.

Oral blending prepares students for phonics instruction by developing an awareness of the separate sounds that make up speech. Oral blending activities then continue in concert with phonics instruction to reinforce and extend new learning. Because these activities involve simply listening to and reproducing sounds, oral blending need not be restricted to the sounds students have been or will be taught in phonics.

The tone of the activities should be playful and informal and should move quickly. Although these activities will provide information about student progress, they are not diagnostic tools. Do not expect mastery. Those students who have not caught on will be helped more by varied experiences than by more drilling on the same activity.

Procedure

The following is a description of the progression of oral blending activities.

Word-Part Blending

Syllables are easier to distinguish than individual sounds (phonemes), so students can quickly experience success in forming meaningful words. Tell students that you are going to say some words in two parts. Tell them to listen carefully so they can discover what the words are. Read each word, pronouncing each part distinctly with a definite pause between syllables. The lists of words that follow are arranged in sequence from easy to harder. They cover different types of cues. Whenever they fit into the sequence, include multisyllabic names of students in the class.

Model

Teacher: dino . . . saur. What's the word?
Students: dinosaur

Example Words

- First part of the word cues the whole word:
  vita . . . min
  vaca . . . tion
  hippopot . . . amus
  ambu . . . lance

- Two distinct words easily combined:
  butter. . . fly
  straw. . . berry
  surf . . . board
  basket . . . ball

- Two distinct words, but the first word could cue the wrong ending:
  tooth . . . ache
  tooth . . . paste
  water . . . fall
  water . . . melon

- First part, consonant + vowel, are not enough to guess whole word:
  re . . . member
  re . . . frigerator
  bi . . . cycle
  bi . . . ology

- Identifying cues in second part:
  light . . . ning
  sub . . . ject
  in . . . sect

- Last part, consonant + vowel sound, carries essential information:
  yester . . . day
  rain . . . bow
  noi . . . sy
  pota . . . to
- Changing the final part changes the word:
  start . . . ing
  start . . . er
  start . . . ed

Blending Initial Consonants

Initial consonant blending prepares students for consonant replacement activities that will come later. Tell students that you will ask them to put some sounds together to make words. Pronounce each word part distinctly, and make a definite pause at the breaks indicated. When a letter is surrounded by slash marks, pronounce the letter's sound, not its name. When you see /s/, for example, you will say "ssss," not "ess." The words that follow are arranged from easy to harder. Whenever they fit into the sequence, include names of students in the class.

Model

Teacher: /t/ . . . iger. What's the word?
Students: tiger

Example Words

- Separated consonant blend, with rest of word giving strong cue to word identity:
  /b/ . . . *roccoli*   /k/ . . . *racker*
  /f/ . . . *lashlight*   /k/ . . . *reature*
- Held consonant that is easy for students to hear, with rest of word giving strong cue:
  /s/ . . . *innamon*   /l/ . . . *adybug*
  /s/ . . . *eventeen*   /n/ . . . *ewspaper*
- Stop consonant that is harder for students to hear preceding vowel, with rest of word giving strong cue:
  /t/ . . . *adpole*   /p/ . . . *iggybank*
  /d/ . . . *ragonfly*   /b/ . . . *arbecue*
- Single-syllable words and words in which the second part gives a weaker cue:
  /s/ . . . *ing*   /l/ . . . *augh*   /v/ . . . *ase*

Blending Final Consonant Sounds

In this phase of oral blending, the last sound in the word is separated.

Model

Teacher: cabba . . . /j/. What's the word?
Students: cabbage

Example Words

- Words that are easily recognized even before the final consonant is pronounced:
  bubblegu . . . /m/   *Columbu . . . /s/*
  crocodi . . . /l/   *submari . . . /n/*
- Multisyllabic words that need the final consonant for recognition:
  colle . . . /j/ (college)   come . . . /t/ (comet)
- Single-syllable words:
  sa . . . /d/   gra . . . /s/ (grass)   snai . . . /l/

Replacing Initial Consonant Sounds

This level of oral blending further develops awareness of initial consonant sounds. The activity begins with a common word then quickly changes its initial consonant sound. Most of the words produced are nonsense words, which helps keep the focus on the sounds in the word. Note that the words are written on the board, but students are not expected to read them. The writing is to help students see that when the sounds change, the letters change, and vice versa.

Model

Teacher: [Writes word on board.] This word is *magazine*. What is it?
Students: magazine

Teacher: Now I'm going to change it. [Erases initial consonant.] Now it doesn't start with /m/; it's going to start with /b/. What's the new word?
Students: bagazine

Teacher: That's right . . . [Writes *b* where *m* had been.] It's *bagazine*. Now I'm going to change it again. . . .

Repeat with different consonant sounds. Then do the same with other words such as *remember, Saturday, tomorrow, lotion,* and *million.* Continue with single-syllable words such as *take, big, boot, cot, seat, look, tap, ride,* and *late.* There are two stages in using written letters:

- The replacement letter is not written until *after* the new "word" with the new sound has been identified.
- Later, the replacement letter is written at **the same time** the change in the initial phoneme is announced. For example, erase *d* and write *m* while you say, "Now it doesn't start with /d/; it starts with /m/."

When the consonants used have already been introduced in phonics, you may wish to alter the procedure by writing the replacement letter and having students sound out the new word. Feel free to switch between the two procedures within a single exercise. If students are not responding orally to written spellings that have been introduced in phonics, do not force it. Proceed by saying the word before writing the letter, and wait until another time to move on to writing before pronouncing.

Blending One-Syllable Words

Students now begin blending individual phonemes to form words. This important step can be continued well into the year. Continued repetitions of this activity will help students realize how they can use the sound/spellings they are learning to read and write real words.

At first, the blended words are presented in a story context that helps students identify the words. They soon recognize that they are actually decoding meaningful words. However, the context must not be so strong that students can guess the word without listening to the phonemic cues. Any vowel sounds and irregularly spelled words may be used because there is no writing involved.

Model

Teacher: When I looked out the window, I saw a /l/ /ī/ /t/. What did I see?

Students: A light.

Teacher: Yes, I saw a light. At first I thought it was the /m/ /ōō/ /n/. What did I think it was?

Students: The moon.

Teacher: But it didn't really look like the moon. Suddenly I thought, maybe it's a space /sh/ /i/ /p/. What did I think it might be?

Students: A spaceship!

When students are familiar with this phase of oral blending, they can move to blending one-syllable words without the story context.

Example Words

- CVC (consonant/vowel/consonant) words beginning with easily blended consonant sounds (/sh/, /h/, /r/, /v/, /s/, /n/, /z/, /f/, /l/, /m/):
  nip   nap
- CVC words beginning with any consonant:
  ten   bug   lip
- Add CCVC words:
  flap   step

- Add CVCC words:
  most   band   went
- Add CCVCC words:
  stamp   grand   scuffs

Replacing Final Consonant Sounds

Final consonant sounds are typically more difficult for students to use than initial consonants.

- Begin with multisyllabic words, and move to one-syllable words.
- As with initial consonants, first write the changed consonant after students have pronounced the new word.
- Then write the consonant as they pronounce it.
- For sound/spellings introduced in phonics instruction, write the new consonant spelling, and have students identify and pronounce it.

Model

Teacher: [Writes word on board.] This word is *teapot*. What is it?

Students: teapot

Teacher: Now I'm going to change it. [Erases final consonant.] Now it doesn't end with /t/; it ends with /p/. What's the word now?

Students: teapop

Teacher: That's right . . . [Writes *p* where *t* had been.] It's *teapop*. Now I'm going to change it again. . . .

Example Words

- Words that are easily recognized even before the final consonant is pronounced:
  picnic   picnit   picnis   picnil   picnid
  airplane   airplate   airplabe   airplafe
- Multisyllabic words that need the final consonant for recognition:
  muffin   muffil   muffim   muffip   muffit
  amaze   amate   amake   amale   amade
- Single-syllable words:
  neat   nean   neap   neam   neaj   nead   neaf
  broom   broot   brood   broof   broop   broon

Replacing Initial Vowels

Up to now, oral blending has concentrated on consonant sounds because they are easier to hear than vowels. As you move to vowel play, remember that the focus is still on the sounds, not the spellings. Use any vowel sounds.

Model

Teacher: [Writes word on board.] This word is *elephant*. What is it?

Students: elephant

Teacher: Now I'm going to change it. [Erases initial vowel.] Now it doesn't start with /e/; it starts with /a/. What's the word now?

Students: alephant

Teacher: That's right . . . [Writes *a* where *e* had been.] It's *alephant*. Now I'm going to change it again. . . .

Example Words

- Multisyllabic words:

  angry   ingry   oongry   ungry   engry
  ivy   avy   oovy   evy   ovy   oivy

- One-syllable words:

  ink   ank   oonk   unk   onk   oink
  add   odd   idd   oudd   edd   udd

Segmentation

Purpose

Segmentation and oral blending complement each other: Oral blending puts sounds together to make words, while segmentation separates words into sounds. While oral blending will provide valuable support for decoding when students begin reading independently, segmentation provides critical support for encoding or spelling.

> *Oral blending will provide valuable support for decoding when students begin reading independently.*

Procedure

Syllable Segmentation

The earliest segmentation activities focus on syllables, which are easier to distinguish than individual sounds, or phonemes. Start with students' names, and then use other words. As with the oral blending activities, remember to move quickly through these activities. Do not hold the class back waiting for all students to catch on. Individual progress will vary, but drilling on one activity is less helpful than going on to others. Return to the same activity often. Frequent repetition is very beneficial and allows students additional opportunities to catch on.

- Say, for example, "Let's clap out Amanda's name. A-man-da."
- Have students clap and say the syllables along with you. Count the claps.
- Tell students that these word parts are called syllables. Don't try to explain; the idea will develop with practice. After you have provided the term, simply say, "How many syllables?" after students clap and count.
- Mix one-syllable and multisyllabic words:
  fantastic   tambourine   good
  imaginary   stand   afraid

Comparing Word Length

Unlike most phonemic awareness activities, this one involves writing or project words on the board. Remember, though, that students are not expected to read what is written. They are merely noticing that words that take longer to say generally look longer when written.

- Start with students' names. Choose two names, one short and one long, with the same first letter (for example, *Joe* and *Jonathan*).
- Write the two names on the board, one above the other, so that the difference is obvious.
- Tell students that one name is *Jonathan* and that one is *Joe*. Have them pronounce and clap each name. Then have them tell which written word they think says *Joe*.
- Move your finger under each name as students clap and say it syllable by syllable.
- Repeat with other pairs of names and words such as *tea/telephone, cat/caterpillar,* and *butterfly/bug*. Be sure not to give false clues. For example, sometimes write the longer word on top, sometimes the shorter one; sometimes ask for the shorter word, sometimes the longer; sometimes ask for the top word, sometimes the bottom; and sometimes point to a word and ask students to name it, and sometimes name the word and ask students to point to it.

Listening for Individual Sounds

Activities using a puppet help students listen for individual sounds in words. Use any puppet you have on hand. When you introduce the puppet, tell students that it likes to play word games. Each new activity begins with the teacher speaking to and for the puppet until students determine the pattern. Next, students either speak for the puppet or correct the puppet. To make sure all students are participating, alternate randomly between having the whole group or individuals respond. The activities focus on particular parts of words, according to the following sequence:

I. Repeating last part of word. Use words beginning with easy-to-hear consonants such as *f, l, m, n, r, s,* and *z.* The puppet repeats only the rime, the part of the syllable after the initial consonant.

Model

Teacher: farm
Puppet: arm

After the pattern is established, students respond for the puppet.

Teacher: rope
Students: ope

Example Words

Use words such as the following:

  mine . . . ine   *soup . . . oup*   *feet . . . eet*

2. Restoring initial phonemes. Now students correct the puppet. Be sure to acknowledge the correction.

Model

Teacher: lake
Puppet: ake
Teacher: No, lllake. You forgot the /l/.
Teacher: real
Puppet: eal
Teacher: What did the puppet leave off?
Students: /r/. It's supposed to be *real.*
Teacher: That's right. The word is *real.*

Example Words

Use words such as the following:

  look . . . ook *mouse . . . ouse*
  sand . . . and

3. Segmenting initial consonants. The puppet pronounces only the initial consonant.

Model

Teacher: pay
Puppet: /p/

Example Words

Use words such as the following:
  moon . . . /m/ *nose . . . /n/* *bell . . . /b/*

4. Restoring final consonants. Students correct the puppet. Prompt if necessary: "What's the word? What did the puppet leave off?"

Model

Teacher: run
Puppet: ru

Students: It's run! You left off the /n/.
Teacher: That's right. The word is *run.*

Example Words

Use words such as the following:
  meet . . . mee *cool . . . coo* *boot . . . boo*

5. Isolating final consonants. The puppet pronounces only the final consonant.

Model

Teacher: green
Puppet: /n/

Example Words

Use words such as the following:
  glass . . . /s/ *boom . . . /m/* *mice . . . /s/*

6. Segmenting initial consonant blends. The sounds in blends are emphasized.

Model

Teacher: clap
Puppet: lap

Next have students correct the puppet.

Teacher: stain
Puppet: tain
Students: It's stain! You left off the /s/.
Teacher: That's right. The word is *stain.*

Example Words

Use words such as the following:
  blaze . . . laze *draw . . . raw*
  proud . . . roud

Discrimination

Purpose

Discrimination activities help students focus on particular sounds in words.

Listening for long-vowel sounds is the earliest discrimination activity. Vowel sounds are necessary for decoding, but young students do not hear them easily. This is evident in students' invented spellings, where vowels are often omitted. Early in the year, students listen for long-vowel sounds, which are more easily distinguished than short-vowel sounds:

- Explain to students that vowels are special because sometimes vowels say their names in words.

- Tell students which vowel sound to listen for.
- Have them repeat the sound when they hear it in a word. For example, if the target-vowel sound is long *e*, students will say long *e* when you say *leaf*, but they should not respond when you say *loaf*.
- Initially students should listen for one long vowel sound at a time. Later they can listen for two vowel sounds. All Example Words, however, should contain one of the target vowels.

Procedure

Listening for Short-Vowel Sounds

These discrimination activities should be done after the short vowels /a/ and /i/ have been introduced. Short vowels are very useful in reading. They are generally more regular in spelling than long vowels, and they appear in many short, simple words. However, their sounds are less easily distinguished than those of long vowels. Thus, the activities focus only on /a/ and /i/. All the words provided have one or the other of these sounds. Either have students repeat the sound of a specified vowel, or vary the activity as follows: Write an *a* on one side of the board and an *i* on the other. Ask students to point to the *a* when they hear a word with the /a/ sound and to point to the *i* when they hear a word with the /i/ sound. Use words such as the following:

bat   mat   sat   sit   spit
pit   pat   pan   pin   spin

Listening for Consonant Sounds in Multisyllabic Words

Discriminating these sounds helps students attend to consonant sounds in the middle of words.

- Say the word *rib*, and have students repeat it. Ask where they hear the /b/ in *rib*.
- Then say *ribbon*, and ask students where they hear the /b/ in *ribbon*.
- Tell students that you will say some words and that they will repeat each word.
- After they repeat each word, ask what consonant sound they hear in the middle of that word. Use words such as the following:

famous   message   picky
jogger   flavor   zipper

Phonemic Play

Purpose

Wordplay activities help students focus on and manipulate sounds, thus supporting the idea that words are made of specific sounds that can be taken apart, put together, or changed to make new words. Through wordplay, students gain important knowledge about language.

Procedure

Producing Rhymes

Many phonemic play activities focus on producing rhymes. A familiar or easily learned rhyme or song is introduced, and students are encouraged to substitute words or sounds. An example is "Willaby Wallaby Woo," in which students change the rhyming words in the couplet "Willaby Wallaby Woo/An elephant sat on you" so that the second line ends with a student's name and that the first line ends with a rhyme beginning with *W*; for example, "Willaby Wallaby Wissy/An elephant sat on Missy."

Generating Alliterative Words

Students can also say as many words as they can think of that begin with a given consonant sound. This is a valuable complement to discrimination activities in which the teacher produces the words and students identify them.

The Alphabetic Principle

The Alphabetic Principle

Purpose

A major emphasis in the kindergarten program is on letter recognition and attending to sounds. Students need to learn the alphabetic principle: that letters work together in a systematic way to connect spoken language to written words. This understanding is the foundation for reading. Students are not expected to master letter/sound correspondence at the beginning of kindergarten, nor are they expected to blend sounds into words themselves. They are expected to become an "expert" only on their Special Letters as they learn how the alphabet works. Through this introduction to the alphabetic principle, students will have the basic understanding required to work through the alphabet letter by letter, attaching sounds to each.

Key concepts of the alphabetic principle include the following:

- A limited number of letters combine in different ways to make many different words.
- Words are composed of sounds, and letters represent those sounds.
- Anything that can be pronounced can be spelled.
- Letters and sounds can be used to identify words.
- Meaning can be obtained by using letters and sounds to determine words.

Procedures for Kindergarten

The following steps can be used for introducing letters and sounds in kindergarten. These steps may be adapted for students at other grades if they do not understand the alphabetic principle. The tone of these activities should be informal, fun, and fast-paced. The purpose of these activities is to familiarize students with how the alphabet works by having them participate in group play with letters and sounds.

I Can Spell Anything

- Reinforce the idea that anything that can be pronounced can be spelled with the letters of the alphabet.
- Tell students that you can spell any word. Have them give you words to spell.
- Write the words on the board, naming each letter as you write it. This shows students that the words contain the letters displayed on the **Alphabet Sound Wall Cards.**

- Have students help you spell the words again by pointing to letters as you say them.
- Encourage students to spell each word letter by letter.

I'm a Letter Expert

- Have **Letter Cards** available for the following set of letters: *b, d, f, h, l, m, n, p, s, t.* You will need two or three cards for each letter. (You will not need the **Alphabet Sound Cards** until later.)
- You will be the letter expert for the vowels.
- Organize the class into groups of two or three, and assign each group a letter. Give each student the appropriate **Letter Card.**
- Tell students that they are now in their Letter Expert groups and that they are going to become experts on their Special Letter's name, shape, and sound.

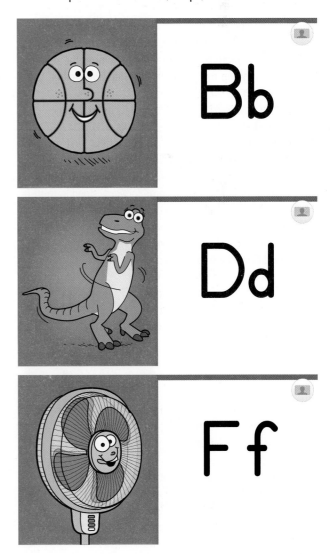

I Can Make Words

- Begin each lesson with a rehearsal of each group's letter name.
- Demonstrate how letters work by writing a word in large letters on the board.
- Tell students the experts for each letter in the word should hold up their *Letter Cards* and name the letter. One member of the group should stand in front of their letter on the board.
- Continue until all letters in the word are accounted for. Remember that you are responsible for the vowels.
- Demonstrate that you can make different words by changing a letter or by changing the letter order.

Identifying Sounds in Words

- Use the *Alphabet Sound Cards* to demonstrate that every letter has at least one sound.
- Give each student the *Alphabet Sound Card* for his or her Special Letter.
- Point out the pictures on the cards. Explain that each card has a picture of something that makes the letter's sound. The picture will help them remember the sound.
- Tell each group the sound for its letter. (Remember, you are the expert for the vowels.)
- Quickly have each group rehearse its letter's name and sound.
- Write a word on the board in large letters. First say the word sound by sound, and then blend the word.
- For each letter/sound in the word, have one student from each Letter Expert group come forward, stand in front of the appropriate letter, and hold his or her card. Although only one member of the group may come forward with the *Letter Card* or *Alphabet Sound Card,* all students in a Special Letter group should say the name or sound of their letter when it occurs in words.
- Say the word again, pointing to the *Alphabet Sound Cards.*
- Ask students who are not already standing to help you hold the vowel cards.
- Vary the activity by changing one letter sound and having an expert for that letter come forward.
- End the activity for each word by saying the sounds in the words one by one and then saying the entire word. Encourage students to participate.

Alphabet Sound Wall Card

Tips

- Remind students to use the picture on the *Alphabet Sound Card* for their Special Letter to help them remember the letter's sound. Students are expected to "master" only their own Special Letter and to share the information with their classmates. At this point in the year, they are not expected to blend and read the words by themselves. These are group activities in which you work with students to help them gain insight into the alphabet.
- Be sure to connect what students learn about the letters and words to the words they work with in *Big Book* selections.
- Occasionally, have students find their special letters in a *Big Book* selection. Play some of the letter replacement and rearrangement games with words encountered in the *Big Books.*

Alphabet Book

Pages 4–5

Developing the Alphabetic Principle

Purpose

The alphabetic principle is the understanding that speech sounds can be mapped onto print. It is the association of sounds with letters and the understanding that speech can be turned into print and print can be turned into speech sounds. Activities associated with the alphabetic principle help kindergarteners develop a more thorough understanding of how sounds "work" in words. In this group of activities, students are introduced to specific letter/sound correspondences, consonants, and short vowels. While students have previously been introduced to vowels and their special characteristics, students' understanding is extended by introducing students to the convention that a vowel has a short sound in addition to its long sound.

With this information and a carefully structured set of activities, students can begin to explore and understand the alphabetic principle in a straightforward and thorough manner. Students not only listen for sounds in specified positions in words; they also link sounds to their corresponding letters. The activities in this group of lessons lay the groundwork for students to work their way through the entire alphabet to learn letter-sound associations and understand how sounds and letters work.

Move students quickly through these activities. Do not wait for all students to master each letter/sound correspondence before going on. They will have more opportunities to achieve mastery. The goal of these activities is for students to obtain a basic understanding of the alphabetic principle.

Procedures

Use these activities to support the development of the alphabetic principle.

Introducing Consonant Letters and Sounds

- Point to the *Alphabet Sound Wall Card,* and ask students what they know about the card (the letter name, the capital and lowercase letter, and so on).
- Turn the card, and point to the picture. Name the picture, and point to and name the letter. Tell students the sound of the letter and how the picture helps them remember the sound. Repeat the sound several times.
- Tell students you will read the short story or an alliterative sentence to help them remember the sound of the letter. Read the story several times, emphasizing the words with the target sound. Have students join in and say the sound.
- After introducing and reviewing a letter/sound correspondence, summarize the information on the *Alphabet Sound Wall Card:* the name of the card, the sound, and the letter.

Generating Words with the Target Sound

Brainstorm to create a list of words that begin with the target sound. Write the words on the board or on a chart. Include any of the students' names that begin with the target sound.

Listening for Initial Sounds

- Give each student a *Letter Card* for the target sound.
- Point to the picture on the *Alphabet Sound Wall Card,* and have students give the sound.
- Tell students to listen for the first sound in each word you say. If it is the target sound, they should hold up their cards. Establish a signal so that students know when to respond.
- Read the list of words, some beginning with the target sound and some beginning with other sounds.

Listening for Final Sounds

The procedure for listening for the final sound of a word is the same as that for listening for the initial sound. Remind students throughout the activity to pay attention to the final sound.

Read a list of words, some ending with the target sound and some ending with other sounds. Avoid words that begin with the target sound.

Linking the Sound to the Letter

- **Word Pairs (initial sounds).** Display pairs of words on the board. One of each pair should begin with the target sound. Say the word beginning with the target sound, and ask students to identify it. Remind them to listen for the target sound at the beginning of the word, to think about which letter makes that sound, and to find the word that begins with that letter. For example,
Target sound: /s/
Word pair: *fit sit*
Which word is *sit?*
- **Word Pairs (final sounds).** Follow the same procedure used for initial sounds. Direct students to think about the sound they hear at the end of the word. As it is often more difficult for students to hear the ending sound, you may need to lead them through several pairs of words. Remind students to listen for the target sound and to think about which letter makes that sound.
- **Writing Letters.** Using either of the handwriting systems outlined in the Level Appendix or the system in use at your school, have students practice writing uppercase and lowercase letters. Remind students about the letter sound, and have them repeat it.

Comparing Initial Consonant Sounds

This activity is exactly like Listening for Initial Sounds except that students must discriminate between two sounds. They are given *Letter Cards* for both sounds and must hold up the appropriate card when they hear the sound.

Comparing Final Consonant Sounds

This activity is exactly like Listening for Final Sounds except that students must discriminate between two sounds. They are given **Letter Cards** for both sounds and must hold up the appropriate card when they hear the sound.

Linking the Consonant Sound to the Letter

In these activities students will link beginning and ending sounds and letters.

- **I'm Thinking of Something That Starts (Ends) with ___ Game.** Begin with the target sound, and add clues until students guess the word. If students give a word that does not begin with the target sound, emphasize the beginning sound, and ask if the word begins with the target sound.
- **Silly Sentences.** Make silly sentences with students that include many words with the target sound. Encourage students to participate by extending the sentences: Mary mopes. Mary mopes on Monday. Mary and Michael mope on Monday in Miami. For older students, have them make silly sentences using the sound at the beginning of their first name. Have them use the dictionary to find more words beginning or ending with the target sound.

Introducing Short-Vowel Sounds

Tell students that vowels are printed in red to remind them that they are special letters. (They are not special because they are printed in red.) They are special because they have more than one sound, and every word in English must have a vowel sound.

- Point to the long Aa **Alphabet Sound Wall Card,** and remind students that this letter is called a vowel. Tell them vowels sometimes say their names in words (for example, *say, day, tray).* When the vowel says its name, the sound is long. Tell them this vowel sound is called long *a.*
- Have students repeat the sound.
- Tell students sometimes vowels say different sounds. Point to the picture of the lamb on the short Aa card, and tell students that *a* also makes the sound heard in the middle of *lamb.* This is the short *a.* Read the short vowel story to help students remember the short *a.*
- Have all students join in saying/a/ /a/ /a/.

Listening for Short-Vowel Sounds Versus Long-Vowel Sounds

- Tell students that you will read words with long *a* and short *a.* Review the two sounds.

- Give students a signal to indicate when they hear the vowel sound. You may want one signal for short *a,* such as scrunching down, and another for long *a,* such as stretching up tall.
- Continue with lists of words such as *add, back, aid, tan, bake,* and *tame.*

Interactive Sound/Spelling Card

Linking the Vowel Sound to the Letter

- **Writing Letters.** Have students practice writing the letter and review the sound of the letter.
- In this activity, students will make words either by adding initial consonants to selected word parts or by adding a different final consonant to a consonant-vowel-consonant combination. Change the beginning of the word or the word ending, but retain the vowel sound to make new words:

Sound/Spelling Wall Card

at	hat	mat	pat
ap	map	tap	tan
am	Sam	Pam	ham

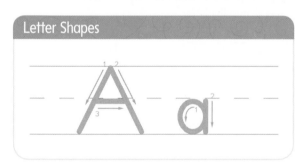

Letter Shapes

Comparing Short-Vowel Sounds

This activity requires students to discriminate between short-vowel sounds in the middle of words. Review the short-vowel sounds.

- Say a word, and have students repeat it. Establish a signal to indicate whether they hear short *a* or short *o* in the middle of the word. For example, they can hold up the appropriate **Alphabet Letter Card** when they hear a sound. Sample words: *cap, cot, rat, rot, rack,* and *rock.*

Linking the Sound to the Letter

- In this activity, write a word on the board, and help students say it.
- Change the word by changing the vowel. Help students say the new word, for example, *map, mop; hot, hat; pot, pat.*
- For a variation of this activity, write the pairs of words, and simply have students say which word is the target word. For example, students see *tap* and *top*. Ask which word *top* is, directing students' attention to the vowel.

Introducing Long-Vowel Sounds

The introduction of short vowels and consonants helps students internalize the alphabetic principle—a sound can be mapped onto a letter. In English, however, some sounds are represented by more than one letter, for example, the /ē/ can be represented by the letter *e* as in *me* but also represented by *e_e* as in *Pete.* Toward the end of kindergarten, students will be introduced to long vowels and two common representations of those sounds. These include the single vowel such as *a* or *e* and the vowel consonant silent *e* (VCe). The introduction of the VCe pattern or unit gives students a wide range of common words to read by the end of kindergarten and sets a solid foundation for first grade.

- If necessary, remind students that vowels are written in red. Point to the long *Aa* card, and tell students that the sound of long *a* is /ā/.
- Have students say the sound with you.
- Tell students that long *a* can be written in more than one way; it can be written as *a* just like short *a* but it can also be written as *a_e.* When we see the blank, it is a clue that another sound and letter needs to be put on the blank or line to make a word.
- Write a_e, and have students give the sound: /ā/. Then write a *t* on the blank, say the sound, and blend the word: *ate.*
- The goal is to have students see the *a_e* or any of the other VCe patterns as a unit.
- While students have been blending and reading short-vowel words, long vowels create a shift in thinking:

Combinations of letters can be used to represent a sound. Here are some easy tips when you are first working with the VCe patterns:

- The VCe patterns are not written on the **Alphabet Sound Cards.** You may want to write the *a_e, e_e, i_e, o_e,* and *u_e* units on the respective long-vowel cards as a reminder for students. Do this as you introduce each long vowel unit. Use an erasable marker so you can reintroduce these special patterns each year.
- Provide maximum support when first using the long-vowel units in blending.
- Write the letter for the first sound, for example, /m/, and have students give the sound.
- Write the unit for /ā/: *a_e.* Tell students this says /ā/. Be sure to write the whole unit.
- Write the final letter ON the blank, for example, *k.* Give the sound for the *k,* and then blend the word.
- Let students hear your voice during the blending, but gradually reduce it so they are doing more of the thinking.
- Help students blend long vowel words as they are reading their **Decodables.**

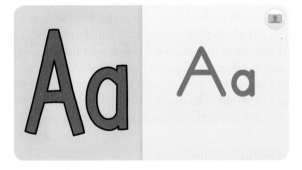

Tips

- Model and support the activities as necessary until students begin to catch on and can participate with confidence.
- To keep students focused on the various activities, have them tell you the task for each activity. For example, after telling students to listen for final sounds, ask students what they will be listening for.
- Actively involve students by giving them opportunities to tell what they know rather than supplying the information for them. *What is the letter name? What is the sound? What words begin with the sound?*
- Keeping students focused on the idea that they are learning about sounds and letters so they can read books themselves makes the lessons more relevant for students.

Introducing Sounds and Letters

Purpose

In *Open Court Reading* students learn to connect sounds to letters in kindergarten using thirty-one *Alphabet Sound Wall Cards.* The purpose of the *Alphabet Sound Wall Cards* is to connect the sounds of the English language with the letter or grapheme representing the sound. These cards are a resource for students to use to remember sound-letter associations for both reading and writing.

Alphabet Sound Wall Cards

Each card contains the capital and lowercase letter and a picture that can be used with or contains the target sound. For instance, the Sausage card introduces the /s/ sound and shows sausages sizzling in a pan. The sound the sausages make sizzling in the pan is /s/ /s/ /s/. The name of the picture on each card contains the target sound at the beginning of the word for the consonants and in the middle for the short vowels. Vowel letters are printed in red, and consonants are printed in black. In addition, the picture associates a sound with an action. This action-sound association is introduced through a short, interactive story found in the *Teacher's Edition,* in which the pictured object or character "makes" the sound of the letter. Long vowels are represented by a tall—or "elongated"— picture of the letters themselves. Short vowels have a green background, and long vowels have a yellow background.

> *The purpose of the Alphabet Sound Wall Cards is to remind students of the sounds of the English language and their letter correspondences.*

Posting the Alphabet Sound Wall Cards

- Display Cards I–26 with the picture sides to the wall. Initially post the first twenty-six cards in alphabetical order so that only the alphabet letters on the back show. When cards are posted this way, they are used early in the kindergarten year to learn the alphabet. As you introduce the sound of each letter, you will turn the card to show the picture and the letter on the other side. The short-vowel cards may be posted as they are introduced later. Because students will be referring to these cards for reading and writing, post them where all students can easily see them.

- Before turning a card, point to the letter. Ask students to tell what they know about the letter. For example, they are likely to know its name if the letter is one with which they have already worked. They might also note that there is an upper- and lowercase for the letter or that the letter is a consonant or a vowel.

- Turn the card, and point to the picture. Tell students the name of the picture (card), and explain that it will help them remember the sound the letter makes.

- Tell students the name and the sound of the letter.

- Read the story that goes with the card. Read it expressively, emphasizing the words with the target sound and the isolated sound when it occurs. Have students join in to produce the sound.

- Repeat the story a few times, encouraging all students to say the sound along with you.

- Repeat the name of the letter and the sound.

- Name each picture, and have students listen for the target sound at the beginning of the word. Ask students to repeat the word and the sound.

- Listening for the sound in different positions in words provides additional work with phonemic awareness. Give each student the letter card for the introduced sound and letter. Read the words from Listening for the Sound, and have students raise their letter card if they hear the target sound at the beginning of the word. For many letters, students will also listen for the sound at the end of words as well.

- To link the sound and the letter, demonstrate how to form the uppercase and lowercase letters by writing on the board or on an overhead transparency. Have students practice forming the letter and saying the sound as they write.

Activities

The pictures and letters on the *Alphabet Sound Wall Cards* also appear on the small sets of individual *Alphabet Sound Cards.* The *Teacher's Edition* specifically suggests that you use the individual *Alphabet Sound Cards* for Workshop and small-group activities for review, reteaching, and practice sessions. Place sets of the cards in the appropriate Workshop area for students to use alone or with partners. Add each small card to the Activity Center after you have taught the lesson in which the corresponding individual *Alphabet Sound*

Card is introduced. Here are some suggestions for activities using the individual *Alphabet Sound Cards:*

1. **Saying sounds from pictures.** The leader flashes pictures as the others say the sound each picture represents.
2. **Saying sounds.** The leader flashes the letters on the cards as the others say the sound that the letters represent.
3. **Naming words from pictures.** The leader flashes pictures. The others say the sound and then say a word beginning with that sound.
4. **Writing letters from the pictures.** Working alone, a student looks at a picture and then writes the letter for the sound that picture represents.
5. **Making words using the pictures.** A student uses the pictures (Sausages, Pig, Timer for *sit*) or the letters to make words.

Card 19: /s/ Sausages

Sue and Sammy had a nice place in the city. On Saturday, Sue and Sammy decided to have sausages for supper. Sammy put seven sausages in a skillet. /s/ /s/ /s/ /s/ /s/ /s/ /s/

Interactive Sound/Spelling Card

Soon the smell of sausages filled the air. /s/ /s/ /s/ /s/ /s/, sizzled the sausages.

"Pull up a seat, Sue," said Sammy. "The sausages are almost ready to serve." /s/ /s/ /s/ /s/ /s/, sizzled the sausages.

Sound/Spelling Wall Card

Sue and Sammy ate the delicious sausages. Soon they wanted more, so Sam put six more sausages in the frying pan. /s/ /s/ /s/ /s/ /s/ /s/, sizzled the sausages.

If you were cooking sausages with Sammy and Sue, what sound would the sausages make as they sizzled? *(Have the students join in:)* /s/ /s/ /s/ /s/ /s/ /s/

Card 20: /t/ Timer

When Tom Tuttle cooks, he uses his timer. Tom Tuttle's timer ticks like this: /t/ /t/ /t/ /t/ /t/ /t/

Interactive Sound/Spelling Card

Tonight Tom Tuttle wants tomatoes on toast. Tom turns on the oven. Tom puts tomatoes on toast in the oven. Tom sets the timer. The timer will ding when Tom's toast and tomatoes are done. Until the timer dings, it ticks: /t/ /t/ /t/ /t/ /t/ /t/.

Tomatoes on toast take ten minutes. /t/ /t/ /t/ /t/ /t/ /t/ Tom can hardly wait. /t/ /t/ /t/ /t/ /t/ /t/ He taps out the time: /t/ /t/ /t/ /t/ /t/ /t/.

What is the sound of Tom Tuttle's ticking timer? *(Have the students join in.)* /t/ /t/ /t/ /t/ /t/ /t/ Ding! Time for dinner, Tom Tuttle!

Sound/Spelling Wall Card

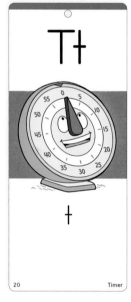

Card 9: /i/ Pig

Interactive Sound/Spelling Card

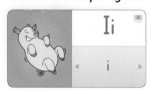

This is Pickles the Pig. If you tickle Pickles, she gets the giggles. This is the sound of her giggling: /i/ /i/ /i/ /i/ /i/.

Tickle Pickles the Pig under her chin. Listen! She's giggling: /i/ /i/ /i/ /i/ /i/. Wiggle a finger in Pickles' ribs. Listen! She's giggling: /i/ /i/ /i/ /i/ /i/.

Sound/Spelling Wall Card

Give Pickles the Pig a wink, and what do you think? First comes a grin. Then listen! She's giggling again: /i/ /i/ /i/ /i/ /i/.

Quick! Tickle Pickles the Pig. What will she say? *(Have the students join in.)* /i/ /i/ /i/ /i/ /i/

Tips

- Throughout the beginning lessons, help students remember that vowels are special by reminding them that vowels sometimes say their names in words. For example, tell them the picture of the *a* on the long *a* **Alphabet Sound Wall Card** is elongated, or tall, because the long *a* says its name. The short *a* **Alphabet Sound Wall Card** pictures the lamb because the lamb makes the short *a* sound, and you can hear the sound in the word *lamb*.
- Throughout the day, students should be encouraged to use the **Alphabet Sound Wall Cards** as a resource to help them with their reading and writing.
- Mastery of letter recognition is the goal students should reach so that they will be prepared to link each letter with its associated sound. If students have not yet mastered the names of the letters, it is important to work with them individually in Workshop, or at other times during the day.
- Both the *Cc* and the *Kk* cards have the same picture—a camera. A camera makes the /k/ sound when it clicks, and the word *camera* begins with the /k/ sound. However, the word *camera* is not spelled with a *k*. Remember, the first sound of the word helps students remember the sound of the letter.
- The picture on the *Qq* card depicts a quacking duck. Make sure that students consistently call it quacking duck, not duck, and that they focus on the /kw/ sound.
- When using *ePresentation* to introduce or review the **Alphabet Sound Wall Cards,** note that the alliterative story and the lively animation will help cement the letter and the sound in students' memory.
- Reinforce with students the letters of the alphabet as well as the sound associated with the letter by having them use the **Individual Alphabet Sound Cards** when working with students independently or in small groups.

Card 17: /kw/ Quacking duck

Quincy the Duck couldn't quite quack like all the other quacking ducks. Oh, he could say /kw/ /kw/ /kw/ /kw/, but it never seemed just right.

Interactive Sound/Spelling Card

When Quincy tried to quack quietly, his quack came out loudly. *(loudly)* /kw/ /kw/ /kw/ /kw/!

When he tried to quack slowly, his quack came out quickly. *(quickly)* /kw/ /kw/ /kw/ /kw/! Quincy just couldn't quack right!

One day Quincy was practicing quacks. His friend Quip quacked along with him. "Repeat after me," said Quip. *(quietly)* /kw/ /kw/ /kw/ /kw/ But Quincy quacked back, *(in normal voice)* /kw/ /kw/ /kw/ /kw/! Quincy still couldn't quack quite right.

Sound/Spelling Wall Card

But Quincy kept quacking. He said, "I won't quit until I quack like the best quackers around." Can you show Quincy how quacking ducks quack? *(Have the students join in.)* /kw/ /kw/ /kw/ /kw/ /kw/

Explicit, Systematic Phonics

The purpose of phonics instruction is to teach students the association between the sounds of the language and the written symbols—spellings—that have been chosen to represent those sounds.

As with all alphabetic languages, English has a limited number of symbols—twenty-six—that are combined and recombined to make the written language. These written symbols are a visual representation of the speech sounds we use to communicate. This is simply a code. The faster students learn the code and how it works, the faster the whole world of reading opens up to them.

Beginning at the kindergarten level, students are introduced to sounds and letters. Students learn that sounds can be mapped onto letters and that those sounds and letters can be blended to read words.

In Grade I, students make the shift from mapping sounds onto letters to mapping sounds onto spellings. Like the introduction of both sounds and letters in kindergarten, the sounds and spellings in Grade I are introduced sequentially and systematically. Each lesson builds on the previous ones. As each sound/symbol relationship is introduced, students learn about and practice with words containing the target sound and letter in kindergarten and sound/spelling in Grade I. This new knowledge is then reinforced through the use of engaging decodable stories specifically written for this purpose.

Learning the written code can be very difficult for some students. When phonics instruction is explicit—students are told the sounds associated with the different written symbols—there is no guesswork involved. They are taught that the sound /b/ is spelled *b*. This systematic, explicit approach affords students the very best chance for early and continuing reading success.

Sound/Spelling Wall Cards

See The Alphabetic Principle for information on the introduction of sounds and letters in pre-kindergarten and kindergarten.

Purpose

The purpose of the *Sound/Spelling Wall Cards* (Grades 1-3) is to help students connect the sounds in English to their spellings. The *Sound/Spelling Wall Cards* are also a reference tool that students should use throughout the day to help them as they read and write. The name of the picture on each card contains the target sound at the beginning of the name for consonants and in the middle for the short vowels. Long vowels are represented by elongated pictures of the vowel. The variant vowels such as /aw/ and /oi/ contain the vowel sound in the name as well. In addition, the picture associates a sound with an action. This association is introduced through an interactive story in which the pictured object or character "makes" the sound. This "action" cue is particularly helpful for students whose primary language is not English. In some cases, the name of the card and the initial sound may be similar to words in other languages. For example, the word for *lion* in Spanish is *león,* which begins with the same sound as the English word. This is not true for other languages. In Russian the word for *lion* is лев and in Japanese it is *raion.* The word for *zipper* in Spanish is *cremallera,* in Russian it is застежка-молния and in Japanese it is *jippa.* But all students can remember the action sounds and use them as a resource for both reading and writing.

> *The faster students learn the code and how it works, the faster the whole world of reading opens up to them.*

Posting the Cards

In Grade I, initially post the first twenty-six cards with the picture to the wall so that only the alphabet letters on the backs show. As you introduce each card, you will turn it to show the picture and the spellings on the front of the card. Some Grade I teachers who have students who are familiar with the cards from kindergarten choose to place the first twenty-six cards (the alphabet) with the pictures facing the class. Because students are familiar with the cards and how to use them, this provides support for writing. Even these first-grade teachers, however, cover the spellings not introduced in kindergarten. In second- or third-grade classrooms in which students are reviewing what they learned the year before, place all the cards with the pictures and the spellings facing forward so students can use these as a resource from the beginning of the school year. Make sure that the cards are positioned so that you can touch them with your hand or with a pointer when you refer to them and so that all students can see them easily. The cards should be placed where students can readily see and reference them throughout the day.

Special Features

Many *Sound/Spelling Wall Cards* contain special features that help students understand how our written language works.

- Vowel spellings are printed in red to draw attention to them. It is the vowels and their different spellings that challenge us all. Consonants are printed in black.
- The blank line in a spelling indicates that a spelling will take the place of the blank in a word. For example, the replacement of the blank with *t* in the spelling *a_e* makes the word *ate*. The blank lines may also indicate the position of a spelling in a word or a syllable. The blank in *h_*, for example, means that the sound /h/ spelled *h_* occurs at the beginning of a word or a syllable.
- The blanks in *_ie_* indicate that the *ie* spelling will not come at the beginning or the end of a word or a syllable as in *babies*, while the blank in *_oy* shows that the *oy* spelling comes at the end of a word or a syllable as in *toy*. Uses of blanks in specific spellings are discussed in the lessons. Please note that when you write or display a spelling of a sound on the board, you should include the blanks.
- The color of the background behind the spellings also helps students with reading and spelling. Consonants have a white background. The colors behind vowel spellings are pronunciation clues. Short-vowel spellings have a green background, which corresponds to the green box that appears before some consonant spellings. Thus, before *ck, tch, dge,* or *x,* there is a green box indicating that a short vowel always precedes that spelling. Long-vowel spellings have a yellow background; other vowel spellings such as *r*-controlled vowels, diphthongs, and variant vowels have a blue background. The color code reinforces the idea that vowels are special and have different pronunciations.
- The purple color bar across some of the cards indicate sounds or spellings that are transferable to Spanish. For example, /b/ spelled *b* and /d/ spelled *d* are both sounds and spelings that also appear in Spanish, and may be easier for English Learners whose first language is Spanish, since these appear in their native language.

Introducing the Sound/Spelling Wall Cards

In first grade, each sound and spelling is introduced by using a see/hear/say/write sequence. In Grades 2 and 3 the same sequence is used in the review of the cards.

1. *See:* Students see the spelling(s) on the *Sound/Spelling Wall Card* and the board or an overhead transparency.
2. *Hear:* Students hear the sound used in words and in isolation in the alliterative story. The sound is, of course, related to the picture (and the action) shown on the *Sound/Spelling Wall Card.*
3. *Say:* Students say the sound.
4. *Write:* Students write the spelling(s) for the sound.

Use the instructional routine for introducing the *Sound/Spelling Wall Cards.*

- Point to the back of the card, and ask students what they know.
- Take down the *Sound/Spelling Wall Card,* turn it, and tell the class the name of the card, the sound, and the spelling.
- Read the alliterative story so students hear the sound used in words as well as in isolation, and say the sound.
- After you present the sound and spelling, have several students go to the board to write the spelling. Have them say the sound as they write the spelling. After they have written the spelling of the sound, give them an opportunity to proofread their own work. Then give the other students the opportunity to help with proofreading by noting what is good about the spelling and then suggesting how to make it better.

Introducing the Sound /s/ spelled *s*

- Point to the back of *Sound/Spelling Wall Card* 19—Sausages, and have students tell you what they know about the card: it is a consonant and there is an upper and lowercase *s* on the card. Turn the card, and tell the class the name of the card: Sausages. Point to the sausages in the picture, and say the word *sausages,* emphasizing the initial consonant sound. Note: teachers often place a sticky note over the other spellings of /s/—*ce, ci_,* and *cy*—in order to help students focus on the single spelling being introduced in the lesson.

- Point to the spelling *s*. Tell students that /s/ is spelled *s*.

- Read the alliterative story, which appears in the Level Appendix of the *Teacher's Editions.* If your students in Grades 2–3 know the cards, have them tell you the name of the card, the sound, the spelling, and the story.

- Display or write *s* on the board, and say the sound. Write the spelling again and ask students to say the sound with you as they write the spelling on write-on boards, on paper, or with their index fingers in the air or in the palm of their hands. Repeat this activity several times.

- Have several students come to the board and write the upper- and lowercase spelling while the others continue to write them on paper or with their fingers. Be sure to encourage students to say the sound as they make the spelling. For students writing at the board, take time to have them proofread their work.

- Have students listen for words beginning with /s/, indicating by some signal, such as thumbs-up or thumbs-down, whether they hear the /s/ sound and saying /s/ when they hear it in a word. Repeat with the sound in various positions in words. Encourage students to tell you and the class words with /s/ at the beginning, as well as at the ends of words.

- Check students' learning by pointing to the card. Have students identify the sound, name the spelling, and discuss how the card can help them remember the sound.

Card 19: /s/ Sausages

Sue and Sammy had a nice place in the city. On Saturday, Sue and Sammy decided to have sausages for supper. Sammy put seven sausages in a skillet. /s/ /s/ /s/ /s/ /s/ /s/ /s/

Soon the smell of sausages filled the air. /s/ /s/ /s/ /s/ /s/, sizzled the sausages.

Interactive Sound/Spelling Card

"Pull up a seat, Sue," said Sammy. "The sausages are almost ready to serve." /s/ /s/ /s/ /s/ /s/, sizzled the sausages.

Sue and Sammy ate the delicious sausages. Soon they wanted more, so Sam put six more sausages in the frying pan. /s/ /s/ /s/ /s/ /s/ /s/, sizzled the sausages.

If you were cooking sausages with Sammy and Sue, what sound would the sausages make as they sizzled? *(Have the students join in:)* /s/ /s/ /s/ /s/ /s/ /s/

Remember that saying the sound, listening to the alliterative story, and listening for the sound (discriminating it from other sounds) in different positions in words are all phonemic awareness activities that have been integrated into phonics.

Sound/Spelling Wall Card

- Difficulty in blending may be the result of not knowing the sounds or not being able to pronounce the sounds. Teach the sounds thoroughly during the introduction of the *Sound/Spelling Wall Card* and during initial sounding and blending. To help ensure success for all students, make certain that every student is able to see the board or screen.

- If students had *Open Court Reading* before, you can ask them if they learned an action to help them remember the sound. If your students do not already have an action they associate with the sound, make some up with your students. They will have fun, and it will be another way for them to remember the sound/spelling relationships.

- If you are using *ePresentation* to introduce the sounds and spellings, note that you can click on the top of the card to see how the sound is formed. You may want to assign cards that pose difficulties to students so that they may watch watch the video and the Sound/Spelling animation at their own pace.

Individual Sound/Spelling Cards

You can use the individual **Sound/Spelling Cards** for review and for small-group preteaching, reteaching, or practice. Students can use them alone or with partners. Here are some suggestions for activities using the individual **Sound/Spelling Cards:**

1. **Saying sounds from pictures.** The leader flashes pictures as the others say the sound each picture represents.

2. **Saying sounds.** The leader flashes the spellings on the cards as the others say the sound that the spellings represent.

3. **Naming spellings from pictures.** The leader flashes pictures. The others name the card, say the sound, and then name as many spellings as they can.

4. **Writing spellings from the pictures.** Working alone, a student looks at a picture and then writes as many spellings for that **Sound/Spelling Card** as he or she can remember.

5. **Saying words from pictures.** The leader presents a series of individual cards, for example, Sausages, Lamb, Timer. The others tell the word by blending the sounds represented—*sat.*

Blending

Purpose

The purpose of blending is to teach students a strategy for figuring out how to read unfamiliar words. Initially students will be blending sound by sound as they learn how to blend. After they understand the process, they will move to whole-word blending and develop the strategy they will use to read unfamiliar words. Ultimately students will sound and blend only those words that they cannot read.

Procedure

Learning the sounds and their spellings is only the first step in learning to read and write. The second step is learning to blend the sounds into words to read them and segment words into sounds to spell them.

Sound-by-Sound Blending

Blending lines are written or displayed on the board as students watch and participate. The lines and sentences should not be written out before class begins. It is through the sound-by-sound blending of the words and the sentences that students learn the blending process. For example, the word students will be blending is *sat.*

- Write the spelling of the first sound in the word. Point to the spelling, and say the sound.

- Have students say the sound with you as you say the sound again. Write the spelling of the next sound. Point to the spelling, and say the sound. Have students say the sound with you as you say the sound again. After you have written the vowel spelling, blend through the vowel (unless the vowel is the first letter of the word), making the blending motion—a smooth sweeping of the hand beneath the sounds, linking them from left to right, for example, *sa.* As you make the blending motion, make sure that your hand is under the spelling that corresponds to the sound you are saying at the moment.

- Then, write the spelling of the next sound—*t.* Point to the spelling, and have students say the sound with you as you touch the spelling. If this is the last sound and spelling in the word, make the blending motion, and have students blend and read the word—*sat.* If this is not the final sound and spelling, continue pointing to the spelling and asking for the sound. For example, in the word *sand,* blend through the vowel, and ask for the sounds for the spellings *n* and *d* before blending the word. After pronouncing the final sound in the word, make the blending motion from left to right under the word as you blend the sounds. Then have students blend the word. Let them be the first to pronounce the word normally.

- Ask the class to read the word again naturally, as they would say or speak it. Then have a student use it in a sentence. Ask another student to extend the sentence, i.e., make it more interesting by giving more information. Help the student by asking an appropriate question about the sentence, using *How? When? Where?* or *Why?* Continue blending the rest of the words in the blending line. At the end of each line, have students reread the words naturally.

Whole-Word Blending

When students are comfortable with sound-by-sound blending, they are ready for whole-word blending.

- Write or display the whole word to be blended on the board.
- Ask students to blend the sounds as you point to each spelling. Unlike sound-by-sound blending, do not stop at the vowel.
- Then have students say the whole word.
- Ask students to use the word in a sentence and then to extend the sentence.
- After blending each line, have students read the words naturally, as they would say them.
- When all of the words have been blended, point to words randomly, and ask individuals to read them.

Blending			
Words			
1 zip	zap	buzz	jazz
2 up	crust	stuff	bug
3 quilt	quiz	van	vest
4 yap	yip	yams	yells

Blending Syllables

In reading, students often encounter multisyllabic words. Some students are intimidated by long words, yet many multisyllabic words are easily read by reading and blending the syllables. Beginning in first grade, students learn about different syllable *generalizations,* open and closed syllables, consonant *-le,* and the like. Students need to remember that each syllable in a word contains one vowel sound. Early in the process, you will need to provide support.

- Have students identify the vowel sounds and spellings in the word.
- Have students blend the first syllable sound by sound if necessary or read the first syllable.
- Handle the remaining syllables the same way.
- Have students blend the syllables together to read the word.

Blending Sentences

Blending sentences is the logical extension of blending words. Blending sentences helps students develop fluency, which is critical for comprehension. Encourage students to reread sentences with phrasing and natural intonation. Sentences are initially blended using the Sound-by-Sound Blending Routine and then the Whole Word Blending Routine.

Write or display the sentence on the board, underlining any high-frequency sight words—words that students cannot decode either because they are irregular or because they contain sounds or spellings that students have not yet learned or reviewed. High-frequency sight words are taught before blending. Write or display the word or words on the board, and introduce them before writing the sentence. Read the word, and have students repeat the word then spell the word. Use each word in a sentence. Point to the word or words, and have students read them again. Some of these words like *of* and *said* will always be nondecodable. Others like *on* and *is* become decodable after the sounds and spellings are taught.

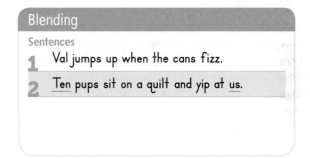

Blending	
Sentences	
1	Val jumps up when the cans fizz.
2	<u>Ten</u> pups sit on a quilt and yip at <u>us</u>.

Tips

- The goal of blending in first grade is not to have students blend words sound by sound for the whole year. Sound-by-sound instruction should begin with maximum instructional support—with teachers and students blending together. As students understand the sound-by-sound blending routine, drop the verbal cues (sound, sound, blend, sound, blend), and simply point to the spellings after they are written, and have the class give the sounds.
- How do you know when to move from sound-by-sound to whole-word blending? When you are writing the final spelling and students are reading the word, it is time to move on to whole-word blending. This often occurs around Unit 3 in first grade.
- Keep in mind, however, that when you introduce more complex long-vowel and variant-vowel spellings, you can always drop back to sound-by-sound blending for the first couple of blending lines in the lesson.

- Even though the entire class may be doing whole-word blending, sound-by-sound blending is an excellent preteaching tool for students needing extra help. After all the sounds and spellings have been introduced, students may be ready to just read the words in the blending lines. Have them read the words, stopping to blend only words they cannot read fluently and automatically.
- In Grades 2 and 3, teachers often begin the phonics review in the Getting Started lessons with sound-by-sound blending and then quickly move into whole-word blending. Again, the goal is to have students reading the words as quickly and automatically as possible. If the majority of the class can do this, then use whole-word blending. Use sound-by-sound blending to preteach the blending lines with students who need more support.

Building for Success

A primary cause of students' blending failure is their failure to understand how to use the *Sound/Spelling Cards.* Students need to practice sounds and spellings when the *Sound/Spelling Cards* are introduced and during initial blending. They also need to understand that if they are not sure of how to pronounce a spelling, they can check the cards. You may need to lead the group almost constantly. Soon, however, leaders in the group will take over. Watch to see which students are having trouble during blending. Include them in small-group instruction sessions. You may want to use the vowel-first procedure to reteach blending lines.

Extra Help

In working with small groups during Workshop, you may want to use some of the following suggestions to support students who need help with blending.

Vowel-First Blending

Vowel-first blending is an alternative to sound-by-sound and whole-word blending for students who need special help. Used in small-group sessions, this technique helps students who have difficulty with the other two types of blending focus on the most important part of each word—the vowels—and do only one thing at a time. These students are not expected to say a sound and blend it with another at virtually the same time. The steps to use in vowel-first blending follow:

1. On the board, write the vowel spelling in each of the words in the line.
   For a short vowel, the line may look like this: *a   a   a*
   For a long vowel, the line may look like this: *ee   ea   ea*
2. Point to the spelling as students say the sound it.
3. Begin blending around the vowels. In front of the first vowel spelling, add the spelling for the beginning sound

of the word. Make the blending motion, and have students blend through the vowel, adding a blank to indicate that the word is still incomplete. Repeat this procedure for each partial word in the line until the line looks like this:

ma__   sa__   pa__
see__   mea__   tea__

4. Have students blend the partial word again as you make the blending motion, and then add the spelling for the ending sound.
5. Make the blending motion, and have students blend the completed word—for example, *mat* or *seed.*
6. Ask a student to repeat the word and to use it in a sentence. Then have another student extend the sentence.
7. Repeat steps 4, 5, and 6 for each word in the line, which might look like this:

mat   sad   pan
seed   meat   team

Tips

- In the early lessons, blend with as much direction and dialogue as is necessary for success. Reduce your directions to a minimum as soon as possible. You have made good progress when you no longer have to say, "Sound—Sound—Blend," because students automatically sound and blend as you write.
- Blending is more than just reading words; it is an opportunity to build vocabulary and to develop oral language.
- Always ask students to use less familiar words in sentences and to extend the sentences. Sentence extension is a technique that can be applied to writing as well. Students will naturally extend sentences by adding phrases to the ends of sentences. Encourage them to add phrases at the beginning or the middle of sentences also.
- Use the vowel-first procedure in small-group preteaching or reteaching sessions with students who are having a lot of trouble with blending. Remember that you must adapt the blending lines in the lessons to the vowel-first method.
- The sight words in the sentences cannot be blended. Students must approach them as words to be memorized. If students have problems reading sight words, tell them the words.
- Cue marks written over the vowels may help students.
  - Straight line cue for long vowels
    EXAMPLES: āpe, mē, fīne, sō, ūse
  - Curved line cue for short vowels
    EXAMPLES: căt, pĕt, wĭn, hŏt, tŭg
  - Tent cue for variations of *a* and *o*
    EXAMPLES: âll, ôff
  - Dot cue for schwa sound with multisyllabic words
    EXAMPLES: saląd, planėt, pencil, wagȯn

Dictation and Spelling

The major reason for developing writing alongside reading is that reading and writing are complementary communicative processes. Decoding requires that students blend the phonemes together into familiar cohesive words. Spelling requires that students segment familiar words into separate phonemes. Both help students develop an understanding of how the alphabetic principle works.

Purpose

The purpose of dictation is to teach students to segment words into individual sounds and to spell words by connecting sounds to spellings. In addition, learning dictation provides students additional opportunities to reflect on the sounds they hear in words.

As students learn about sounds and spellings, they are learning the standard spellings that will enable others to read their writing. As students learn to encode (spell), they develop their visual automaticity for spelling words and hence increase their writing fluency. Reinforcing the association between sounds and spellings through dictation gives students a spelling strategy that leads to writing independently.

Dictation is an instructional experience; it is not a test. Students should be encouraged to ask for as much help as they need. The proofreading technique is an integral part of dictation. Students correct their own errors. During dictation walk around the room observing students and identifying those who may need reteaching. Provide reinforcement and feedback as well.

There are two kinds of dictation: Sounds-in-Sequence Dictation and Whole-Word Dictation. The two types differ mainly in the amount of help they give students in spelling the words. The instructions vary for each type.

Procedure

Sounds-in-Sequence Dictation

Sounds-in-Sequence Dictation gives students the opportunity to spell words sound by sound, left to right, checking the spelling of each sound as they write. (Many students write words as they think they hear and say the words, not as the words are actually pronounced or written.)

- Pronounce the first word to be spelled. Use the word in a sentence, and say the word again (word/sentence/word). Have students say the word.
- Tell students to think about the sounds they hear in the word. Ask, "What's the first sound in the word?"
- Have students say the sound.
- Point to the *Sound/Spelling Card,* and direct students to check the card. Ask what the spelling is. Students should say the spelling and then write it.
- Proceed in this manner until the word is complete.
- **Proofread.** You can write the word on the board as a model, or have a student do it. Check the work by referring to the *Sound/Spelling Cards.* If a word is misspelled, have students circle the word and write it correctly, either above the word or next to it.

Whole-Word Dictation

Whole-Word Dictation gives students the opportunity to practice this spelling strategy with less help from the teacher.

- Pronounce the word, use the word in a sentence, and then repeat the word (word/sentence/word). Have students repeat the word. Tell students to think about the word and each sound in the word. Remind students to check the *Sound/Spelling Cards* for spellings and to write the word.
- **Proofread.** Write or have a volunteer write the word on the board as a model. Check the word by referring to the *Sound/Spelling Cards.*

Dictation and Spelling		
Words		
1 bump	fuzz	vent
2 yes	cut	zest
3 quit	strum	yelp

Sentence Dictation

Writing dictated sentences helps students apply this spelling strategy to extend writing and supports the development of fluent and independent writing. Dictation of a sentence also helps students apply conventions of written language, such as capitalization and punctuation.

- Say the complete sentence aloud.
- Depending on the time of year, dictate one word at a time, following the routine for Sounds-in-Sequence or Whole-Word Dictation.

Continue this procedure for the rest of the words in the sentence. Remind students to put a punctuation mark at the end. Then proofread the sentence. When sentences contain sight words, the sight words should be dictated as whole words. Students should be encouraged to check the high-frequency sight words posted in the room if they are unsure how to spell them.

Proofreading

Whenever students write, whether at the board or on paper, they should proofread their work. Proofreading is important because it helps students learn by self-correction, and it gives them an immediate second opportunity for success. Students should proofread by circling—not by erasing—each error. After they circle an error, they should write the correction beside the circle. This type of correction allows you and students to see the error as well as the correct form. Students also can see what needs to be changed and how they have made their own work better.

You may want to have students use a colored pencil to circle and write in the correction. This will make it easier for them to see the changes. It is also the same skill students will use as they proofread their writing.

Proofreading Routine

- Write—or have a student write—the word or sentence on the board or on an overhead transparency.
- Have the other students tell what is good; for example, it is spelled correctly.
- Have students check their words and identify whether anything can be made better, the word needs to be spelled differently, or the handwriting needs to be improved.
- If there is a mistake, have the student circle it and write it correctly—make it better.

The Word Building Game (Grades K and 1)

The Word Building game gives students a chance to apply their segmentation abilities and to practice using the sounds and spellings they are learning. It lays the foundation for Dictation. The game is a fast-paced activity in which students spell related sets of words with the teacher's guidance. (Each successive word in the list differs from the previous one usually by one sound.)

For the Word Building game, students use their *Letter Cards* to build the words. (As an alternative they can use pencil and paper.) You will be writing at the board.

Give students the appropriate *Letter Cards.* For example, if the list for the Word Building game is *am, at,* and *mat,* they will need their *a, m,* and *t Letter Cards.*

- Say the first word, such as *am,* and use it in a sentence. Have students repeat the word. Ask students for the first sound in the word, and then check the *Sound/Spelling Cards* for the spelling. Touch the first sound's card, in this case the Lamb card, and have students say the sound. Continue the process with the second sound, and then write the word on the board. Have students compare their words with your word, make changes as needed, and then blend and read the word with you.
- Students will then change the first word to make a different word. Say the next word in the list, (at). Segment the sounds of the word, and have students find the *Letter Cards* that correspond. Write the new word (at) under the first word (am) on the board, and have students change their cards to spell the new word. Have them compare their words to yours and make changes as needed. Blend and read the word with students. Continue in a like manner through the word list.

Word Analysis

Purpose

As students move into the upper grades and encounter more complex and longer words, the understanding of morphology and the morphological units that make up words is important for fluent reading, vocabulary development, and comprehension.

Word Analysis activities support the development of fluency as students learn to identify and read meaningful chunks of words rather than individual spellings. Word Analysis also supports the development of vocabulary as students learn how inflectional endings change a word's tense, number, and so on and how affixes can be added to a base word to create or derive a new but related meaning.

Morphemes are the smallest units that have semantic meaning. Morphemes may be free or bound. A free morpheme can stand alone, such as the words *dog, man,* or *woman.* A bound morpheme, on the other hand, is a unit of meaning that must be combined with another morpheme to make a meaningful word. For example, in *rewrite* the prefix *re-* means "to do again", and in *dogs* the *-s* changes the meaning to plural. Both *re-* and *-s* are bound morphemes because they must combine with other words to create new words.

Learning about word structure helps the reader on several levels. Being able to identify key word parts not only helps with the pronunciation of longer, unfamiliar words but it also helps with meaning. In Word Analysis, students learn how to deconstruct words—to identify the base word or root of the word as well as the affixes attached to the word. When affixes occur at the beginning of a word, they are called *prefixes,* and when affixes occur at the end of a word, they are called *suffixes.* The prefix, base word, root, and suffix are all morphemes. They all contain units of meaning.

For example, in the word *restatement,* there are three morphemes: the prefix *re-,* the base *state* and the suffix *-ment.*

prefix	base	suffix
re-	*state*	*-ment*

Suffixes, in particular, can impact the base or root word in different ways. Suffixes such as *-s* and *-ed* can change the tense of a verb; suffixes such as *-s* can change the number of a noun to make it a plural. Derivational morphemes, in contrast, can be added to words to create or derive another word, for example the addition of *-ness* to the adjective *sad* creates the new noun *sadness,* or the addition of *-ly* changes the adjective *sad* to an adverb, *sadly.*

COMMON LATIN ROOTS	COMMON GREEK ROOTS
aud: *auditory, auditorium, inaudible, audible, audition*	**auto:** *automatic, autograph, autobiography, automobile*
dict: *dictate, predict, contradict, prediction*	**bio:** *biology, biography*
ject: *reject, inject, project, object, projection, objection*	**graph:** *graphite, geography, graphic, photograph, phonograph*
port: *transport, import, export, portable, support, report*	**hydr:** *hydrogen, hydrant*
rupt: *rupture, erupt, eruption, disrupt, interruption*	**meter:** *speedometer, odometer, thermometer, metronome*
scrib/script: *scribe, describe, manuscript, inscription, transcript, description, prescription*	**ology:** *geology, zoology, phonology*
spect: *spectator, inspect, inspector, respect, spectacle, spectacular*	**photo:** *photography, photocopy, photosynthesis, photogenic*
struct: *structure, construct, instruct, destruction, reconstruction*	**scope:** *telescope, stethoscope, microscope, microscopic, periscope*
tract: *tractor, traction, attract, subtraction, extract, retract, attractive*	**tele:** *telephone, television, telegraph*
vis: *vision, visual, visit, supervisor, invisible, vista, visualize, visionary*	**therm:** *thermos, thermostat*

Word analysis includes the study of the following:

- **Compound words** are made of two words that combine to form a new word. Compounds can be open or closed.
- **Base words and roots** focus on learning about the basic element of words. Base words and roots are the foundations upon which the meaning of a word is formed. A base may be a real word as in *audio,* meaning "sound," but it can also be used with a suffix to become *audible,* changing the noun to an adjective. Although *audible* can have other elements, it does not need other elements to be complete. Most roots, however, do need other elements. Roots such as *duct, anthrop,* and *cred* require affixes to form the words *deduct, anthropology,* and *incredible,* respectively. Knowledge of root words and affixes provides students with critical tools for understanding derived words.
- **Prefixes** include any morpheme that is attached to the beginning of a root or a base word and changes the meaning of that word. Prefixes do not change the form of the word, only the meaning. Common prefixes include: *con-, com-, ad-, de-, di-, dis-, per-, re-, sub-, hyper-, un-,* and so on as well as numbers (*bi-, tri-, uni-, mono-, octo-,* and so on).
- **Suffixes** include any morpheme that is attached to the end of a base word or root and that changes the meaning of that word. Suffixes often change the function or part of speech of the word and often require a spelling change in the base word or root as well. For example, the addition of *-ial* to *colony* changes a noun to an adjective.

Other examples of suffixes that change the word form include the following:

- Noun suffixes: *-age, -al, -ance, -ant, -ate, -ee, -ence, -ent, -er, -or, -ar, -ese, -ess, -hood, -ice, -ism, -ist, -ment, -ness, -sion, -tain, -tion, -ure*
- Suffixes that form adjectives: *-able, -al, -er, -est, -ette, -let, -ful, -fully, -ible, -ic, -ical, -ish, -ive, -less, -ous, -some, -worthy*
- Suffixes that form adverbs: *-ly, -wards, -ways, -wide, -wise*
- Suffixes that create verb forms: *-ate, -ed, -en, -ing, -ise, -ize, -yze*
- Inflectional endings are a special set of suffixes that change the number (singular to plural), case, or gender when added to nouns and change tense when added to verbs.

Teaching Word Analysis

- Have students read the words in a line. Note that sometimes students are intimidated by longer words. Understanding syllable breaks helps when reading these longer words. The chart on the preceding page includes information on syllable "generalizations." These may help students when reading longer words during Word Analysis activities and in the reading of the selections.
- Explain that words can be made of several individual parts.
- Examine the words in each line for meaningful parts, base words, roots, and affixes.
- Identify the root or base word, and discuss the meaning.
- Underline and discuss the meaning of the prefix or suffix or both. If there is a prefix and a suffix, begin with the prefix. Tell students a prefix is a group of letters that is attached to the beginning of a base or root word. These letters have a specific meaning. For example, *un-* means "not" or "the opposite of," *non-* means "not," and *re-* means "again." A suffix is a group of letters that comes at the end of the base word or root and changes the meaning of the word. For example, *-er* changes a verb to a noun or the person doing the action as in *sing* and *singer,* or *-al* or *-ial* change nouns to adjectives as in *colony* and *colonial.*
- Reassemble the word, thinking about the meaning of the word parts.
- Say the word.
- Use the word in a sentence.
- In addition to working with roots and base words and affixes, Word Analysis lessons also focus on compound words, synonyms, homonyms, and homophones.

Decoding

Words

1	acceptable	respectable	forgettable	huggable
2	erasable	valuable	movable	adorable
3	reality	similarity	curiosity	generosity
4	rarity	creativity	activity	sincerity

WORD	BREAK INTO SYLLABLES	SYLLABLE GENERALIZATIONS
puppet	pup-pet	Closed. If a word has two consonants in the middle, divide the word between the two consonants. The first syllable is closed, and the vowel pronunciation is short.
music	mu-sic	Open. If a word has a VCV pattern, break the syllables before the consonant, which makes the first syllable an open syllable and the first vowel long.
closet	clos-et	Some VCV patterns have the break after the consonant, which makes the first syllable a closed syllable and the vowel pronunciation short.
hundred	hun-dred	When there is a VCCCV pattern, the break is usually between the consonants. The first syllable is closed, and the vowel pronunciation is short.
coward	cow-ard	When there are two diphthongs, the syllable break comes between them.
chaos	cha-os	When there is a VV pattern, the syllable break comes between the vowels, and the first vowel is usually long.
handle	han-dle	Consonant plus -le. If a word has an -le (or -el) at the end, it usually forms a separate syllable and is pronounced with the consonant and /ə/ /l/.
excitement reform	ex-cite-ment re-form	Prefixes and suffixes are separate syllables.
entertain hurdle	en-ter-tain hur-dle	R-controlled vowels. In most syllables where the vowel is followed by an r, the vowel sound is r-controlled.
complete	com-plete	Final e. When there is a vowel, consonant, and then an e at the end, the vowel before the consonant is pronounced long, and the e is silent.

Connecting Word Analysis to Vocabulary

For students to develop a deeper understanding of words, they should have multiple experiences with them. There are any number of activities that students can do to help them use words and internalize their meanings. The following activities can be used with the whole class or in small groups during Workshop.

- Give a word, and ask the student to find it in the line and to give a definition.

- Give a word, and ask the student to add a prefix or a suffix and to tell the meaning of the new word and the new part of speech.

- If the word is a multiple-meaning word, have the student point to the word, and then have the student give one meaning and use it in a sentence. Then have a second student give another meaning and use it in a sentence. (Be sure that the words that are used are truly multiple-meaning words and not words that can be used as different parts of speech, for example, a verb and a noun that have the same basic meaning.)

- Give two words, and have the student point to them. Ask what is the difference between these two words. For example, *hot* and *cold* are antonyms. The same could be done for synonyms, homonyms, and homophones. This gets students to use the vocabulary and do the thinking. Point to two words, and have students tell how they are alike and different. For example, *history, historical,* and *historian* all have the same root. All three words have a common root, but *history* and *historian* are nouns, and *historical* is an adjective.

- Give students a word, and have them point to the word. If it is a singular noun, have them change it to a plural or vice versa. If it is a verb, have students change the tense, or if it is an adjective, change it into an adverb if appropriate. In all cases, be sure that students spell the new word.

- Give students a word, have them point to and read the word, and then give the part of speech.

- Have small groups of students play a game with the Word Part Cubes. Divide teams into 2-3 students, and have them roll a prefix cube, a base word or root cube, and a sufix cube. See how many words, if any students can come up with. Make the game more challenging by having students roll more than one cube from each category.

- Give a student a word, and have him or her use the word in a sentence. Have the class decide if the sentence truly shows the meaning of the word. For example, if the word is *camouflage,* and the student says, "Animals use camouflage," have the class add to the sentence to show the meaning: "Animals use camouflage to protect themselves from predators."

- Give students a word with a base word, and ask them to point to the word and read it and then to tell the root of the word.

- Give students a word with a Greek or Latin root. Have them point to and read the word, and then have them identify the root. Challenge students to think of other words that have the same root.

- Give students a word with a prefix or suffix. Have a student point to and read the word and then identify the prefix or suffix and tell the meaning of the affix. Then, if appropriate, have the student or a different student replace the affix with a different one and tell the meaning of the new word.

- When appropriate, give students a word, and have them give a synonym or antonym. When appropriate, work on gradations of words. For example, if the word is *hot* then the opposite is *cold.* Gradations would be *hot, warm, tepid, cool, cold.* These kinds of activities expand vocabulary.

- Give two words that are connected in some way, for example, *colony* and *colonial.* Have students come to the board, point to the words, and read them. Then have them tell why or how the words are connected.

- Have students find other words that follow comparable patterns to those taught in the lesson. If *colony, colonial, colonist* is a line in Word Analysis, many students could find related nouns and use them with affixes (*history, historical, historian).* Challenge students to think more about words.

Tips

- Be sure students understand the limits of structural analysis. The *un-* in *unhappy* is a prefix, but the *un* in *under* and *uncle* is not.

- Help students realize that many words are related and that using their knowledge of a word can help them understand related words.

- Encourage students to use their knowledge of word structure during all reading to clarify unfamiliar words.

Developing Oral Language			
Words			
1 careful	thankful	cheerful	colorful
2 delightful	thoughtful	beautiful	merciful
3 endless	worthless	flawless	fearless
4 powerless	speechless	penniless	merciless

Fluency

Fluency is the ability to read or access words effortlessly with seemingly little attention to decoding. Fluent readers decode words not only automatically but accurately. In addition, fluent readers group words into meaningful units, utilize punctuation to guide their voices, and use expression appropriately to help them comprehend what they are reading. Fluent readers also adjust their reading rate as necessary.

To become proficient readers who fully understand what they read, the entire process of decoding must become automatic. Readers need to be so familiar with the sound/spellings, with common meaningful units like prefixes and suffixes, and with the most common nondecodable sight words that they automatically process the spellings and word chunks. This enables them to read words effortlessly and expend most of their energy on comprehending the meaning of the text.

> ### *Automaticity is a key component of fluency.*

The concept of fluency is introduced in the early grades, even before students are reading. When reading aloud, teachers are modeling fluency and using expression and intonation to support meaning. In kindergarten, emergent readers learn about concepts of print that support fluency: learning about spaces and ending punctuation, reading from left to right, and automatically recognizing high-frequency sight words. Students apply this knowledge to reading *Pre-Decodables.*

As students learn to connect sounds to letters and spellings, they begin reading *Decodables,* which help build automaticity and accuracy. While fluency begins in kindergarten and first grade, many students continue to need practice in building fluency in second and third grades. Initially students can use the *Decodable Stories* in Grades K–3, but fluency practice should include materials from a variety of different sources, including selections from the *First Readers* in Grades K and I as well as the *Student Anthologies* in Grades I–3.

At all grade levels using *Pre-Decodables, Decodables, First Readers, Student Anthologies,* or any other materials, students need to appreciate that fluency is about meaning. Take time to ask questions after students have read, talk about new and interesting words, and discuss any problems students encountered.

Building Fluency: Reading Pre-Decodables (K–1)

Purpose

Pre-Decodables play an important role in students' early literacy development by providing them with meaningful "reading" experiences and expanding their awareness of the forms and uses of print. By following along as you read aloud a *Pre-Decodable,* students learn about the left-to-right and top-to-bottom progression of print on a page, the clues that indicate the beginnings and endings of sentences, the connections between pictures and words, and important book conventions such as front and back covers, authors' and illustrators' names, title pages, and page numbers.

The *Pre-Decodables* provide students with opportunities to apply their growing knowledge of letter names, shapes, and sounds and to become familiar with individual words. In addition, students practice reading high-frequency sight words. The automatic recognition of these words, the identification of ending punctuation, and reading with expression support the development of foundational fluency skills.

Through retelling the story in a *Pre-Decodable,* predicting or wondering about what will happen, and asking and responding to questions about the book, students not only learn about the relationship between spoken and written language, they learn to think about what they are reading.

About the Pre-Decodables

Each *Pre-Decodable* contains a story that engages students' interest as it provides them with opportunities to practice what they are learning in their lessons. These "pre-decodable" stories each contain several high-frequency words that most students already have in their spoken vocabularies and that are a basic part of all meaningful stories. Learning to identify high-frequency words quickly, accurately, and effortlessly is a critical part of students' development as fluent, independent readers. The inside back cover of each *Pre-Decodable* contains a cumulative list of all high-frequency words previously introduced.

Pre-Decodable Routine

- Before reading a *Pre-Decodable,* take time to familiarize students with any new high-frequency words in the book and to review previously introduced words. To reinforce the idea that it is important to know these words because they are used so often in print, always point out the words in context. For example, focus students' attention on the words in *Big Book* selections or on signs and posters around the classroom.

- Give each student a copy of the book. Tell students that you will read the book together. Hold up your book. Read the title. If the title has a rebus picture, point to it, and tell students what it is. Then point to the word beneath it, and explain that the picture represents that word. Point to and read the names of the author and illustrator, reminding students that an author writes a book, and an illustrator draws the pictures. Page through the book, pointing to and naming the rebus pictures. Have students say the name of each rebus. To avoid confusion, always tell them the exact word that a rebus represents. Do not encourage them to guess at its meaning.

- Give students time to browse through the book on their own, commenting on what they see in the illustrations and making predictions about what they think the book will be about. Encourage them to comment on anything special they notice about the story, the illustrations, or the words in the book.

- Help students find page 3. Read the book aloud without stopping. As you read, move your hand beneath the words to show the progression of print. Pause at each rebus as you say the word it represents, pointing first to the rebus then to the word beneath it.

- Reread the book. This time, ask students to point to and read the high-frequency words.

- Tell students to follow along in their books as you read the story again. Read the title aloud, and then have students read it with you. Reread page 3. Point to each rebus picture, and ask a volunteer to "read" it. Point to the word beneath the picture, and remind students that the picture shows what the word is. Continue through each page of the book, calling on volunteers to "read" and stopping as necessary to clarify and help students with words.

- After reading, answer any questions students might have about the book. Encourage them to discuss the illustrations and to explain what is happening in each one.

Building Fluency: Reading Decodables (K–3)

Purpose

The most urgent task of early reading instruction is to make written thoughts intelligible to students. This requires a balanced approach that includes systematic instruction in phonics as well as experiences with authentic literature. Thus, from the very beginning, *Open Court Reading* includes the reading of literature. At the beginning of first grade, when students are learning phonics and blending as a tool to access words, the teacher reads aloud. During this time students are working on using comprehension strategies and skills and discussing stories. As students learn to decode and blend words, recognize critical sight words, and develop some level of fluency, they take more responsibility for the actual reading of the text.

This program has a systematic instruction in phonics that allows students to begin reading independently. You may want to refer to pages 42-50 to review this instruction, which is supported by the *Open Court Reading Decodables.*

About the Decodables

The *Open Court Reading Decodables* are designed to help students apply, review, and reinforce their expanding knowledge of sound/spelling correspondences. Each story supports instruction in new phonic elements and incorporates elements and words that have been learned earlier. There are eight-page and sixteen-page *Decodables.* Grade K has eight-page *Decodables.* In Grade I, the eight-page books focus on the new element introduced in the lesson, while the sixteen-page books review and reinforce the elements that have been taught since the last sixteen-page book. They review sounds from several lessons and provide additional reading practice. Grades 2–3 have eight-page *Decodable Stories* in Getting Started, and eight- and sixteen-page stories in Units I–3 in Grade 3 and Units I–6 in Grade 2.

The primary purpose of *Decodables* is to provide practice reading the words with the target sound or sounds, which is why both a Core Set and a Practice Set of *Decodables* is available for each grade. It is important that students also attach meaning to what they are reading. Questions are included in the *Teacher's Edition* to check both understanding and attention to words.

Decodable Routine

Preparing to Read

- Introduce and write or display on the board any high-frequency sight words or story words introduced or reviewed in the story. Tell students how to pronounce any new high-frequency words. Then point to each new word, and have students spell and say it. Have them read any previously introduced sight words in the Word Bank list. All the *Open Court Reading Decodables* contain high-frequency words that may not be decodable. For example, the word *said* is a common high-frequency word that is not decodable. Including words such as *said* makes the language of the story flow smoothly and naturally. Students need to be able to recognize and read these words quickly and smoothly.

- Read the title. At the beginning of the year, you may need to read the title of the book to students, but as the year goes on, you should have a student read it whenever possible.

- Browse the story. Have students look through the story, commenting on whatever they notice in the text or illustrations and telling what they think the story will tell them.

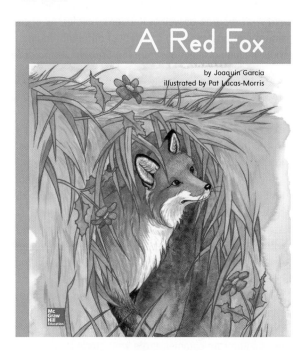

Reading the Story

After browsing, students will read the story a page at a time. These stories are designed to support the application of sound and spelling knowledge. Students should also understand what they are reading, and they should feel free to discuss anything

in the story that interests them. Any areas of confusion are discussed and clarified as they arise, as described below.

- Have students read a page to themselves. Then call on one student, groups of students, or the class to read the page aloud.

- If a student has difficulty with a word that can be blended, help her or him blend the word. Remind the student to check the *Sound/Spelling Cards* for help. If a word is not decodable or cannot be blended using the sound/spellings learned so far, pronounce the word for the student.

- If a student has trouble with a word or sentence, have the reader call on a classmate for help and then continue reading after the word or sentence has been clarified. After something on a page has been clarified or discussed, have a different student reread that page before moving on to the next page.

- Repeat this procedure for each page.

- Reread the story twice more, calling on various students to read or reading it in unison. These readings should go more quickly, with fewer stops for clarification.

Responding to the Story

After the story has been read aloud a couple of times, have students respond as follows:

- Ask students which words are difficult and how they figured them out. They may mention high-frequency words they did not recognize, words they had to blend, or words whose meanings they did not know.

- Have students retell the story in their own words, describe what they liked about it, or tell what they found interesting or surprising.

- Questions are provided in the *Teacher's Edition.* These questions are designed to focus students' attention on the words and not just the pictures. Ask students the questions, and have all students point to the answer in the story rather than having one student respond orally. Having students point to the answers is important. First, it ensures that all students are engaged in finding the answer, not just one. Second, by pointing to the answer, you know that students know the answer from reading and not just from having heard it read. Third, locating information in a text is an important skill. Finally, by pointing to the answer, you can quickly monitor who is understanding the story and who may still need more support during Workshop.

- Have students reread the story with partners. Circulate among the pairs, listening to individual students read. This allows you to monitor students' reading and to identify any students who may need additional help during Workshop.

Building Fluency beyond Decodables

For some students, fluency develops naturally, seemingly without instruction. Other students, however, benefit from more explicit instruction. There are students who can decode and read words but lack the critical phrasing, intonation, and expression that support meaning. Teach the text characteristics that support fluency, model them for students, and then provide students regular opportunities to practice fluency. Instruction can focus on any or all of the following areas:

- Discuss and model ending punctuation and what this means in terms of expression and intonation. This should be modeled and then discussed with students. Begin with ending punctuation, and then move to internal punctuation such as commas and semicolons. During modeling,
  - pause longer at a period or other ending punctuation.
  - raise your voice at a question mark.
  - use expression when you come to an exclamation point.
  - pause at commas or other internal punctuation such as semicolons.
  - when you come to quotation marks, think of the character and how he or she might say his or her words.
  - pause at an ellipsis.
  - pause at dashes.

- Discuss and model words written in a special way—typographical signals such as underlined words, boldfaced words, or those in all caps—need to be read with expression and changed in intonation for emphasis.
- Talk about reading rate. Oral reading should be done at a normal speaking rate. Students should not be reading so fast that someone listening could not hear the individual words and make sense of what is being read.
- Discuss and model intonation. Let students hear how voices change with different ending punctuation, how voices change when reading dialogue, and how intonation changes with cues from the author. In dialogue, think of the difference between "screamed Jennifer" versus "pleaded Jessie."
- Work on phrase cue boundaries. A good way to teach this is by using an overhead of what students are reading. Mark natural phrase boundaries—for example, clauses, prepositional phrases, subject phrases, verb phrases, and so on, with slashes. For example, *In the summertime,/Josh likes to play baseball/ at the park/down the street from his house.* Have students listen to you read the text,

noticing how you paused at the markers. Then have students read the sentences naturally, using the markers as guides. Scaffold the instruction. In the beginning, mark the boundaries, and have students practice reading using the already marked passages. As students become comfortable, have them mark what they are reading with boundary markers. Gradually fade out the markers or slashes.

Fluency instructions is built into every lesson in **Open Court Reading** and is available daily. Fluency develops over time, and students should be given repeated opportunities to practice fluency with a variety of different texts. After students have read a text, take time to go back and discuss any new vocabulary or interesting words that students encountered.

> ## Fluency is not an isolated activity; it supports comprehension.

There are a number of techniques for practicing fluency: repeated readings, partner reading, listening to recordings of the readings available for the **Decodables, First Readers,** and **Student Anthologies**, as well as Reader's Theater. All of these techniques can be done with a variety of different reading materials, including selections from the **Student Anthologies,** or other reading materials.

- Repeated readings increase reading rate, accuracy, and comprehension by providing students with multiple exposures to words and spelling patterns. In addition, it helps students improve their ability to break sentences into meaningful phrases and to use intonation. It is effective with both older and younger students. Repeated readings involve the students reading segments of text between 50 to 200 words, depending upon students' ability. Students should practice repeated readings with a variety of different text types. While repeated readings can be done with materials from **Open Court Reading,** using segments from science and social studies texts helps students in the upper grades apply their reading knowledge across the curriculum. The goal is to have students read the text fluently and automatically at a per-minute rate commensurate with grade-level norms.
- Recorded readings help build confidence and are excellent support for English Learners. The recordings allow students to hear good models of reading from a variety of text types and to develop their awareness of phrasing and prosody, or expressive reading. Students read along with the text, aloud or subvocalizing. When the student is comfortable with the text, the student

Fluency

Accuracy

REMIND students that accuracy means reading without mistakes. Accurate reading is necessary for full comprehension of a text.

Model reading page 240 of "All about Earthquakes!" with accuracy. Demonstrate pausing at a potentially unfamiliar word, such as *skyscrapers*, and sounding it out, then rereading the entire sentence accurately.

Have students take turns reading the page several times with a partner. Tell them the more they read, the more their accuracy will improve.

Inquiry

Step 4—Revise Conjectures

COLLECT MORE INFORMATION Display for students the most current version of your conjecture. If your research led you to change it, review the reasons for the revision. Remind them that once they revise a conjecture, they will usually do more research and continue exploring.

Say, *If, for example, our conjecture is* Scientists are working on ways to stop some earthquakes, *we might want to see if we can find any other current research about stopping earthquakes. Since our previous research had information about a study done in 2014, we might want to focus on only looking at information from that year and later. In this instance, the Internet might be the best place to find information, as many books would be out of date.*

Due to the potentially scientific nature of this unit's Inquiry research, suggest as well to students the possibility of making their own scientific observations related to the class conjecture, and recording those observations as a way to recall information from the experience. As students utilize any technical texts in their research, scaffold for them as needed if the texts are at the high end of their reading abilities.

Discuss the best places to find the right types of information for your class conjecture, depending on how your conjecture has changed.

Teacher Tip

INQUIRY During Workshop, have students meet in their small groups to work on their Inquiry activities.

All about Earthquakes!

DAY 3 LESSON 4

ePresentation

Fluency

People want to be safe from tsunamis and earthquakes, so scientists closely watch plate movements and monitor vibrations. This helps scientists warn people of dangers. Buildings and other structures are safer now too. Tall skyscrapers sway during earthquakes instead of falling down. Bridges bend and bridge towers absorb earthquakes' energy.

Scientists use special tools to study earthquakes.

240

Unit 2 • Lesson 4 • Day 3   T239

should practice reading the text independently and then read a portion of it to the teacher. The recordings available digitally in ***Open Court Reading*** can help students develop fluency with selections in the ***Student Anthologies.***

- Reader's Theater legitimizes practicing fluency because it involves reading a script. While students do not memorize the script the way actors do in a play, they must be able to read the script fluently so the audience—the rest of the class—can enjoy the play. Several students can work together on a single play or playlet. They will need to practice reading the script several times before presenting it to the class. Reader's Theater also provides students with a writing opportunity. Using a selection from their ***Student Anthologies,*** students can write a playlet, and then practice it for Reader's Theater.

- Radio Reading, like Reader's Theater, connects reading aloud to real-life situations. Students, with copies of the text, read aloud in front of the class as if they were news broadcasters. Informational text works particularly well for this. Students can practice, and then once a week, several students can be the radio announcers. Students can also write weekly news reports and read them.

- Partner Reading involves students reading with a partner. They can take turns reading pages or the entire selection. While one student reads, the listening-partner should note misread words and then discuss them with the partner after the reading. If the pairs are reading for one-minute-fluency checks, the nonreading partner can be responsible for timing the reading. Selections should be read multiple times with the goal being that students achieve a higher fluency rate on successive readings.

Assessing Fluency

Fluency should be assessed periodically to determine students' growth and to monitor progress. Listening to students read regularly is key. Fluency assessment should include not just reading rate but decoding accuracy, prosody (phrasing and intonation), and expression. In addition, checks should be done using various text types.

Generally accepted procedures for assessment include the following:

- Use a passage of approximately 250 words at the student's reading level. In the first half of first grade, use the appropriate ***Decodable*** in the Practice set. Have two copies—one for the student to read and one for you to mark.

- Have the student read the passage for one minute. Use a timer, if possible, so you do not have to keep watching a stopwatch or the minute hand on a clock. You can also record the reading. The goal is to have students read the text aloud in a natural way, the way they would speak the words. This is not a race! Use the following scoring conventions. Mark any errors made by the reader.

Descriptive Statistics for Oral Reading Fluency by Season for Grades 1–3 (Medians)

		Fall	Winter	Spring
Grade	Percentile	WCPM[1]	WCPM	WCPM
1	90		81	111
	75		47	82
	50		23	53
	25		12	28
	10			
2	90	106	125	142
	75	79	100	117
	50	51	72	89
	25	25	42	61
	10	11	18	31
3	90	128	146	162
	75	99	120	137
	50	71	92	107
	25	44	62	78
	10	21	36	48

[1]WCPM = words correct per minute

SOURCE
From "Curriculum-Based Oral Reading Fluency Norms for Students in Grades 1 Through 6" (2005) by Jan E. Hasbrouck and Gerald Tindal. *Behavioral Research and Teaching.*

- Draw a line through any misread word, and count it as an error.
- Circle any words the student omits or refuses to read, and count them as errors.
- Indicate with a caret any extra words the student inserts.
- Draw an arrow between words the student reverses, and count as one error.
- Put two check marks above a word that a student repeats, but do not count it as an error.
- Draw a box around the last word a student reads in the one-minute time frame.

To calculate the student's accuracy rate, count the total number of words read in one minute. Subtract the number of errors from the total number of words read, and use that number to find the number of correct words read per minute.

For example, to calculate the rate:
Total words read – errors = words correct per minute
75 words read – 10 errors = 65 words per minute

For example, to calculate the accuracy:
Number of words ÷ the total number of words = percent of accuracy
145 (words correct) ÷ 156 (total number of words) = 93%

In addition, watch for and note the following:

- Expression
- Ability of the reader to read words in natural syntactic clusters

Assessing accuracy, pace or rate, and expression provides information for instruction.

In addition to the qualitative information, some teachers like to use rubrics in their evaluation of fluency.

- **Level 1:** Reads basically word by word. Reading is labored with difficulty in reading words automatically and fluently. There is little expression. Words are sounded out.
- **Level 2:** Reads in limited phrases of two words, but grouping of words is not natural. There is still some word-by-word reading. There is little or no appropriate expression or intonation.
- **Level 3:** Reads in phrases with most having appropriate breaks. There is attention to punctuation and syntax. Much of the reading has appropriate expression and intonation.
- **Level 4:** Reads in larger meaningful chunks. Reads with appropriate phrasing, intonation, and expression. Reader demonstrates understanding of the piece.

Interpreting Fluency Data

First compare the student's number of correct words per minute with accepted fluency norms.

Then examine the student's accuracy percentage. Reading accuracy should remain constant or gradually increase within and between grades until it stabilizes at 90 percent or higher. Compare the student's accuracy percentage after each assessment to ensure that his or her accuracy percentage is holding constant or improving.

Next examine the types of errors the student made, and consider what they mean for instruction.

- Inserting extra words suggests that the student understands what is being read but is reading perhaps impulsively or carelessly.
- Refusing to attempt to read words suggests that the student may be uncertain of his or her abilities, unwilling to take risks, or needs additional work with decoding at the sound/spelling or morpheme level. Look at the words the student does not read. Are they one-syllable words or multisyllabic words?
- Misreading routine CVC and CVCe words suggests that the student may need more work with the sounds and spellings. In some cases, a student may be able to read words with common sounds and spellings but needs more work with long vowels, diphthongs, and digraphs.
- Looking for patterns in errors is key.
- Using or not using intonation, expression, and phrasing but reading quickly and accurately suggests that students need to think about how words combine to make meaning and how our expression can support understanding.

Tips

- Use Workshop time for building fluency. Introduce different ways to practice fluency one at a time.
- Set up a listening area for Workshop that students can use to listen to the selection.
- Make sure *Pre-Decodables, Decodables,* and *Student Anthologies* are available to students.
- Have simple timers available for students to check their fluency rate.
- Introduce one element of fluency at a time, such as rate, automaticity, intonation, prosody, and so on.
- Encourage students to chart their fluency growth. If students are doing repeated reading, have them chart the number of words read each day for several days so they can see their fluency improving.
- When students have developed some degree of fluency with a *Pre-Decodable* or *Decodable* or selection from the *First Reader* or *Student Anthology,* send the materials home for additional practice.
- Use a range of materials to practice building fluency throughout the day. Remember, fluency practice can be as short as one minute several times a day.

Fluency

Prosody

REMIND students that reading a text with proper phrasing helps to communicate its meaning more clearly. Model reading the poem with proper phrasing and intonation.

After you read the entire poem, reread the first stanza. Have students repeat the lines after you, mimicking your phrasing and intonation. Continue to read the rest of the poem in this manner to help students build fluency with reading poetry.

Reading Aloud

Purpose

Research has shown that students who are read to are more likely to develop the skills they need to read successfully on their own. In this program there are *Big Books,* picture books, and excerpts for reading aloud.

While there are *Big Books* in Kindergarten and Grade I, in every grade level of *Open Court Reading* there are opportunities for teachers to read aloud to students. At the beginning of each unit is a Read Aloud selection tied to the unit theme, and it is usually above the students' independent reading level. This Read Aloud selection allows students the opportunity to think about the unit theme before reading selections on their own.

Reading aloud at any age serves multiple purposes. Reading aloud

- provokes students' curiosity about text.
- conveys an awareness that text has meaning.
- demonstrates the various reasons for reading text (to find out about the world, to learn useful new information and new skills, or simply for pleasure).
- exposes students to the "language of literature," which is more complex than the language they ordinarily use and hear.
- provides an opportunity to teach the problem-solving strategies that good readers employ. As students observe you interacting with the text, expressing your own enthusiasm, and modeling your thinking aloud, they perceive these as valid responses and begin to respond to text in similar ways.

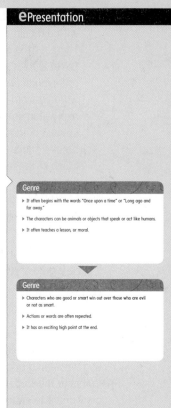

LESSON 1 · DAY 1 Reading and Responding

Objectives: Students will
- discuss the elements of a folktale.
- listen attentively.
- build vocabulary.

Build Background

Background Information

TELL students that in this unit they will read selections about animals in a variety of habitats. They will learn how these animals interact, how they spend their days, and how they adapt, or change their behavior, to live in certain environments.

Tell students that they are going to listen to a tale in which the author imagines the creation of the first armadillos. The text is part of a collection of fantasy stories about the origins of animals that was published by British author Rudyard Kipling in 1902. Kipling's *Just So Stories* describes how animals changed or acquired certain features because of magical occurrences or interference by humans. One tells how the camel got its hump, another explains how the leopard got its spots, and so on.

Genre

TELL students that *The Beginning of the Armadillos* is a folktale. Then discuss the following elements of a folktale:

- It often begins with the words "Once upon a time" or "Long ago and far away."
- The characters can be animals or objects that speak or act like humans.
- It often teaches a lesson, or moral.
- Characters who are good or smart win out over those who are evil or not as smart.
- Actions or words are often repeated.
- It has an exciting high point at the end.

Comprehension Strategy

MODEL the comprehension strategy Clarifying as you read. Stop periodically to identify something unclear or confusing in the text. Then explain how you can clarify the information by using context clues, reading further in the text, rereading, or consulting outside sources.

ePresentation

Genre
- It often begins with the words "Once upon a time" or "Long ago and far away."
- The characters can be animals or objects that speak or act like humans.
- It often teaches a lesson, or moral.

Genre
- Characters who are good or smart win out over those who are evil or not as smart.
- Actions or words are often repeated.
- It has an exciting high point at the end.

T12 Unit 4 · Lesson I · Day I

Procedures

The following set of general procedures for reading aloud is designed to help you maximize the effectiveness of any Read Aloud session.

- **Read-Aloud sessions.** Set aside time each day to read aloud.
- **Introduce the selection.** Tell students that you are going to read a story aloud to them. Tell its title, and briefly comment on the topic. To allow students to anticipate what will happen in the story, be careful not to summarize.
- **Build Background.** Build background knowledge by telling students the genre, and also by giving them any necessary background information needed to understand the story. Say, "Let's talk a little about _____." If the story is being read in two (or more) parts, before reading the second part, ask students to recall the first part.
- **Introduce Vocabulary.** Introduce any vocabulary necessary for understanding the Read Aloud.

Reading and Responding

The Beginning of the Armadillos

from Just So Stories by Rudyard Kipling
retold by Zachary Swift

In the very middle of the High and Far-Off Times was a Stickly-Prickly Hedgehog, and he lived on the banks of the turbid Amazon, eating shelly snails and things. And he had a friend, a Slow-Solid Tortoise, who lived on the banks of the turbid Amazon, eating green lettuces and things.

But also, and at the same time, there was a Painted Jaguar, and he lived on the banks of the turbid Amazon too; and he ate everything that he could catch. When he could not catch deer or monkeys he would eat frogs and beetles; and when he could not catch frogs and beetles he went to his Mother Jaguar, and she told him how to eat hedgehogs and tortoises.

She said to him, graciously waving her tail, "My son, when you find a Hedgehog you must drop him into the water and then he will uncoil, and when you catch a Tortoise you must scoop him out of his shell with your paw."

One night, Painted Jaguar found Stickly-Prickly Hedgehog and Slow-Solid Tortoise sitting under the trunk of a fallen tree.

"Now attend to me," said Painted Jaguar, "because this is very important. My mother said that when I meet a Hedgehog I am to drop him into the water and then he will uncoil, and when I meet a Tortoise I am to scoop him out of his shell with my paw. Now which of you is Hedgehog and which is Tortoise? To save my spots, I can't tell."

"Are you sure of what your Mummy told you?" said Stickly-Prickly Hedgehog. "Perhaps she said that when you uncoil a Tortoise you must shell him out of the water with a scoop."

"And perhaps your Mummy said that when you water a Hedgehog you must drop him into your paw," said Slow-Solid Tortoise.

"I don't think it was at all like that, and you are making my spots ache," said Painted Jaguar, "I only want to know which of you is Hedgehog and which is Tortoise."

"I shan't tell you," said Stickly-Prickly, "but you can scoop me out of my shell if you like."

"Aha!" said Painted Jaguar, "now I know you're Tortoise." Painted Jaguar darted out his paddy-paw just as Stickly-Prickly curled himself up, and of course Jaguar's paddy-paw was just filled with prickles. He knocked Stickly-Prickly away into the woods and put his paddy-paw into his mouth. As soon as he could speak he said, "Now I know he isn't Tortoise at all. But"—and then he scratched his head with his un-prickly paw—"how do I know that this other is Tortoise?"

 English Learner

COGNATES If students' native language is a Romance language, they may recognize the following cognate verbs that appear in *The Beginning of the Armadillos*: *painted, jaguar, tortoise, solid, paw, minute, anxious, turbid, useful, escape, fascinating, practice, exercise, precise,* and *tremendous* (Spanish: *pintado, jaguar, tortuga, sólido, pata, minuto, ansioso, túrbido, útil, escaparse, fascinante, practicar, ejercicio, preciso, tremendo*).

- **Go over the Essential Question.** This question should be uppermost in students' minds as they listen to the story being read aloud. Make sure to have students answer this question after the story is read.
- **Read the story expressively.** Occasionally react verbally to the story by showing surprise, asking questions, giving an opinion, expressing pleasure, or predicting events. Expressive reading not only supports comprehension but serves as a model for fluency. See the Thinking Aloud section for suggestions.
- **Use Comprehension Strategies.** While reading aloud to students, model the use of comprehension strategies in a natural, authentic way. Remember to try to present a variety of ways to respond to text. These include visualizing, asking questions, predicting, making connections, clarifying, and summarizing.
- **Retell.** When you have finished reading the story, call on volunteers to retell it.
- **Discuss.** After reading, discuss with students how the selection connects with the unit theme, and revisit the Essential Question for the story.
- **Reread.** You may wish to reread the selection on subsequent occasions, focusing the discussion on the unit theme.

Thinking Aloud

The following options for modeling thinking aloud will be useful for reading any story aloud. Choose responses that are most appropriate for the selection.

- React emotionally by showing joy, sadness, amusement, or surprise.
- Ask questions about ideas in the text. This should be done when there are points or ideas that you really do wonder about.
- Identify with characters by comparing them to yourself.
- Show empathy with or sympathy for characters.
- Relate the text to something you already know or something that has happened to you.
- Show interest in the text ideas.
- Question the meaning or clarity of the author's words and ideas.

Responding to Text

At reasonable stopping points, ask students general questions to get them to express their own ideas and to focus their attention on the text. These types of generic questions will help students discuss their reactions to the reading and demonstrate their comprehension.

- What do you already know?
- What seems really important here? Why do you think so?
- Was there anything that you did not understand? What?
- What new ideas did you learn?
- What surprised you in the story?
- Use discussion starters to engage students in talking about text. Model these and others in the beginning, and then encourage students to use them.
  - I like the part where _____.
  - I didn't like the part where _____.
  - _____ reminds me of _____.
  - I learned _____.
  - My favorite character was _____ because _____.

Vocabulary

Purpose

Strong vocabulary skills are correlated to achievement throughout school. The purpose of vocabulary instruction is to introduce students to new words (and ideas) and to teach them a range of strategies for learning, remembering, and incorporating unknown vocabulary words into their existing reading, writing, speaking, and listening vocabularies.

Words chosen for inclusion in *Open Court Reading* are based upon the vocabulary research of Andy Biemiller, who has developed a comprehensive database of words students with large vocabularies know by the end of sixth grade. Biemiller's work identifies words that all students need to know and provides evidence that students from various backgrounds acquire these word meanings in roughly the same order. For practical purposes, this means that a child with an average-sized vocabulary of 6,000 root word meanings at the end of Grade 2 knows mainly the same word meanings as a Grade 4 child who knows about 6,000 root word meanings. It appears that for students with small vocabularies, improving vocabulary mainly means moving them through the sequence faster. Because vocabulary knowledge is so critical to comprehension, vocabulary instruction is integrated throughout *Open Court Reading*.

Part 1: Foundational Skills

- In Grades K–1, students are using words they blend in sentences to develop vocabulary and oral language. These words may include affixes or inflectional endings. Learning about affixes and inflectional endings helps students see the relationship between base or root words and various forms of the base or root. Reviews of blending lines focus on using words based on teacher clues as well as finding synonyms and antonyms.
- In Grades 2–3, Word Analysis develops vocabulary and the understanding that words can be deconstructed and related through known elements to determine meaning. Students learn to analyze word parts or study word relationships to enable them to secure new vocabulary quickly and efficiently. Types of words they would study include the following:
  - **Antonyms** Words with opposite or nearly opposite meanings (*hot/cold*)
  - **Synonyms** Words with similar meanings (*cup, mug, glass*)
  - **Greek and Latin Roots** Words with different beginnings or endings that have Greek or Latin roots (*civil, biology*)

- **Multiple Meanings** Words that have more than one meaning (*run, dressing, bowl*)
- **Shades of Meaning** Words that express degrees of a concept or quality (*like, love, worship*)
- **Levels of Specificity** Words that describe at different levels of precision (*living thing, plant, flower, daffodil*)
- **Compound Words** Words comprised of two or more words (*daylight*)
- **Homographs** Words that are spelled the same but have different meanings and come from different root words (*bear, count*)
- **Homophones** Words that sound the same but have different spellings and meanings. (*mane/main, to/two/too*)
- **Base-Word Families** Words that have the same base word (*care, careless, careful, uncaring*)
- **Prefixes** An affix attached before a base word that changes the meaning of the word (*misspell*)
- **Suffixes** An affix attached to the end of a base word that changes the meaning of the word and often the part of speech (*careless*)
- **Classification and Categorization** Sorting words with related meanings (*colors, shapes, animals, etc.*)

Part 2: Reading and Responding

- Selection Vocabulary instruction focuses on teaching the meaning of specific words necessary for understanding the selection.
- Before reading the selection, the teacher orally introduces the definitions of the concept vocabulary word as well as any vocabulary words critical to understanding the selection. Definitions and examples are given, and students use the words in sentences. Suggestions are made throughout the reading to discuss new and interesting words. Work from Biemiller suggests that clarifying words in the context of reading is an effective technique for expanding student vocabulary. Suggestions for which words to stop and clarify are given. Vocabulary activities found throughout the lesson reinforce and extend vocabulary knowledge.
- During reading, students monitor their understanding of words and text. When they do not understand something, they stop and clarify what they have read. Students will use these same skills—context clues, apposition, and structural elements or word analysis—to clarify the meanings of additional words encountered while reading. Determining the meanings of words while reading

prepares students for the demands of independent reading in and out of school.

- After reading, students develop vocabulary with the introduction of the remainder of the selection vocabulary words. They also review any interesting words they identified and discussed during reading. They record any of these words in their Writer's Notebooks and are encouraged to use these words in discussion and in writing. This is followed by guided vocabulary practice in which students discuss the definitions of critical words; learn to apply critical skills such as context, word analysis, and apposition; review the definitions of the vocabulary; and use the vocabulary words in a variety of oral and written activities. Vocabulary review activities are found throughout the lesson.
- From the middle of Grade I on, students review the selection vocabulary words by reading the words in a new context as part of the Apply Vocabulary portion in the *Student Anthology.*

Part 3: Language Arts

During writing, students are encouraged to use their new vocabulary in writing.

General Strategies

There is no question that having students read and reading to students are effective vocabulary instructional strategies. Most word learning occurs through exposure to words while listening and reading. Multiple exposures to words, particularly when students hear, see, say, and write words, is also effective. Word play, including meaning and dictionary games, helps develop a word consciousness as well.

Vocabulary Strategies for Unknown Words

Different strategies have been shown to be particularly effective for learning completely new words. These strategies—word analysis, apposition, and context clues—can be used in the selection or in the Apply Vocabulary section of the *Student Anthologies.*

Context Clues Some words can be inferred from context and can be learned with repeated exposure to words while reading and listening. Although using context can be useful, it is not the most effective way to learn new words. Also, as students move into content area reading, context becomes a less effective tool for determining the meaning of unfamiliar words.

Syntax How a word is used in a sentence may provide clues to its meaning. This is particularly effective with homographs. "The lead pipe is a hazard to the community." Here *lead* is an

adjective and is pronounced with a short *e*. In "He will *lead* the troops into battle," *lead* has a very different meaning, is a verb, and is pronounced with a long *e*.

Apposition Sometimes a word is defined within the text. In an appositive, the definition of a word is often set off by commas for the reader.

Word Analysis Examining the affixes and roots of a word often provides clues to the meaning of the word. Knowing the meaning of at least part of the word can provide a clue to its entire meaning. For example, *unenforceable* can be broken down into meaningful word parts, each of which can be used to help students understand the meaning of the larger word. Word analysis is a particularly important tool in content area reading and may be the most effective strategy.

In addition, other strategies can be used to learn new words, including the following:

Key Word This strategy involves providing or having students create a mnemonic clue for unknown vocabulary. For example, the word *mole* is defined in chemistry as a "gram molecule." By relating *mole to molecule,* students have a key to the meaning of the word.

Definitions Copying a definition is not a highly effective strategy for learning new words. Defining words and then using them in a variety of activities helps solidify meanings and deepen understanding. It is not uncommon for the meaning of the vocabulary words to be unclear when students use the words in sentences. For example, a typical sentence a student might give for the word *camouflage* is "The octopus uses camouflage." The word *camouflage* is used correctly, but there is no real indication that the student knows the meaning of the word. Having students extend the sentence to explain why or how helps clarify the meaning: "The octopus uses camouflage to protect itself from predators" or "The method of camouflage an octopus uses when it is in danger is to change its shape and color."

Contextual Word Lists Teaching vocabulary in context is another way to secure understanding of unknown words. Grouping words by subject area such as science, social studies, math, descriptive words, new words, and so on enables students to connect word meanings and to build vocabulary understanding.

Figurative Language Idioms, metaphors, similes, personification, puns, and novel meanings need to be specifically taught, especially for English Learners.

Derivational Word Lists Presenting groups of words derived from a particular language or with specific roots or affixes is an effective way to reinforce meanings and spellings of foreign words and word parts.

Developing Vocabulary

Routine

After students read the selection, display the selection vocabulary words, pronunciations, and parts of speech, and discuss these with students. Have students use context, apposition, or word analysis to verify the meaning of the words in the selection, providing clarification as needed. If students cannot determine the meaning of the word using one of these skills, they can consult the glossary or dictionary, or you can give them the meaning of the word.

As as class, review the selection vocabulary words by completing the oral vocabulary activities as well as the *Skills Practice* pages that go along with the vocabulary words. Then have students read the vocabulary story in the Apply Vocabulary section of their *Student Anthologies.* As they read, students may notice that the highlighted vocabulary words may not match the selection vocabulary words exactly; instead, the highlighted word may be a form of the vocabulary word with a prefix or suffix added that may change the part of speech or the meaning of the word. Discuss these new forms of the vocabulary words with students. Also discuss the concept vocabulary word with students and its connection to the theme.

For further vocabulary practice, have students complete the activity on the Apply Vocabulary page. Provide examples and clarification as necessary. Extend students' vocabulary with additional activities in the *Teacher's Edition.* Daily practice with the selection vocabulary will give students the repeated exposure to the words necessary for students to internalize the meaning of the words.

Following are suggestions for modeling the use of context clues, apposition, or word analysis to determine the meaning of a word.

Modeling Using Context Clues

Have students read the selection vocabulary word used in context in the selection or in the Apply Vocabulary section. Explain to students that they can use context clues, or other words in the sentence or passage, to determine the meaning of the highlighted vocabulary word. For example, if the word is *products,* the context might include the following:

When bees help plants, they are also helping people. One example of this is that bees pollinate cotton plants, and people use cotton to design and make clothes. People also eat many foods that come from plants. Some bees make a special food from plants that people enjoy—honey! People use honey in food, drinks, and home products.

Have students look for clues in the sentences that might help them understand the meaning of the highlighted word. Point out that the sentence in which the word *products* appears talks about things made with honey. The earlier part of the paragraph tells about people making clothes and bees creating honey. These are all clues that *products* are things that are made or created. Look on the next page at the other selection vocabulary word, *design,* as it appears in the **Student Anthology**. Use the same strategy and look for context clues to use with your class.

II. Selection Vocabulary Routine

Develop Vocabulary

- Display the vocabulary words, pronunciations, and parts of speech.
- For each vocabulary word, discuss the definition.
- Have students use the context in the selection or the parts of the word to verify the meaning of the word.
- Provide examples and clarification as needed.

Practice Vocabulary

- As a class, review the selection vocabulary words by completing the vocabulary activity orally.
- Have students complete the vocabulary *Skills Practice* pages individually.

Apply Vocabulary

- Have students read the vocabulary story in their *Student Anthologies.*
- Review the selection vocabulary words and discuss the new forms of the words and any meanings that may have changed.
- Discuss the concept vocabulary word and its connection to the theme.

Extend Vocabulary

- Have students turn to the second page of the Apply Vocabulary spread in their *Student Anthologies.*
- Tell students to follow the directions for the Extend Vocabulary activity.
- After each student has completed the activity, continue the activity as a class using the content provided in the *Teacher's Edition.*

Review Vocabulary

- Complete the vocabulary activity to help students review the words.
- Provide examples and clarification as needed.

Modeling Using Apposition

Have students read the selection vocabulary word used in context in the selection or in the Apply Vocabulary section. Explain to students that they can use apposition to determine the meaning of the word. In apposition, the word is followed by the definition, which is set off by commas. For example, for the word *absorbs,* the sentence might read:

Each one *absorbs,* or takes in, sunlight and turns it into energy.

It should be clear to students that by using apposition, they can figure out that the meaning of the word *absorbs* is "takes in." However, you should still use the same word in another sentence so students do indeed know the meaning of *absorbs.*

Modeling Using Word Analysis

Word analysis is the strategy that students will most likely use to figure out the meanings of most words. Have students read the selection vocabulary word used in context in the selection or in the Apply Vocabulary section. Explain to students that they can use word analysis, or parts of the word, to determine

the meaning of the highlighted word. For example, for the Selection Vocabulary word *unaware,* the sentence might read:

The tiny frog was unaware that he was being watched.

Even if students do not know the meaning of the word *aware,* they should be able to figure out that the word *unaware* means "not aware," because they should know the meanings of common prefixes. Confirm with students that *unaware* means "does not know." Use the word *unaware* in another sentence to consolidate the meaning for students.

Semantic Mapping Having students create a semantic map of an unknown word after learning its definition helps them learn the word's meaning. Have students write the new word and then list in a map or a web all the words they can think of that are related to it.

Semantic Feature Analysis A semantic feature analysis helps students compare and contrast similar types of words within a category to help secure unknown words. Have students chart, for example, the similarities and differences between types of sports, including new vocabulary such as *lacrosse* and *cricket.*

Bees help by drinking nectar from flowers. As a bee drinks, it brushes against the plant's pollen, and some of the pollen sticks to the bee. When the bee flies to the next plant, some of the old pollen rubs off onto the flower, and new pollen sticks to the bee.

Bees carry pollen in different ways. One way is by pollen sticking to little hairs all over the bees. Even their eyes have hair! These hairs make bees look fuzzy. Bees also carry pollen in special parts of their back legs called pollen baskets. Their bodies are adapted to help them do their work.

86

When bees help plants, they are also helping people. One example of this is that bees pollinate cotton plants, and people use cotton to design and make clothes. Without bees, cotton plants would have a difficult time reproducing. People also eat many foods that come from plants. Some bees make a special food from plants that people enjoy—honey! People use honey in food, drinks, and home products.

Many animals also like honey. Badgers, bears, and some kinds of birds seek out bee homes in order to snack on honey and honeycomb.

Honeybees use the nectar they drink to make honey. One bee can drink from 50 to 100 flowers in one trip—no wonder bees are so busy! The bees save the honey, and in the winter when there are no flowers, they have a tasty meal.

87

Comprehension and Close Reading

Purpose

The primary aim of reading is comprehension. Without comprehension, neither intellectual nor emotional responses to reading are possible—other than the response of frustration. Reading is about problem solving. Expert readers bring their critical faculties to bear on everything they read. They generally understand most of what they read, but just as importantly, they recognize when they do not understand, and they have at their command an assortment of strategies for monitoring and furthering their understanding and for accessing complex text.

A significant amount of research shows that the close reading of complex text, regardless of whether a students is a struggling or advanced reader, leads to significant gains in reading proficiency. Text complexity is determined by a number of factors, including vocabulary, the structure of a selection, the language conventionality and clarity within a selection, and the knowledge demands placed on the reader. Students must have the tools to read closely complex text from across the curriculum.

When students closely read complex text, they understand the text's key ideas and details because they have thoroughly read the text and comprehended its meaning. In order to do this, students may need to reread a passage or the entire selection thoughtfully and deliberately in order to reflect on what the passage covers. Students may come across difficult vocabulary or sentence structure. They will need to think about, reread, or associate a context with the meanings of individual words or sentences when vocabulary or language becomes complex. In addition, students should reflect on the development of the ideas within a text from beginning to end to understand how an author might state and defend an argument or use narrative features in telling a tale.

> *The goal of comprehension strategy instruction is to have students understand what they are reading as they are reading it.*

The goal of comprehension strategy instruction is to have students understand what they are reading as they are reading it. Ultimately, the goal is to turn responsibility for using strategies over to students as soon as possible. Research has shown that students' comprehension and learning problems are not a matter of mental capacity but rather their inability to use strategies to help them learn. Expert readers use a variety of strategies to help them make sense of the text and to get the most out of what they read. Trained to use a variety of comprehension strategies, students dramatically improve their learning performance. To do this, the teacher models strategy use through *Big Books* and *Student Anthologies* and gradually incorporates various kinds of prompts and possible student think-alouds as examples of the types of thinking students might do as they read to comprehend what they are reading.

Setting Reading Goals

Even before they begin reading and using comprehension strategies, good readers set reading goals and expectations. Readers who set goals and have expectations regarding the text they are about to read are more engaged in and notice more about what they read. Having determined a purpose for reading, they are better able to evaluate a text and know whether it meets their needs. Even when the reading is assigned, as in the *Student Anthologies,* the reader's engagement is enhanced when he or she has determined ahead of time what information might be gathered from the selection or how the selection might interest him or her.

Comprehension Strategies

Successful readers are active readers who interact with the text. Descriptions of strategies expert readers use to comprehend text are listed below.

Asking Questions

Asking questions allows the reader to constantly check his or her understanding and to follow the writer's train of thought. Good readers ask questions that may prepare them for what they will learn. If their questions are not answered in the text, they may try to find answers elsewhere and thus add even more to their store of knowledge. Certain types of questions occur naturally to a reader, such as to clear up confusion or to wonder why something in the text is as it is. Intentional readers take this somewhat informal questioning one step further by formulating questions with the specific intent of checking their understanding. They literally test themselves by thinking of questions a teacher might ask and then by determining answers to those questions. Students should think to themselves the following:

1. What do I already know about this topic?
2. What else would I like to know about this topic?

3. What questions do I think the author will answer as I read this selection?
4. How does this information connect to what I already know about the topic?
5. How does this connect to the unit theme?
6. What is not making sense in this selection?
7. What is interfering with my understanding?

Answering Questions

Students must not only ask questions as they read, but they should actively try to find answers to their questions in the text or outside of it. If their questions are not answered in the text, students may try to find answers elsewhere and thus add even more to their store of knowledge. As students read, they should consider the following:

1. How does this information answer my question?
2. Does this information completely answer my question?
3. Do I have more questions after finding some answers?
4. If I cannot find the answers to my questions within the text, where else can I go to find the answers?

Clarifying

Monitoring understanding is key to reading. It allows readers to make sure they understand what they read. They note the characteristics of the text, such as whether it is difficult to read or whether some sections are more challenging or more important than others are. In addition, when readers become aware that they do not understand, they stop and take appropriate action, such as rereading or adjusting their reading speed, to understand the text better.

As they read, good readers stay alert for problem signs such as loss of concentration, unfamiliar vocabulary, or lack of sufficient background knowledge to comprehend the text. This ability to self-monitor and identify difficult aspects of the text is crucial to becoming a proficient reader.

Clarifying may occur at the word, the sentence, the paragraph, or the whole-text level. At the word level, the reader might

- apply decoding skills to sound out unknown words.
- apply context clues in text to figure out the meanings of words.
- use structural elements to figure out the meanings of words.
- ask someone the meanings of words.
- check a dictionary or glossary to understand words not clarified by clues or rereading.

Suggestions for Clarifying

▶ Reread the text

▶ Read on in the text

▶ Look up a word

▶ Make connections to prior knowledge

At the passage level, complex sentences may require the reader to look for the main idea in the sentence, to pull out clauses that may interfere with the main idea, or to ask for help. When faced with unfamiliar concepts, readers often ask for clarification from someone. Students should think about the following to clarify understanding:

1. Does this selection make sense? If not, what do I not understand?
2. If I do not know a word, how can I figure it out? Will word analysis, context clues, or apposition help me figure out the meaning? If I am still confused, should I ask someone or look it up in the dictionary or glossary?
3. If a sentence is long and complicated, have I reread it as well as the sentences before and after it to see if the meaning is clarified? Have I read the sentence part by part to see exactly what is confusing? Have I tried to restate the sentence in my own words?
4. If the paragraph is long and includes many facts and details, have I reread the paragraph more slowly? Have I looked for and found the meanings of words that I do not know? Have I discussed the paragraph with someone to help clarify? Have I tried to restate the information in my own words to make sure I understand it?

Making Connections

Making connections between the text and what is known from personal experience or previous reading deepens our understanding of text and expands our understanding. Comprehension is enhanced when we relate what is read to what is known. Students should think about the following:

1. Does this selection remind me of something else I have read or seen?
2. What personal connections can I make to this selection?
3. How does this selection connect with other selections I have read, either in this unit or other units?
4. How does this selection connect to events in our world today?
5. How does this selection relate to events or topics I have studied in social studies or science?

Predicting

Predicting what will happen in the story allows the reader to summarize what has been read so far, to identify clues and events in the text, and to use prior knowledge and personal experience to make inferences about what will happen next. Predictions are not wild guesses. They are made based on information provided by the author as well as the reader's background knowledge. Students should think the following:

1. What do I predict will happen next?
2. What evidence from the selection supports my prediction?
3. What evidence from my personal experience or knowledge supports my prediction?

Confirming Predictions

When reading fiction, readers make predictions about what they are reading and then confirm or revise those predictions as they go. Students should think to themselves the following:

1. How was my prediction confirmed? What information supported my prediction?
2. Was my prediction not confirmed? What really happened?
3. What clues did I miss that might have helped me make a more accurate prediction?

The responsibility for using strategies by students should begin as soon as they understand that reading is about problem solving and making sense of text and that these strategies will help them do both.

Summarizing

Periodically it is important to summarize and check our understanding as we read. Sometimes readers reread to fill in gaps in their understanding. They use the strategy of summarizing to keep track of what they are reading and to focus their minds on important information. The process of putting the information in one's own words not only helps good readers remember what they have read but also prompts them to evaluate how well they understand the information. Sometimes the summary reveals that one's understanding is incomplete, in which case it might be appropriate to reread the previous section to fill in the gaps.

The strategy of summarizing is particularly helpful when readers are reading long or complicated text. When to stop and summarize depends on the difficulty of the text as well as the type of text. Often in content area reading, it makes sense to stop and summarize the key ideas after each section. In narratives, the reader often stops to summarize after an episode has been read. Many of us will automatically summarize what has happened if we have put down a book and are about to continue reading it again. Students should think to themselves the following:

1. What is this selection about?
2. How can I state what I have just read in my own words?
3. How should I organize my summary?
4. Have I included any information that should be deleted from my summary?
5. Have I repeated any information that should be deleted from my summary?

Visualizing

Creating a mental image about the text involves not just the literal interpretation of the author's words but going beyond the literal to incorporating prior knowledge and experiences that deepen understanding. Readers form mental images as they read. They picture the setting, the characters, and the action in a story.

Visualizing can also be helpful when reading expository text. Visualizing helps readers understand descriptions of complex activities or processes. When a complex process or an event is being described, the reader can follow the process or the event better by visualizing each step or episode. Sometimes an author or an illustrator helps the reader by providing illustrations, diagrams, or maps. If no visual aids have been provided, it may help the reader to create one. Creating mental images helps the reader create pictures that can be stored efficiently in his or her long-term memory. Students should think to themselves the following:

1. What picture do the words from this selection create in my mind?
2. What can I see, hear, smell, taste, and/or feel in my mind?
3. Which specific words from the selection help me visualize the feelings, actions, and settings?
4. How does my mental picture help me understand what I am reading?
5. How do the author's descriptions help extend my understanding beyond the text?

Procedures

Modeling and Thinking Aloud

One of the most effective ways to help students understand and use critical comprehension strategies is to make strategic thinking public. Modeling these behaviors and encouraging students to think aloud as they attempt to address comprehension problems and to understand text can demonstrate for everyone in a class how these behaviors are put into practice. Suggestions for think-alouds are provided throughout the *Teacher's Edition.*

The most effective models you can offer will be those that come from your own reading experiences. What kinds of questions did you ask yourself? What kinds of things surprised you the first time you read a story? What kinds of new information did you learn? What kinds of things were confusing until you reread or read further? Drawing on these questions and on your students' questions and comments as they read will make the strategic reading process more meaningful to students. Below are suggestions for modeling each of the comprehension strategies.

Before Reading

Modeling Setting Reading Goals. To model setting reading goals, engage students in the following:

- **Build background.** As you approach a new text, give students pertinent background information, such as words, definitions, or concepts that students will need to know in order to understand the selection.
- **Browse the text.** To get an idea of what to expect from a text, look at the title and the illustrations. When students are reading fiction, they will browse the text to look for Clues, Problems and Wonderings.
  - Possible clues will support comprehension—for example, genre, content, author, setting, and so on—potential problems might include things such as difficult words or dense paragraphs as well as unfamiliar concepts; and wonderings are the things students are curious to find out about from their reading—questions about the selection. Wonderings are students' purposes for reading.

Clues/Problems/Wonderings		
C	P	W
Many birds depend on the cactus for shelter.	pleats cavity	How much longer can the cactus survive without water?

- When students read nonfiction, they will use a KWL chart—this is what I know (K), this is what I want to find out (W), and this is what I have learned (L). Both these activities—Clues, Problems, and Wonderings and KWL—engage students in thinking before reading the selection by having them activate their own background knowledge, identify potential problems, and set purposes for reading. Have students glance quickly at the selection, looking briefly at the illustrations and the print. Have them tell what they think they might be learning about as they read the selection. Early in the year, model the thinking involved with these activities and then begin to turn the responsibility for completing them over to students.

During Reading

Modeling—or thinking aloud—about how to use strategies to solve problems is a powerful tool for teaching comprehension. While think-aloud models are included in all lessons, relate your own thinking and experiences to the lesson and the think-alouds. Early in the process you will need to model thinking about how, when, and why to use the strategies. Encourage students to stop and use them as well; engage them in thinking!

- **Modeling Summarizing.** Summarizing while reading fiction helps the reader check for understanding, consolidate learning, and anticipate content. The strategy of summarizing the plot and then predicting what will happen next enhances a student's reading of fiction. The same procedure can be used to the student's advantage in reading nonfiction. In informational text, it is particularly logical to stop and summarize at the end of a section before going on to the next one. Appropriate times to stop and summarize include the following:

For Fiction
- When a narrative text has covered a long period of time or a number of events
- When an especially critical scene has occurred

For Informational Text
- When a complex process has been described
- When many facts have been presented

For Either
- Any time there is the potential for confusion about what has happened or what has been presented in the text
- When returning to a selection

- **Modeling Clarifying.** A reader may need clarification at any point in the reading. Model this strategy by stopping at points that confuse you or that may confuse your students. Indicate that you are experiencing some confusion and need to stop and make sure you understand what is being read. Difficulty may arise from a challenging or unknown word or phrase. It may also stem from the manner in which the information is presented. Perhaps the author did not supply needed information. As you model this strategy, vary the reasons for stopping to clarify so that students understand that good readers do not simply skip over difficult or confusing material—they stop and determine what they do not understand, and then they reread or slow down their reading speed to help them understand the text.

Differentiated Instruction: Clarifying

AL Work with students to stop and clarify and ideas, words, or phrases that they find confusing on pages 42–43. Help students identify any words or concepts that are unknown or not clear.

OL For additional practice, review a book students are using for researching animal homes. Prompt them to clarify ideas that seem confusing, as well as unknown words and phrases.

BL For a challenge, have students share how they clarified unknown words or confusing ideas in a book on their own.

- **Modeling Asking Questions.** Learning to ask productive questions is not an easy task. Students' earliest experiences with this strategy take the form of answering teacher-generated questions. However, students should be able to move fairly quickly to asking questions like those a teacher might ask. Questions that can be answered with a simple *yes* or *no* are not typically very useful for helping them remember and understand what they have read. Many students find it helpful to ask questions beginning with *Who? What? When? Where? How?* and *Why?* As students become more accustomed to asking and answering questions, they will naturally become more adept at phrasing their questions. As their question asking becomes more sophisticated, they progress from simple questions that can be answered with explicit information in the text to questions that require making inferences based on the text.

- **Modeling Predicting.** Predicting can be appropriate at the beginning of a selection—on the basis of the titles and the illustrations—or at any point while reading a selection. At first, your modeling will take the form of speculation about what might happen next, but tell students from the start what clues in the text or illustrations helped you predict to make it clear that predicting is not just guessing. You can also help students with sentence frames to get them started with their own predictions. When a student makes a prediction—especially a far-fetched one—ask on what in the selection or in his or her own experience the prediction is based. If the student can back up the prediction, let the prediction stand; otherwise, suggest that the student make another prediction on the basis of what he or she already knows. Often it is appropriate to summarize before making a prediction. This will help students consider what has come before as they make their predictions about what will happen next. When reading aloud, stop whenever a student's prediction has been confirmed or contradicted. Have students tell whether the prediction was confirmed. If students seem comfortable with the idea of making predictions but rarely do so on their own, encourage them to discuss how to find clues in the text that will help them.

Predicting Sentence Frames

▶ I predict _____ because _____.

▶ The clues the author gave are _____, so I _____ what I predict.

▶ My prediction was confirmed because _____.

▶ I want to revise my prediction because _____.

- **Modeling Making Connections.** To model making connections, share with students any thoughts or memories that come to mind as you read the selection. Perhaps a character in a story reminds you of a childhood friend, allowing you to better identify with interactions between characters. Perhaps information in an article on Native American life in the Old West reminds you of an article that you have read on the importance of the bison to Native Americans. Sharing your connections will help students become aware of the dynamic nature of reading and show them another way of being intentional, active learners.

- **Modeling Visualizing.** Model visualizing by describing the mental images that occur to you as you read. A well-described scene is relatively easy to visualize, and if no one does so voluntarily, you may want to prompt students to express their own visualizations. If the author has not provided a description of a scene, but a picture of the scene would make the story more interesting or comprehensible, you might want to model visualizing as follows: "Let's see. The author says that the street was busy, and we know that this story is set during the colonial period. From what I already know about those times, there were no cars, and the roads were different from the roads of today. The street may have been paved with cobblestones. Horses would have been pulling carriages or wagons. I can almost hear the horses' hoofs going clip-clop over the stones." Remind students that different readers may picture the same scene quite differently, which is fine. Every reader responds to a story in her or his own way.

If your students have not previously engaged in the sort of strategic thinking aloud that is promoted throughout *Open Court Reading,* you will have to do all or most of the modeling at first, but encourage students to participate as soon as possible. Remember, however, the goal is for students to use these strategies independently as they read both in and out of school. In addition to the think-alouds for the teachers, there are also prompts to encourage students to do the thinking. Students should begin assuming responsibility for using these strategies as soon as they understand that reading is about problem solving and making sense of text and that these strategies will help them do both.

Most students are unaccustomed to thinking aloud. They will typically stay mute as they try to determine an unfamiliar word or to deal with a confusing passage. When this happens, students should be encouraged to identify specifically with what they are having difficulty. A student might identify a particular word, or he or she may note that the individual words are familiar but that the meaning of the passage is unclear.

Active Response

Not only are good readers active in their reading when they encounter problems, but they respond constantly to whatever they read. In this way they make the text their own. As students read they should be encouraged to

- make as many connections as they can between what they are reading and what they already know.
- visualize passages to help clarify their meanings or simply to picture appealing descriptions.
- ask questions about what they are reading. The questions that go through their minds during reading will help them examine, and thus better understand, the text. Doing so may also interest them in pursuing their own investigations. The questions may also provide a direction for students' research or exploration.
- summarize and make predictions as a check on how well they understand what they are reading.

Reading Aloud

At the beginning of the year, students should be encouraged to read selections aloud. This practice will help you and them understand some of the challenges posed by the text and how individual students approach these challenges.

Reading aloud helps students build fluency, which in turn will aid their comprehension. Students in Grades K–3 can use *Decodables* to build fluency, while students in Grades I–3 can use the literature from the *Student Anthologies.* Fluent second graders read between 79 and 117 words per minute with accuracy and understanding, depending on the time of the year (fall/spring). Fluent third graders can be expected to read between 99 and 137 words per minute.

Make sure that you set aside time to hear each student read during the first few days of class—the days devoted to Getting Started are perfect for this—so that you can determine students' abilities and needs. Workshop is also a good time to listen to any students who do not get to read aloud while the class is reading the selection together.

Tips

- Remember that the goal of all reading is comprehension. If a story or article does not make sense, the reader needs to choose whatever strategies will help make sense of it. If one strategy does not work, the reader should try another.
- Always treat problems encountered in text as interesting learning opportunities rather than something to be avoided or dreaded.
- Encourage students to think aloud about text challenges.
- Encourage students to help each other build meaning from text. Rather than telling each other what a word is or what a passage means, students should tell each other how they figured out the meanings of challenging words and passages.
- Assure students that these are not the only strategies that can be used while reading. Any strategy that they find helpful in understanding text is a good, useful strategy.
- Encourage students to freely share strategies they have devised on their own. You might want to write these on a large sheet of paper and tape them onto the board.
- An absence of questions does not necessarily indicate that students understand what they are reading. Be especially alert to students who never seem to ask questions. Be sure to spend tutorial time with these students occasionally, and encourage them to discuss

specific selections in the context of difficulties they might have encountered and how they solved them as well as their thoughts about unit concepts.

- Observing students' responses to text will enable you to ascertain not only how well they understand a particular selection but also their facility in choosing and applying appropriate strategies. Use the comprehension rubrics to evaluate students' understanding of and ability to use the different reading strategies. Note the following:
  - Does the student choose from a variety of strategies or use the same few over and over?
  - Is the student able to justify his or her strategy choice?
  - Is the student able to identify alternative strategies or resources when current strategies fail?
  - Is the student refining his or her own use of strategies?
- Encourage students to use the reading strategies throughout the day in all their reading activities.

Becoming familiar and comfortable with these self-monitoring techniques gives readers the confidence to tackle material that is progressively more difficult. A good, mature reader knows when understanding what he or she is reading is becoming a problem and can take steps to correct the situation. He or she has internalized the strategies, values them, and uses strategies automatically.

Access Complex Text

Purpose

An important purpose of writing is to communicate thoughts from one person to another. The goal of instruction in accessing complex text is to make students aware of the purpose and organization behind the structure of a written piece. If the reader can discern the complexity of the structure, he or she will be more able to understand the author's logic and to gain knowledge both of the facts and the intent of the selection. By keeping the organization of a piece in mind and considering the author's purpose for writing, the reader can go beyond the actual words on the page and make inferences or draw conclusions based on what was read. Strong, mature readers utilize these "between the lines" skills to get a complete picture of not only what the writer is saying but what the writer is trying to say.

Effective skills for accessing complex text include the following:

Cause and Effect

What made this happen? Why did this character act the way he or she did? Knowing the causes of events helps the reader see the whole story. Using this information to identify the probable outcomes (effects) of events or actions will help the reader anticipate the story or article.

Classify and Categorize

The relationships of actions, events, characters, outcomes, and such in a selection should be clear enough for the reader to see the relationships. Putting like things or ideas together can help the reader understand the relationships set up by the writer.

Differentiated Instruction: Classify and Categorize

AL If students have difficulty using information in the selection to classify and categorize, then have them classify items in the classroom by color or shape.

OL If students could use more practice, then ask them to classify and categorize animals into categories such as pets and wild animals.

BL If students need a challenge, then ask them to think of other ways to classify and categorize the information in the selection.

Compare and Contrast

Using comparison and contrast is one of the most common and easiest ways a writer gets his or her reader to understand a subject. Comparing and contrasting unfamiliar thoughts, ideas, or things with familiar thoughts, ideas, and things gives the reader something within his or her own experience base to use in understanding.

Fact and Opinion

Learning to distinguish fact from opinion is essential to critical reading and thinking. Students learn what factors need to be present for a statement to be provable. They also learn that an opinion, while not provable itself, should be based on fact. Readers use this knowledge to determine for themselves the validity of the ideas presented in their reading.

Main Idea and Details

An author always has something specific to say to his or her reader. The author may state this main idea in different ways, but the reader should always be able to tell what the writing is about. To strengthen the main point or main idea of a piece, the author provides details to help the reader understand. The reader needs to know what kinds of details he or she is dealing with before making a judgment about the main idea.

Making Inferences

Readers make inferences about characters and events to understand the total picture in a story. When making inferences, readers use information from the text, along with personal experience or knowledge, to draw conclusions about what was read and to gain a deeper understanding of a story event and its implications.

Sequence

The reader cannot make any decisions about relationships or events if he or she has no idea in which order the events take place. The reader needs to pay attention to how the writer is conveying the sequence. Is it simply stated that first this happened and then that happened? Does the writer present the end of the story first and then go back and let the reader know the sequence of events? Knowing what the sequence is and how it is presented helps the reader follow the writer's line of thought.

Writer's Craft

When students analyze the way an author created the literary experience—why he or she said things in certain ways with certain words, phrases, and styles, and why the text was structured the way it was, they are looking at the writer's crafting of the selection. Students approach text differently when they look at the writer's craft. Their focus shifts from understanding the text to reading text for the sake of gaining new information, new experiences, and interesting viewpoints. Examining the writer's craft means turning text inside out to see how it is made, how it is held together, and what makes it work.

As students progress through *Open Court Reading*, the texts they encounter become increasingly complex, providing richer opportunities for understanding the writer's craft. Students' awareness of the skills that make up this craft will build developmentally over time, as techniques they were once only able to recognize become ones they can analyze, evaluate, and choose to use in their own compositions.

Writer's Craft should happen after readers have immersed themselves in the text. During the first reading of the selection, students employ comprehension strategies to understand, appreciate, and learn from a text. During the second reading, students will not only try to understand the text complexity of the selection, but they will also look more

closely at what an author has done to create a particular experience with words.

Solidify the connection between how an author writes and how readers make sense of a selection by encouraging students to incorporate different author techniques into their own writing. As they attempt to use these devices, they will get a clearer understanding of how to identify them when they are reading.

Many students never progress beyond producing a written text that duplicates their everyday speech patterns. Mature writers, however, take composition beyond conversation. They understand the importance of audience and purpose for writing. They organize their thoughts, eliminating those that do not advance their main ideas, applying what they have learned in reading, and elaborating on those that do so that their readers can follow a logical progression of ideas in an essay or story. Mature writers also know and can use the conventions of grammar, usage, spelling, and mechanics. They proofread and edit for these conventions, so their readers are not distracted by errors.

Good writers are good readers. They know the structure of text, the techniques of writers, and the importance of clarity of thought. Students who analyze a writer's craft can get inside the process of creating text, not just to better appreciate texts but also to become more skilled and informed writers. They are, in fact, reading with a writer's eye. When students understand what authors have done to put together interesting, effective, and engaging texts, they will be more able to do the same when they write. When students read literature with a writer's eye, they begin to understand something of the craft, which allows them to try their hand at writing. In other words, as we give students more cognitive control over the writing process, we give them the power to write through their reading. Not surprisingly, this is a two-way street. As students become more attuned to reading like writers, they will become more appreciative and critical of texts and learn to take an active rather than a passive stance toward reading.

Below are a number of examples that help students understand how a writer crafts a selection, whether fiction or nonfiction.

Author's Purpose

Everything is written for a purpose. That purpose may be to entertain, to persuade, or to inform. Knowing why a piece is written—what purpose the author had for writing the piece—gives the reader an idea of what to expect and perhaps some prior idea of what the author is going to say.

Genre Knowledge

Readers learn to recognize the differences between narratives, informational texts, and persuasive texts. Subgenres of fiction may include realistic fiction, fantasy, fairy tales, folktales, plays, poems, biographies, and so on. Readers determine why an author chose to write in one of the basic genres.

Language Use

Readers learn to recognize the way authors communicate important details and events in a story. Language use may includes rhyme, repetition, sentence structures (simple, compound, declarative, interrogative, imperative, and exclamatory), alliteration, simile, metaphor, exaggeration, onomatopoeia, personification, sensory details, descriptive words, effective adjectives and adverbs, dialogue, and formal vs. informal language.

Point of View (Informational or Persuasive Text)

The author's point of view in an informational text is the position or perspective that the author takes on the subject he or she is writng about. The author may arrange topics in a certain sequence, or the author might present facts in such a way so as to inform or to persuade his or her audience.

Point of View (Narrative/Fiction)

Point of view in a narrative involves dentifying who is telling the story. If a character in a narrative is telling the story, that character uses his or her point of view to describe the action in the story and tell what the other characters are like. This is called *first-person point of view*. If the narrative is told in *third-person point of view,* someone outside the story who is aware of all of the characters' thoughts, feelings, and actions is relating them to the reader.

Essential Question How do animals change as they grow older?

Insects Grow and Change
by Katie Sharp

Insects are animals. All animals grow and change. Some insects do not change very much from when they are born. This grasshopper does not change a lot.

Other insects change a great deal as they grow. They look different at each stage in their lives. Sometimes they change inside a protective case called a chrysalis that they form around themselves.

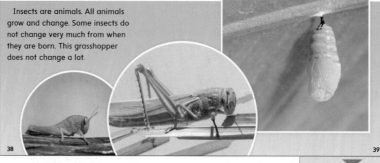

38   39

⊙ Writer's Craft

Genre Knowledge

◯ **READ** pages 38 and 39. Review with students that authors of informational text help explain what they are writing about by giving readers facts that they can check in other sources. Ask, *What facts has the author given on these pages that readers can check?* Possible Answer: *Readers can check whether grasshoppers change a lot as they get older. They can check whether some insects look different in each stage of their lives.*

Language Use

🔵 **DISCUSS** with students the information that the author provides about insects' life cycles. Ask, *What words does the author use to tell about insects that change as they grow that might be unfamiliar to readers?* The words *stage* and *chrysalis* might be unfamiliar. *Why does the author use words like these in her writing?* The words are important for readers to know if they want to understand how insects change. Help students identify and define other academic or scientific terms in the selection that are important for the writer to include and for the reader to learn about this topic.

🔵 Teacher Tip	👥 Differentiated Instruction
VOCABULARY To help students understand what a *chrysalis* is, call attention to the photo on page 39 and have students say the name.	**OL** **LANGUAGE USE** Reinforce for students the idea that the kind of text an author writes determines how he or she will use language by having students discuss the poems that they have read and the way that the poets' used words to create mental pictures that appeal to the feelings of readers. Then have students contrast this language use with what they have read in their informational and explanatory text selections.

Unit 3 • Lesson 3 • Day 4   **T237**

Story Elements: Character

A character is a person or creature that interacts with others within a story. There are different kinds of characters in stories, and different ways to describe them. Readers learn to identify the different characteristics of the characters (physical features, character types such as heroes or villains, personality types, feelings, and motivations), and the ways that the author describes the characters, such as with descriptive details, dialogue, and illustrations.

Story Elements: Plot

Readers learn to recognize the overall structure, or plot, of the story. A plot usually includes a beginning, a problem that must be solved, the climax or highest point of the story, a resolution of the problem, and an ending. Authors may use of sequence, cause and effect, details, and dialogue to build the plot.

> Sammy spotted a ptarmigan. All summer the ptarmigans had been hard to see because their brown feathers blended in so well with the landscape. Lately, though, their brown feathers were being replaced by white ones.
>
> "Have you seen any warblers?" Sammy trilled.
>
> "Nope," clucked the ptarmigan. "I bet they've flown south. Warblers always fly south."
>
> "Is that what you do?" asked Sammy.
>
> "Don't have to," said the ptarmigan.
>
> "There's lots of food for me here. And I grow special feathers for winter. Soon I'll be almost completely white."
>
> "Everybody will be able to see you!" said Sammy. "Won't that be dangerous?"
>
> "Silly Sammy," chuckled the ptarmigan. "I'll be almost invisible once the snow comes. But you, Sammy, you'd better start flying south."

Ptarmigans

Ptarmigans are some of the only birds that can live year-round in the far north. Along with their white winter camouflage, they grow a thick undercoat of down and "boots" of feathers to keep their toes cozy. To stay warm at night and during snowstorms, they dig "snow caves" for shelter.

Writer's Craft

Language Use: Descriptive Words

HAVE students reread the first paragraph of the story. Ask them whether they see any descriptive words that help them visualize the setting of Sammy's Arctic home. **Possible Answer:** *The text says that the frost "twinkled and sparkled" on the leaves. These specific verbs help me picture exactly what the frosty trees looked like as the sun shone on them. When the author writes that Sammy "shivered," I can picture his tiny body shaking with excitement and cold.*

Story Elements: Plot

ASK students to identify the problem or conflict of this story's plot. **Possible Answer:** *The problem is that it is time for Sammy to migrate to Panama, but he is all alone and does not know how to get there.* **Then ask** how Sammy has set out to solve the problem. **Possible Answer:** *He asks other birds and animals along the way if they know which direction to go—and sometimes follows them or hitches a ride.*

Story Elements: Character

ASK students to explain how specific aspects of the illustration on page 121 combine with the text to emphasize the character of the ptarmigan. **Possible Answer:** *The illustration shows a bird with thick, warm-looking feathers all around its lower half. This illustration helps me understand the description of the undercoat in the sidebar, but it also adds to the ptarmigan's attitude. He speaks to Sammy with confidence. I would feel confident if I had those feathers to stay warm in winter.*

Teacher Tip

CHARACTER Discuss with students the personality traits displayed by other characters in the story. Create a chart that lists traits and text evidence for as many characters as possible.

Unit 4 • Lesson 6 • Day 4 **T371**

Story Elements: Setting

The setting of a story is composed of three pieces: the place where the story occurs;, the timeframe or when the story takes place, and the amount of time that passes within the story from the beginning to the end.

Text Features

Text features are usually used in informational texts and they help readers make sense of what they are reading. Text features may include headings, illustrations, photos, captions, diagrams, charts, maps, punctuation, font size or color, and numbered or bulleted lists.

Procedures

Read the Selection

First, have students read the selection using whatever skills they need to help them make sense of the selection. Then discuss the selection to assure that students did, indeed, understand what they read. Talk about any confusion they may have, and make any necessary clarifications.

Reread

Revisiting or rereading a selection allows the reader to note specific techniques that authors use to organize and present information in narrative and informational texts. When students have a basic understanding of the piece, have them reread the selection in whole or in part, concentrating on selected accessing complex text and writer's craft skills. Students learn to appreciate that writers use different structures, for example, cause and effect or compare/contrast, to organize their work and that recognizing these structures can help readers understand what they have read. It is these same structures that students will use in their own writing.

Limit this concentration on specific comprehension/writing skills to one or two that can be clearly identified in the piece. Trying to concentrate on too many things will just confuse students and make it harder for them to identify any of the organizational devices used by the writer. If a piece has many good examples of several different aspects, then go back to the piece several times over a span of days.

Reading Big Books

Purpose

Many students come from homes where they are read to often, but a significant number of other students have not had this valuable experience. *Big Books* (Grades K and I) offer all students crucial opportunities to confirm and expand their knowledge about print and reading, to develop vocabulary, and to enjoy literacy experiences. They are especially useful for shared reading experiences in the early grades.

The benefits of reading *Big Books* include engaging even nonreaders in

- unlocking the books' messages.
- developing print awareness.
- participating in good reading behaviors.
- observing what a good reader does: remarking on the illustrations and the title, asking questions about the content and what might happen, making predictions, and clarifying words and ideas.
- promoting the insights about print, for example, that a given word is spelled the same way every time it occurs as high-frequency words are identified.
- reinforcing the correspondence between spoken and written words and spelling patterns.
- enjoying the illustrations and connecting them to the text to help students learn to explore books for enjoyment and information.
- learning about different genres and the language of print.
- developing vocabulary and academic language.
- interpreting and responding to literature and expository text before they can read themselves.

Procedure

During the first reading of the *Big Books,* you will model reading behaviors and comprehension strategies similar to those that will later apply to their own reading. This focus on strategies encourages students to think about the ideas in the stories, to ask questions, and to learn new vocabulary. During the second reading, you will address print awareness and teach accessing complex text skills such as classifying and categorizing, sequencing, or making inferences, which help the reader organize information and focus on the deeper meaning of the text. At first, teachers should expect to do all of the reading but should not prevent students from trying to read on their own or from reading words they already know.

- **Activate Prior Knowledge.** Read the title of the selection and the author's and illustrator's names. At the beginning of each *Big Book,* read the title of the book and discuss what the whole book is about before going on to reading the first selection. Initiate a brief discussion of any prior knowledge students have that might help them understand the selection.

> **Big Books** *offer all students opportunities to confirm and expand their knowledge about print and reading.*

- **Browse the Selection.** Explain to the class that browsing means to look through the pages of the story to get a general idea of what the story is about, to see what interests them, and to ask questions. Ask students to tell what they think the story might be about just from looking at the illustrations. This conversation should be brief so that students can move on to a prereading discussion of print awareness.

- **Develop Print Awareness.** The focus of browsing the *Big Books* is to develop awareness of print. Urge students to tell what words or letters they recognize rather than what they expect the selection to be about. To develop print awareness, have students look through the selection page by page and to comment on whatever they notice in the text. Some students may know some of the words, while others may recognize only specific letters or sounds. The key is to get students to look at the print separately from the illustrations even before they have heard the actual text content. This process isolates print awareness so that it is not influenced by content. It also gives you a clearer idea of what your students do or do not know about print.

- **Read Aloud.** Read the selection aloud expressively, using intonation and pauses at punctuation. Not only does this enable students to hear and enjoy the text as it is read through once, it serves as an early model for fluency. Good fluency and expression support comprehension. As you read, you will stop periodically to model behaviors and comprehension strategies that all students will need to develop to become successful readers—for example, asking questions; clarifying unfamiliar words, first by using the pictures and later by using context; or predicting what might happen next.

- **Reread.** Read the selection expressively again. During the second reading of the stories, you will focus on teaching accessing complex tex skills. Also, to develop print awareness, point to each word as it is read, thus demonstrating that text proceeds from left to right and from top to bottom and helping advance the idea that words are individual spoken and written units. Invite students to identify the rhyming words in a poem or to chime in on repetitive parts of text as you point to the words. Or students can read with you on this second reading, depending on the text. As students' knowledge of words and phonics grows, they can participate in decoding words and reading high-frequency sight words.

- **Discuss Print.** Return to print awareness by encouraging discussion of anything students noticed about the words. Young students should begin to realize that you are reading separate words that are separated by spaces. Later, students will begin to see that each word is made of a group of letters. Students should be encouraged to discuss anything related to the print. For example, you might ask students to point to a word or to count the number of words on a line. Or you might connect the words to the illustrations by pointing to a word and saying it and then asking students to find a picture of that word.

- **Responding.** Responding to a selection is a way of insuring comprehension. Invite students to tell about the story by asking them what they like about the poem or story or calling on a student to explain in his or her own words what the poem or story tells about. Call on others to add to the telling as needed. For nonfiction selections, this discussion might include asking students what they learned about the topic and what they thought was most interesting.

Tips for Using Big Books

- Make sure the entire group is able to see the book clearly while you are reading.
- If some students are able to read words, encourage them to do so during the rereading.
- Encourage students to use their knowledge of print.
- Encourage students' use of academic language as they talk about reading. Students should be comfortable using strategic reading words such as *predict* and *clarify* and book and print words such as *author* and *illustrator.*
- Allow students to look at the *Big Books* whenever they wish.
- Provide small versions of the *Big Books* for students to browse through and to try to read at their leisure.
- The reader of the *Big Book* should try to be part of the collaborative group of learners rather than the leader.

Collaborative Conversation and Discussion

Discussion enables students to share what they are learning, to voice their confusions, and to compare perceptions of what they are learning. Discussion deepens and makes their learning more meaningful. Discussion also creates a natural environment for conversational opportunities that foster oral communication and use of academic language.

Purpose

Through discussions, students are exposed to points of view different from their own and learn how to express their thoughts and opinions coherently. Through discussion, students add to their own knowledge that of their classmates and learn to explain themselves coherently. They also begin to ask insightful questions that help them better understand what they have read and all that they are learning through their inquiry/research and explorations. The purpose of classroom discussion is to provide a framework for learning.

> *The purpose of classroom discussion is to provide a framework for learning.*

Procedure

Reflecting on the Selection

After students have finished reading a selection, provide an opportunity for them to engage in discussion about the selection. Students should

- check to see whether the questions they asked before reading as part of Clues, Problems, and Wonderings and KWL (What I Know, What I Want to Know and What I Have Learned) have been answered. Encourage them to discuss whether any unanswered questions should still be answered. If unanswered questions are related to the theme, add those questions to the **Concept/Question Board.**
- respond to the Essential Question.
- discuss any new questions that have arisen because of the reading. Encourage students to decide which of these questions should go on the **Concept/Question Board.**
- share what they expected to learn from reading the selection and tell whether expectations were met.
- talk about whatever has come to mind while reading the selection. This discussion should be an informal sharing of

impressions of, or opinions about, the selection; it should never take on the aspects of a question-and-answer session about the selection.

- give students ample opportunity to ask questions and to share their thoughts about the selection. Participate as an active member of the group, making your own observations about information in a selection or modeling your own appreciation of a story. Be especially aware of unusual and interesting insights suggested by students so that these insights can be recognized and discussed. To help students learn to keep the discussion student-centered, have each student choose the next speaker instead of handing the discussion back to you.

Clues/Problems/Wonderings		
Clues	Problems	Wonderings
A warbler is a bird because it builds a nest in a tree and it flies back and forth.	alighted examined	Will Shima find out that the warbler is sneaking into his house?

Recording Ideas

As students finish discussions about their reactions to a selection, they should be encouraged to record their thoughts, feelings, reactions, and ideas about the selection or the subject of the selection in their Writer's Notebooks. This will not only help keep the selections fresh in students' minds; it will strengthen their writing abilities and help them learn how to write about their thoughts and feelings.

Students may find that the selection gave them ideas for their own writing, or it might have reminded them of some person or incident in their own lives. Perhaps the selection answered a question that has been on their minds or raised a question they had never thought before. Good, mature writers—especially professional writers—learn the value of recording such thoughts and impressions quickly before they fade. Students should be encouraged to do this also.

Handing Off

Handing off (Grades 1–3) is a technique of turning over to students the primary responsibility for generating and sustaining discussion. Often, students who are taking responsibility for controlling a discussion tend to have all "turns" go through the teacher. The teacher is the one to whom attention is transferred when a speaker finishes, and the teacher is the one who is expected to call on the next speaker—the result being that the teacher remains the pivotal figure in the discussion.

Having students "hand off" the discussion to other students instead of the teacher encourages them to retain complete control of the discussion and to become more actively involved in the learning process. When a student finishes his or her comments, that student should choose (hand off the discussion to) the next speaker. In this way, students maintain a discussion without relying on the teacher to decide who speaks.

When handing off is in place, the teacher's main roles are to

- start the discussion with a question or questions
- occasionally remind students to hand off,
- help students when they get stuck,
- encourage them to persevere on a specific point,
- guide them back to a discussion, and
- monitor the discussion to ensure that everyone gets a chance to contribute. The teacher may say, for example, "Remember, not just boys (or girls)." or "Try to choose someone who has not had a chance to talk yet."

Discuss the Selection

▸ Why is it important for humans and animals to be able to communicate?

▸ How might honeyguides deal with the challenges they face due to many Boran people moving into cities?

It is not unusual early in the process for students to roam from the topic and selection. To bring the discussion back to the topic and selection, be a participant, raise your hand, and ask a question or make a statement that refocuses students' thinking and discussion.

For handing off to work effectively, a seating arrangement that allows students to see one another is essential. It is hard to hold a discussion when students have their backs to each other. A circle or a semicircle is effective. In addition, all students need to have copies of the materials being discussed.

Actively encourage this handing-off process by letting students know that they, not you, are in control of the discussion.

If students want to remember thoughts about, or reactions to, a selection, suggest that they record these in the Response Journal section of their Writer's Notebooks. Encourage students to record the thoughts, feelings, or reactions that are elicited by any reading they do.

Exploring Concepts within the Selection

To provide an opportunity for collaborative learning and to focus on the concepts, you may want to have students form small groups and spend time discussing what they have learned about the concepts from this selection. Topics may include new information that they have acquired, new ideas that they have had, or new questions that the selection raised.

Students should always base their discussions on postings from the **Concept/Question Board** as well as on previous discussions of the concept. The small-group discussions should be ongoing throughout the unit; during this time, students should continue to compare and contrast any new information with their previous ideas, opinions, and impressions about the concepts. How does this selection help confirm their ideas? How does it contradict their thinking? How has it changed their outlook?

As students discuss the concepts in small groups, circulate around the room to make sure that each group stays focused upon the selection and the concepts. After students have had some time to discuss the information and the ideas in the selection, encourage each group to formulate some statements about the concept that apply to the selection.

Differentiated Instruction: Discuss the Selection

AL Give students the following sentence stems to help them join the conversation by building on the comments of others: *I agree with your point because _____. I understand what you mean, but I think _____. I think it is also true that _____.*

OL Challenge students to respond to at least one comment from a fellow classmate during the discussion.

BL Challenge students to make a list of topics to cover in the discussion.

Sharing Ideas about Concepts

Have a representative from each group report and explain the group's ideas to the rest of the class. Then have the class formulate one or more general statements related to the unit concepts and write these statements on the **Concept/Question Board.** As students progress through the unit, they will gain more and more confidence in suggesting additions to the **Concept/Question Board.**

- **Visual Aids** During this part of the discussion, you may find it helpful to use visual aids to help students as they

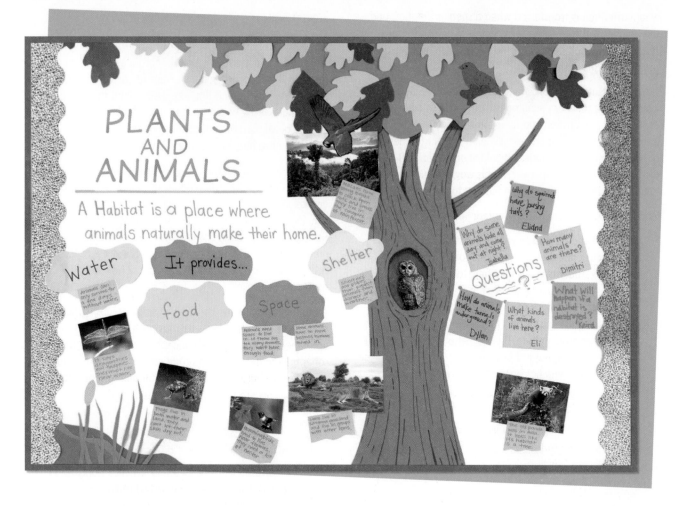

build the connections to the unit concepts. Not all units or concepts will lend themselves to this type of treatment; however, aids such as time lines, charts, graphs, and pictographs may help students see how each new selection adds to their growing knowledge of the concepts.

Encourage students to ask questions about the concepts that the selection may have raised. Have students list on the **Concept/Question Board** those questions that cannot be answered immediately and that they want to explore further.

Exploring Concepts across Selections

As each new selection is read, encourage students to discuss its connection with the other selections and with the unit concepts. Also encourage students to think about selections that they have read from other units and how they relate to the concepts for this unit.

Ultimately, this ability to make connections between past knowledge and new knowledge allows any learner to gain insights into what is being studied. The goal of the work with

concepts and the discussions is to help students to start thinking in terms of connections—how is this like what I have learned before? Does this information confirm, contradict, or add a completely different layer to that which I already know about this concept? How can the others in the class have such different ideas than I do when we just read the same selection? Why is so much written about this subject?

> *Through discussions, students are exposed to points of view different from their own and learn how to express their thoughts and opinions coherently.*

Learning to make connections and to delve deeper through self-generated questions and substantive discussions give students the tools they need to become effective, efficient, lifelong learners.

Tips

- Create an environment that facilitates discussion. Have students sit in circles or some other configuration so everyone can see each other.
- When students are discussing the selection, they should have their books with them, and students should feel free to refer to them throughout the discussion.
- Discussions offer a prime opportunity for you to introduce, or seed, new ideas about the concepts. New ideas can come from a variety of sources: Students may draw on their own experiences or on the books or videos they are studying; you may introduce new ideas into the discussion; or you may invite experts to the class.
- If students do not mention an important idea that is necessary to the understanding of some larger issue, you may "drop" that idea into the conversation and, indeed, repeat it several times to make sure that it does get picked up. This seeding may be subtle ("I think that might be important here") or quite direct ("This is a big idea, one that we will definitely need to understand and one that we will return to regularly").
- To facilitate this process for each unit, you must be aware of the unit concepts and be able to recognize and reinforce them when they arise spontaneously in discussions. If central unit concepts do not arise naturally, then, and only then, will you seed these ideas by direct modeling. In order to do this, you need to actively participate in the discussion. The more you turn over discussions to students, the more involved they will become, and the more responsibility they will take for their own learning. Make it your goal to become a participant in, rather than the leader of, class discussions.
- Help students see that they are responsible for carrying on the discussion. After a question is asked, always wait instead of jumping in with a comment or an explanation. Although this wait time may be uncomfortable at first, students will come to understand that the discussion is their responsibility and that you will not jump in every time there is a hesitation.
- As the year progresses, students will become more and more adept at conducting and participating in meaningful discussions about what they have read. These discussions will greatly enhance students' understanding of the concepts that they are exploring.

Teacher Tip

DISCUSSION Remind students that it is important to be respectful during discussions. They can do this by listening to others with care and by speaking about the topic one at a time. Provide support as they learn to build on each other's conversations in a respectful way.

Discussion Starters and Questions

The following examples of discussion starters can be modeled initially, but then the responsibility for using them should be turned over to students. The starters provide the opportunity for open-ended discussions by students.

- I didn't know that . . . .
- Does anyone know . . . .
- I figured out that . . . .
- I liked the part where . . . .
- I'm still confused about . . . .
- This made me think . . . .
- I agree with _____ because . . . .
- I disagree with _____ because . . . .
- The reason I think _____ is . . .
- I found _____ interesting because . . . .
- I learned . . .
- What I learned in this selection reminds me of what we read in _____ because . . .
- This author's writing reminds me of . . .
- I had problems understanding _____ because . . .
- I wonder why the author chose to . . .
- I still do not understand . . .
- I was surprised to find out . . .
- I like the way the author developed the character by . . .
- The author made the story really come alive by . . .
- I still have a question about _____.

In addition to these open-ended discussion starters, students should be encouraged to ask open-ended questions. When students ask questions, other students should respond to the question before moving on to another idea or topic.

One student asking a question often helps to clarify something for the whole class and places a value on asking questions as a critical part of learning.

- Why did the author . . .?
- What did the author mean when he or she wrote . . .?
- Who can help me clarify . . .?
- Who can help me figure out . . .?
- How does this piece connect to the unit theme?
- What does this section mean?

Inquiry

Even in elementary school, students can produce works of genuine research—research that seeks answers to real questions or solutions to real problems.

Inquiry—research, investigation, and exploration—forms the heart of the *Open Court Reading* program. To encourage students to understand how reading and writing are tools for learning that can enhance their lives and help them become mature, educated adults, they are asked in each unit to use the content they are learning in the unit as the basis for further inquiry, exploration, and research. The unit information is simply the base for their investigations.

There are two types of units in the *Open Court Reading* program—units based on universal topics of interest such as friendship or creativity, and content units that provide students a very solid base of information upon which they can begin their own inquiry and research. Units delving into science-related areas such as animal habitats, light and sound, and extreme weather, or into social studies units that address American history, rules we follow, or citizenship invite students to become true researchers by exploring personal areas of interest driven by problems or questions raised by students. Based upon common areas of interest, students conduct Inquiry in small collaborative groups and then present their findings to their classmates. In this way, students recognize the importance of sharing knowledge and gain much more knowledge of the unit theme than they would have simply by reading the selections in the unit.

The selections in the units are organized so that each selection will add more information or a different perspective to students' growing bodies of knowledge.

Inquiry through Reflective Activities

Purpose

The units in *Open Court Reading* that deal with universal topics tend to be explored through reflective activities. These units—such as Off to School, Teamwork, or Art on the Move—are organized to help students expand—perhaps even change—their perspectives of familiar concepts. As they explore and discuss the concepts that emerge from reading selections related to each unit topic, students are involved in activities that extend their experiences and offer opportunities for reflection. Such activities include writing, drama, art, interviews, debates, and panel discussions. Students will choose the activities and presentation format best suited to explore or investigate their research questions. Throughout each unit, students may be involved in a single ongoing investigative activity, or they may participate in a number of different activities. They may choose to produce a final written project or a multimedia presentation. They will share with the rest of the class the new knowledge that they have gained from their investigations. Workshop provides an ideal time for students to work individually or in collaborative groups on their investigation and/or projects.

The Inquiry activities will be those of students' own choosing, thereby allowing them to explore the unit concepts more fully. They are free, of course, to make other choices or to devise activities of their own.

Procedure

Choosing an Area to Investigate

While students may work on activities alone, in pairs, or in small groups in later units, have them work as a whole class, at least for the first unit or two. This will give you time to model the steps of the Inquiry process and allow students time to understand what should be happening in each step. Over time, as students become more comfortable with the process, they should decide what concept-related question or problem they wish to explore. Generally, it is better for students to generate wonderings, questions, or problems after they have engaged in some discussion at the beginning of each unit. This should be done, however, before they have had a chance to consult source materials. The goal is to have students ask questions that will drive their inquiry. This approach is more likely to bring forth ideas that students actually wonder about or wish to understand. Students may also look at the questions posted on the **Concept/Question Board** or introduce fresh ideas inspired by material they have just finished reading.

In later units, Inquiry pairs or groups may develop based upon common areas of interest or common questions that appear on the **Concept/Question Board.** Students who share a common interest for inquiry should work together to develop a common question to explore. Some students may need your assistance in deciding upon, or narrowing down, a question or a problem so that it can be explored more easily. A good way to model this process for students is to make webs for a few of your own ideas on the board and to narrow down these ideas to a workable question or problem.

Organizing the Group

After a question or a problem has been chosen, students may choose an activity that will help them investigate that problem or question. For example, if students in Grade 3 are exploring the question "How do Native American tribes show respect to the natural world?" they may want to create a conjecture about how some Native Americans show respect for nature through traditional songs and dances or by supporting efforts to preserve wild places for various plants and animals. To collect specific information, students may want to conduct an interview with someone knowledgeable about a particular tribe's customs, or they may also want to do some additional reading about Native American traditions, explore resources on the Internet, and so on. Students will also need to learn what to look for as well as how to take notes from their various resources. They will revise their conjecture if necessary. Lastly, students need to decide how, or if, they want to present their findings. For instance, after collecting information and revising their conjectures, students may want to create a slideshow that shows the different ways in which Native American tribes show respect for nature, and then present the slideshow for all to see and discuss.

Deciding How to Investigate

The following suggestions may help you and your students choose ways in which to pursue their investigations. For units on universal topics that are more literary in nature, students may want to do one of the following activities to pursue answers to their questions.

- Conduct an information search to pursue a question or a problem. Discussion or writing may follow.
- Write and produce an original playlet or puppet show based on situations related to the concepts.
- Play a role-playing game to work out a problem related to the concepts.
- Stage a panel discussion with audience participation on a question or problem.
- Hold a debate on an issue related to the concept.
- Write a personal-experience story related to the concepts.
- Invite experts to class. Formulate questions to ask.
- Conduct an interview with someone on a subject related to the concepts.
- Produce and carry out a survey on an issue or a question related to the concept.
- Produce a picture or photo-essay about the concept.

You may want to post this list in the classroom so that groups have access to it as they decide what they want to investigate and how they want to proceed. Encourage students to explore other possibilities as well and to add these ideas to the list.

EXAMPLE: In the Teamwork unit in Grade 2 of *Open Court Reading,* students read "The Mice Who Lived in a Shoe." This selection is about how a family of mice work together with their extended family and friends to build a new house. During the class

discussion, some students may note that it may not have been a good idea for Pa to ask everyone to draw his or her dream house. As the discussion continues, other students may conclude from the story that it was a good idea for Pa to ask the question and to consider everyone's ideas for the final design. Students may then relate this story to their own sense of teamwork, and how working together gives everyone a sense of value and accomplishment.

Students choose some reflective activities that will help them learn more about teamwork and that will answer some of their questions about the unit concepts. These questions may relate to how people who are very different from one another can work together toward a common goal. Other students may want to find out how different animal species demonstrate teamwork or perhaps how both people and animals can work as a team. Some students may be interested in going to the library to find books about how to train dogs or other animals. Other students may want to interview dog trainers. Review with students what they know about interviewing. They should proceed by performing the following:

- Researching examples of interviews to see what they might look like and how to build in space to write answers
- Preparing a list of questions to ask
- Preparing a list of subjects to interview, deciding how to record the interview (by audio recording, video recording, or taking written or keyed notes)
- Contacting in advance the person(s) they want to interview
- Deciding whether to photograph the person and, if so, getting permission to do so in advance—collecting the equipment necessary for conducting the interview
- After they conduct the interviews, students decide how they wish to present the information that they have collected.

EXAMPLE: You may wish to distribute relevant resources to small groups of students or to the entire class to review. Then you will need to walk the entire class through the process of reading and note-taking. Model for students how to collect information by taking good notes. You may want to proceed with the following:

- Display a two-column chart with "Words" as the heading in column 1 and "Images" as the heading in column 2.
- Read aloud a few sentences from a relevant book or Internet site.
- Discuss with students the most important point or points contained in the information you read aloud to them.
- Write each phrase that students identify in the Words column, and then draw a simple sketch for each conept in the Images column. Be sure to write phrases only and not complete sentences.

- Point out that neither you nor they are copying things verbatim from the resources at hand; instead, you are writing down the most important points.
- Continue modeling note-taking for students.
- After you have completed taking notes, write the word "Summary" and then have students summarize all the information you have written.

After students collect the information, they will need to organize the information to revise their conjecture, if necessary. Then guide then through the process of pulling together their research and presenting it to the class. Encourage students to plan, draft, revise, and edit/proofread their work until they are completely satisfied with it.

Not all questions on the **Concept/Question Board** will be explored in depth. Throughout the unit, students can continue discussing teamwork and raising and posting new questions. Remind them that as they read further, they may think of additional ways to explore the unit concepts. Students should sign or initial their questions or ideas so that they can identify classmates with similar interests and exchange ideas with them. The teacher should encourage students to feel free to write an answer or a note on someone else's question or to consult the Board for ideas for their own explorations. From time to time, the teacher should post his or her own questions on the **Concept/ Question Board**.

Tips

- Workshop is an ideal time for students to work on their Inquiry activities.
- Some students work better within a specified time frame. Whenever they are beginning a new activity, discuss with students a reasonable period of time within which they will be expected to complete their investigations. Post the completion date somewhere in the classroom so that students can refer to it and pace themselves accordingly. At first, you may have to help them determine a suitable deadline, but eventually they should be able to make this judgment on their own.
- Have students use the resources in *eInquiry* to help them on their investigation activities.
- Some teachers like to do the Inquiry for the first unit with a common question decided upon by the whole class. Then students break into small groups and work on different ways to explore the question. One group may do a literature search while another might conduct a survey. The end results in students sharing new knowledge that addresses the common research question.

Inquiry through Research

Purpose

Students come to school with a wealth of fascinating questions. Educators need to capitalize on this excitement for learning and natural curiosity. A classroom in which the teacher is the only person who asks the questions and defines the assignments, only correct answers are accepted, and students are not allowed to make errors and consider alternative possibilities to questions can quickly deaden this natural curiosity and enthusiasm. The purpose of the inquiry and research aspect of this program is to capitalize on students' questions and natural curiosity by using a framework or structure based upon the scientific method. This structure helps students ask questions and preserve the open-ended character of real research, which can lead to unexpected findings and to questions that were not originally considered.

> *Students come to school with a wealth of fascinating questions. Educators need to capitalize on this excitement for learning and natural curiosity.*

The conventional approach to school research papers can be found, with minor variations, in countless textbooks and instructional resources. This approach consists of a series of steps such as the following: Select a topic or choose a topic from a list suggested by the teacher, narrow the topic to something of interest, collect materials, take notes, outline, and write. By following these steps, a student may produce a presentable paper, but the procedure does not constitute research in a meaningful sense. Indeed, this restrictive approach may give students a distorted notion of what research is. We see students in universities and even in graduate schools still following this procedure when they write research papers or literature reviews; we see their dismay when their professors regard such work as mere cutting and pasting and ask them what their original contribution is.

Elementary school students can produce works of genuine research—research that seeks answers to real questions or solutions to real problems—when they are provided the opportunity, taught how to ask good questions and develop conjectures, and work collaboratively to find information or data that will support or refute their conjecture. Being able to collect, analyze, and evaluate information are critical twenty-first century skills. In the adult world, as knowledgeable consumers, productive members of a sophisticated workforce, and lifelong learners, students will be expected to identify problems, raise questions, analyze new information, and make informed decisions based on this information. Preparing students for the analytic demands of adult life and teaching them how to find answers are goals of education.

Process

To make the research productive, the following important principles are embodied in this approach:

1. Research is focused on problems, not topics.
2. Questions and wonderings are the foundation for inquiry and research.
3. Conjectures—opinions based on less than complete evidence or proof—are derived from questions and guide the research; the research does not simply produce conjectures.
4. New information and data are gathered to test and revise conjectures.
5. Discussion, ongoing feedback, and constructive criticism are important in all phases of the research but especially in the revising of problems and conjectures.
6. The cycle of true research is essentially endless, although presentations of findings are made from time to time; new findings give rise to new problems and conjectures and thus to new cycles of research.

Routine

While working with the science and social studies units, students are encouraged to use this framework to keep their research activities focused and on track. Within this framework, there is flexibility. Students may begin with a question, develop a conjecture, and begin collecting information only to find that they need to redefine their conjecture. Like the writing process, there is a recursive nature to this framework. Students may go through these steps many times before they come to the end of their research. Certainly for adult researchers, this cycle of question, conjecture, research, and reevaluation can go on for years and, in some cases, lifetimes.

This cycle uses the following process:

1. Decide on a problem or question to research. Students should identify a question or problem that they truly wonder about or wish to understand and then form research groups with other students who have the same interests.
   - My problem or question is _____.

2. Formulate an idea or conjecture about the research problem. Students should think about and discuss with classmates possible answers to their research problems or questions and meet with their research groups to discuss and record their ideas or conjectures.
   - My idea/conjecture/theory about this question or problem is _____.
   - I think the answer to my question is _____ .

3. Identify needs and make plans. Students should identify knowledge needs related to their conjectures and meet with their research groups to determine which resources to consult and to make individual job assignments. Students should also meet periodically with the teacher, other classmates, and research groups to present preliminary findings and to make revisions to their problems and conjectures on the basis of these findings.
   - I need to find out _____ .
   - To do this, I will need these resources: _____
   - My role in the group is _____ .
   - This is what I have learned so far: _____
   - This is what happened when we presented our findings _____

4. Reevaluate the problem or question based on what we have learned so far and the feedback we have received .
   - My revised problem or question is _____ .

5. Revise the idea or conjecture.
   - My new conjecture about this problem is _____.

6. Identify new needs and make new plans.
   - Based on what I found out, I still need to know _____ .
   - To do this, I will need these resources: _____
   - This is what I have learned: _____
   - This is what happened when we presented our new findings: _____

Choosing a Problem to Research

Choosing a problem to research takes time and begins to develop through discussion and reading.

1. Discuss with students the nature of the unit. Explain to students that the unit they are reading is a research unit and that they will develop and present the results of their research. They are free to decide what problems or questions they wish to explore, with whom they want to work, and how they want to present their finished products. Their presentation may be a piece of writing, a poster, a play, or any other format to present the results of their investigations and research. They may work individually, with partners, or in small groups.

2. Discuss with students the schedule you have planned for their investigations: how long the project is expected to take, how much time will be available for research, when the first presentation will be due. This schedule will partly determine the nature of the problems that students should be encouraged to work on and the depth of the inquiry students will be encouraged to pursue.

3. Have students talk about things they wonder about that are related to the unit subject. For example, in the Grade I unit Stars and Stripes, students might wonder how something becomes a symbol. Conduct a free-floating discussion of questions about the unit subject.

4. Brainstorm possible questions for students to think about. It is essential that students' own ideas and questions be the starting point of all inquiry. Helpful hint: For the first research unit, you might wish to generate a list of your own ideas, having students add to this list and having them choose from it.

5. Using their wonderings, model for students the difference between a research topic and a research problem or question by providing several examples. For example, have them consider the difference between the broad topic *California* and the problem *Why do so many people move to California?* Explain that if they choose to research the topic *California,* everything they look up under the subject heading or index entry *California* will be related in some way to their topic. Therefore, it will be quite difficult to choose which information to record. This excess of information also creates problems in organizing research. Clearly, then, this topic is too broad and general. Choosing a specific question or problem, one that particularly interests them, helps them narrow their exploration and advance their understanding. Some possible ideas for questions can be found in the unit introduction. Ideas can also be generated as you and your students create a web of their questions or problems related to the unit concept. For example, questions related to the topic *California* might include the following: Why do so many people move to California? How have the different groups of people living in California affected the state?

6. A good research problem or question not only requires students to consult a variety of sources but is engaging and adds to the groups' knowledge of the unit concepts. Furthermore, good problems generate more questions. Help students understand that the question *Why do so many people move to California?* will need many resources to contribute to an answer to the question, and all information located needs to be evaluated in terms of usefulness in answering the question.

7. Remember that this initial problem or question serves only as a guide for research. As students begin collecting information and collaborating with classmates, their ideas

will change, and they can revise their research problem or question. Frequently, students do not sufficiently revise their problems until after they have had time to consider their conjectures and to collect information.

8. As students begin formulating their research problems, have them elaborate on their reasons for wanting to research their stated problems. They should go beyond simple expressions of interest or liking and indicate what is puzzling, important, or potentially informative, and so forth about the problems they have chosen.

9. At this stage, students' ideas will be of a very vague and limited sort. The important thing is to start them thinking about what really interests them and what value it has to them and the class.

10. Have students present their proposed problems or questions, along with reasons for their choices, and have an open discussion of how promising proposed problems are. As students present their proposed problems, ask them what new things they think they will be learning from their investigations and how that will add to the group's growing knowledge of the concepts. This constant emphasis on group knowledge building will help set a clear purpose for students' research.

II. Form research groups. To make it easier for students to form groups, they may record their problems on the board or on self-sticking notes. Final groups should be constituted in the way you find best for your class—by self-selection, by assignment on the basis of common interests, or by some combination of methods. Students can then meet during Workshop to agree on a precise statement of their research problem, the nature of their expected research contributions, and lists of related questions that may help later in assigning individual roles. They should also record any scheduling information that can be added to the planning calendar.

Using Technology

Students and teachers can access the Web site **connected.mcgraw-hill.com** to find information about the themes in their grade level. In addition, students may access activities in *eInquiry* that will give them direction and tools to help them in their investigations.

What does Inquiry look like in the classroom?

Inquiry is a new concept for many students and develops over an extended period of time. The following series of vignettes are an example of what Inquiry might look like in a third-grade classroom that is studying the third-grade unit Extreme Weather.

Lesson 1

Developing Good Research Questions

For the unit on extreme weather, Ms. Hernandes introduced the theme through the read-aloud selection "Wind" and then had the class read the selection "Storm Chasers." Now she is focusing on having her students generate some questions. To maximize the number of resources available to her students to do their inquiry, she talked with the librarian at her local library as well as local high school teachers who are knowledgeable in the area of extreme weather. Both were able to provide resources for the class.

Ms. Hernandes began with a discussion of weather. She had prepared some basic questions to get the class started.

- How is weather important to us?
- What are some different types of extreme weather?
- How can we prepare for different types of weather?
- When did people first start to measure weather?
- Why do you think people want to control weather?
- How can technology help us to understand weather?
- What kinds of risks are involved in studying extreme weather?
- Why are some people, plants, or animals more affected by weather than others are?

The teacher felt that using open-ended questions like these would help get her students talking about what they know about weather as well as give her an opportunity to informally assess students' background knowledge.

Students were able to provide some basic information such as the following:

- Weather affects the way we dress, live, and work.
- Extreme weather could be a drought in one area, a hurricane in another, or a blizzard in another area.
- We can measure weather by using thermometers, barometers, or other types of technology.
- People want to control the weather so it does not get too extreme.
- Technology helps us understand weather because it can create record data and go into places that would not be safe for humans.
- People might get into dangerous situations by studying tornadoes or hurricanes.
- Sometimes different species have different tolerances for extreme situations in their habitat.

But there were some basic misunderstandings that arose during the conversation, such as the following:

- Everyone knows what to do when there is bad weather.
- Bad weather goes away, and then everything is okay again.

- Because chasing storms and studying extreme weather is exciting, it is worth the risk.

By discussing extreme weather in such general terms, students were able to share basic information.

To move students to the next level—asking questions— Ms. Hernandes began by thinking aloud about things related to the unit that interested her.

"I really am curious about how extreme weather forms. And I also wonder about ways we can protect ourselves from extreme weather." Ms. Hernandes encouraged her students to share some of their wonderings or things they are curious about and helped lead students to generate additional questions. Some student wonderings included the following:

- I wonder how certain animals survive in places with extremely hot weather.
- How did changes in Earth's weather lead to the extinction of dinosaurs?
- How do people protect buildings from hurricanes or tornadoes?
- How did people survive in Arctic regions before the invention of electricity?
- What would happen if the weather was always the same where we lived?
- What would happen if the weather was the same all across the globe?
- Why do people always talk about the weather?
- How do umanned machines measure changes in Earth's weather?

Lesson 2

Forming Conjectures

Ms. Hernandes and her class have been reading about extreme weather for the past week. Many students read different trade books during Workshop to learn more about weather. Every day at the end of Workshop, they shared some of their new questions. Some students even started bringing in articles from newspapers and magazines and posting them on the **Concept/Question Board.**

By now there are a number of questions on the **Concept/Question Board,** and Ms. Hernandes wants to work with the class to move from asking questions to forming conjectures. She began by modeling or thinking aloud and sharing some of her own thoughts: "When I watch the weather report on television, I know that the reporter uses radar to predict what is going to happen. I wonder if in the future everyone will have some kind of handheld device to help us predict the weather."

The focus is on asking questions. She recognized that students' questions needed to be refined to lead to functional conjectures. The class discussed what makes a good question.

- Questions or wonderings should be things that students are truly curious about.
- Questions should be generated without consulting an encyclopedia or a reference source.
- Good questions cannot be answered with a simple *yes* or *no.*
- Questions should help students deepen their understanding of the unit theme rather than focus on a character or incident in a specific story.
- A good research question often begins with *how.*

To help move students toward developing some good questions for inquiry, the class reviewed all the questions and grouped them together. They discussed these groups of questions and decided to think of a good representative question. The class worked over the next couple of days to think of a question they were all interested in. Ms. Hernandes and the class talked about their questions and how to refine them. For example, one question the class raised earlier was "How do unmanned machines measure changes in Earth's weather?" Ms. Hernandes wrote the question on the board and discussed it with her students. They talked about what possible answers they might find. Then she guided the class to change the focus of the question to "Why are unmanned drones more effective than people when studying some types of weather?"

Because a goal of Inquiry is to have students move from asking questions to forming conjectures, Ms. Hernandes explained to the class that they were now going to take their question and develop a conjecture. Developing a conjecture simply means thinking of what they think the best answer is, given what they know now and have read so far. Ms. Hernandes modeled this by using the question students raised in the earlier lesson, "Why are unmanned drones more effective than people when studying some types of weather?" Ms. Hernandes thought aloud about possible answers to this question and guided the class to change the question into some conjectures such as the following:

- Unmanned drones can safely reach dangerous areas.
- Unmanned drones eliminate human error.
- Stormchasers are often volunteers and have jobs, while unmanned drones are always available.

Ms. Hernandes discussed the possible conjectures with students. As as class, they selected the conjecture "Unmanned drones can safely reach dangerous areas."

Lesson 3

Forming Conjectures

Identifying Needs and Making Plans

The class conjecture was "Unmanned drones can safely reach dangerous areas." Ms. Hernandes put the conjecture on the board for students to see. She guided the class to see that this did not really relate to extreme weather, so as a class, they revised the conjecture to "Unmanned drones are more effective than people when studying some weather because they can safely reach dangerous areas."

During the week, Ms. Hernandes continued working with the class on Inquiry. To help the group get started on identifying needs and materials related to their conjecture, Ms. Hernandes asked the following questions:

- What information will we need to help us decide if our conjecture is accurate?
- Where can we find this information?
- Who can help us find information related to our conjecture?
- What people in our school might be able to help us?
- What family members might know something about this?
- What words could we plug in on the Internet to help us get more information?

During the rest of this week, students started collecting different resources and reading various books during Workshop. Ms. Hernandes guided students to take notes using their own words, double-checking their summaries against the original, and writing down information such as the title, author, and copyright information or Website URLs about the sources. Ms. Hernandes also helped students conduct effective Internet searches by focusing on key terms such as "why use weather drones" rather than using the entire conjecture. Also, she cautioned students to look for reputable sources at *.gov* or *.org* Websites and to crosscheck source dates, because often new research is available.

Lesson 4

Revising Plans as Necessary

Collecting Data and Information

Now that students have started collecting material, they need to identify individual job assignments so they are not duplicating efforts. At the beginning of this week, Ms. Hernandes took time to have students meet in their groups. During this time she met with the small groups to track their progress, discuss any problems, and help them focus their research efforts.

The groups had been working with the conjecture "Unmanned drones are more effective than people when studying some weather because they can safely reach dangerous areas." However, while one of the small groups had found information supporting the conjecture, another had found some more current research that did not entirely support the conjecture. Ms. Hernandes put the conjecture on the board for students and then drew a Venn diagram. In the first oval she wrote "the main way meteorologists measure hurricanes from within is by sending in hurricane hunters." In the second oval she wrote "weather drones can give general information by flying high over hurricanes; hurricane hunters can give detailed information by flying deep into hurricanes." In the overlap, she wrote "planes that go into hurricanes carry specialized equipment."

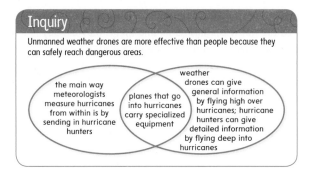

Ms. Hernandes discussed this information with her class and concluded that because the most current information indicated that drones and hurricane hunters serve different purposes, perhaps it was time to change the conjecture to make it more accurate. The group agreed to change it to "Unmanned weather drones are more effective than people at accomplishing certain tasks." She led students to use their synthesized information to confirm or refute the conjecture, and then guided them to revise the conjecture as needed.

The class continued to gather more information. Ms. Hernandes then helped them to organize the information into related groups, again using a Venn diagram to synthesize relevant pieces of inforamtion.

Lesson 5

Continuing Working and Planning Final Presentation

At this point students are beginning to conclude their investigations and are thinking about ways to present their findings. At this point, Ms. Herndandes helped divide students into groups so that different groups would present different parts of the research to the rest of the class. As groups practiced presenting their information, Ms. Hernandes modeled constructive comments such as the following: "Your points are clearly made." "Your charts and graphs help us understand each of your points." "Each one of you presented different pieces of information that all connect to your conjecture." "How was your conjecture supported?"

After the lesson, Ms. Hernandes took time to reflect and realized that it was very hard for her students to give constructive feedback. She knew that this is an area they would need to work on. She would have to continue modeling but also thought about having groups exchange conjectures and provide feedback in writing to each other. This might reduce anxiety as well as give students time to reflect on the questions and conjectures and to develop some thoughtful feedback.

During this week, Ms. Hernandes took time to discuss possible ways that students could present their findings. The class brainstormed other ideas including the following:

- Writing a story
- Creating a poster illustrating a process
- Performing an experiment related to the research
- Planning to create a Webpage
- Staging a panel discussion with audience participation

Students returned to their groups to decide how they wanted to present their findings.

Lesson 6

Final Presentation

Students have been busy working on completing their investigations and developing their presentations. While the class decided on a single research question at the beginning of the unit, know that as the Inquiry process develops over the course of the year, different groups will develop their own conjectures. In this unit, because the class had a single conjecture that guided their research, Ms. Hernandes divided the class into groups for presentation purposes only. Each group will be presenting different information. Ms. Hernandes has created a simple web with the class's research question in the center and circles around the question. After groups present their work, the class will discuss what information was found to address the research question. As presentations are made, students will also be encouraged to make connections not only to the question but to each other's findings.

Throughout the unit, Ms. Hernandes recognized that students need more work on asking questions of each other and providing constructive feedback. She plans on modeling questions and comments as groups complete their presentations. Some examples include the following:

- How does what you presented support or refute your conjecture?

- Would you clarify . . .
- It would be helpful if . . .
- Have you thought about . . .
- Your visuals really helped me better understand your ideas.
- That was a great idea. Where can we find more information on it so we can learn more about it?
- What other questions did you think of as you were researching your conjecture?

Overall, Ms. Hernandes felt that this first attempt at Inquiry with the entire class focusing on a single question but generating multiple conjectures made Inquiry manageable for students and herself. Ms. Hernandes is now thinking about how to plan the next Inquiry unit so there are multiple questions as well as multiple conjectures. From the final presentations, she has really begun to appreciate how Inquiry incorporates all the reading and writing skills she has been teaching and how it takes students to the next level of learning—delving deeper into ideas that personally interest them, taking time and responsibility to learn about something, working collaboratively, and sharing new ideas and information.

Tips

- Inquiry takes time to develop. You may want to do the first unit as an entire class.
- Provide time throughout the unit for students to work on Inquiry. Use Workshop as well as computer and library time to support Inquiry.

- Helpful hint: Students' initial responses may indeed be topics instead of problems or questions. If so, the following questions might be helpful: What aspect of the topic really interests you? Can you turn that idea into a question?
- If students are careful about the problems or questions they choose to research, they should have few problems in following through with the research. If the problem is too broad or too narrow, they will have problems.
- Monitor student progress. Meet with groups during Workshop throughout the unit to check on progress and help resolve any concerns or problems.
- Have students take sufficient time in assessing their needs—both knowledge needs and physical needs in relation to their research. Careful preplanning can help the research progress smoothly with great results.
- Encourage students to reevaluate their needs often so they are not wasting time finding things they already have or ignoring needs that they have not noticed.
- Interim presentations of material are every bit as important, if not more so, than final presentations. It is during interim presentations that students have the opportunity to rethink and reevaluate their work and change direction or to decide to carry on with their planned research.
- Connect Inquiry to learning in the content areas. Have students apply their Inquiry skills to learning science, social studies, and the arts.

Inquiry Planner

USE the steps below to have students research the theme Extreme Weather.

	Steps	Examples
LESSON 1	Develop Questions	Why are unmanned drones more effective than people when studying some types of weather?
LESSON 2	Create Conjectures	Unmanned drones can safely reach dangerous areas. Unmanned drones eliminate human error. Storm chasers are often volunteers and have jobs, while unmanned drones are always available.
LESSON 3	Collect Information	I need to learn more about how unmanned drones research the weather. To do this, I will look for information in books and online. I will also e-mail a local weather station to interview them.
LESSON 4	Revise Conjectures	Unmanned weather drones are more effective than people at accomplishing certain tasks.
LESSON 5	Develop Presentations	My group will create a web page with information about why unmanned drones are more efficient at researching weather. It will show videos taken by unmanned weather drones and have links to more information.
LESSON 6	Deliver Presentations	Groups will present their research findings. The class should discuss the presentation and ask any new questions they have about the information presented.

Listening and Speaking Skills

Some people are naturally good listeners, and others have no trouble speaking in front of groups. Many people, however, need explicit instruction on how to tune in for important details and how to organize and make an oral presentation. While some people naturally critique what they read, hear, and see, many others need specific guidance to develop skills for analyzing what they encounter in images and the media. The abilities to listen appropriately and to speak in conversations and in groups, as well as to critically evaluate the information with which they are presented, are fundamental skills that will serve students throughout their lives.

Purpose

In addition to reading and writing, listening and speaking is an integral part of *Open Court Reading.* Through the development of listening and speaking skills, students gain flexibility with and confidence in communicating orally, visually, and in writing. When speaking and listening skills are neglected, many students have difficulty speaking in front of groups, organizing a speech, or distinguishing important information they hear. Speaking in front of groups can create anxiety—even for many adults. Much of this anxiety would not exist if listening and speaking skills were taught from the early years.

Many of the listening and speaking skills are very similar to reading or writing skills. For example, listening for details is the same type of skill as reading for details. Preparing an oral report employs many of the same skills as preparing a written report. Learning to use these skills effectively gives students flexibility in how they approach a task. Furthermore, listening and speaking are naturally reinforced in all aspects of learning as students listen and respond to each other during discussions, writing, and Inquiry.

Procedure

Listening and speaking skills are integrated throughout the lessons in *Open Court Reading.* The following skills are taught and reviewed throughout the year so that students encounter the skills again and again:

- **Listening.** Listening skills include comprehending what one hears and listening for different purposes, such as to identify sequence or details, to summarize or make inferences, or to follow directions.

- **Speaking.** Speaking skills include speaking formally and conversationally, using appropriate volume, giving oral presentations, and using effective grammar. Speaking skills also include using descriptive words, figurative language, and formal and informal language.
- **Interaction.** Interaction instruction focuses on a combination of listening and speaking skills. These include asking and responding to questions; nonverbal cues such as eye contact, facial expression, and posture; and contributing to and interacting in group settings.
- **Presenting Information.** The presentation skills include sharing ideas, relating experiences or stories, organizing information, and preparing for speeches. These skills are often included in the Writing instruction so that students can prepare their stories or information in written or oral form. These skills are an integral part of the Inquiry process as students share their ideas, questions, conjectures, and findings.

Tips

- Identify the parallels among the language arts skills: providing written and oral directions, telling or writing a narrative, and so on. Encourage students to see that they have choices for communicating. Discuss the similarities and differences between varying forms of communication, and determine whether one is preferable in a given situation.
- Ensure that all students have opportunities to speak in small groups and whole-class situations.
- Provide and teach students to allow appropriate wait time before someone answers a question.
- Encourage students (as they are able) to take notes to help them remember what they heard so they can better respond.
- Remind students to use visuals when appropriate in their presentations to support their presentations and to help keep the listeners' attention.
- Set up simple class rules to show respect for the listener and speaker. These rules should be used during Inquiry, handing off, or any time of the day and should foster respect for the speaker and listeners.
  - Students should speak in a voice loud and clear enough for everyone in the class to hear.
  - Students should raise their hands and not interrupt.

- If someone asks a question, then the person who responds should address the question before going on to another idea or topic.
- The speaker should look at the audience, and the audience should look at the speaker.

Rubrics

Rules for speaking and listening should be set for your students at the beginning of the year, so that everyone understands what is expected of both listeners and speakers. You will have multiple opportunites to model the expected behavior during Handing Off. In addition, share with students the following rubrics that are available in the Level Appendix of the *Teacher's Editions* so that students may see how they will be evaluated for both speaking and listening.

Speaking and Listening Rubrics

The following rubrics can be used to measure students' speaking and listening abilities during collaborative conversations. **SRA Open Court Reading** provides a four-point rubric for speaking and a four-point rubric for listening. These rubrics can be used at any point during the lesson when students are demonstrating their speaking and listening skills. The rubrics identify the types of behavior students use when they are actively listening or when they are speaking and presenting information appropriately.

Speaking Rubric

1 The student speaks in conversational language with mispronunciations of words. Run-on and incomplete sentences are common, and the student's vocabulary is marked by the frequent use of words such as *things* and *stuff* rather than academic language. The student's voice is barely audible, and his or her stance is informal. The student makes no eye contact and uses no pictures or illustrations.

2 The student speaks in a mixture of academic and conversational language with mispronunciations of words. Most of the student's sentences are simple or run-on sentences, and his or her vocabulary is primarily conversational with little use of academic language. Content includes irrelevant facts. The student's voice is soft and hard to hear, and his or her stance is informal. The student makes no eye contact even when pictures or illustrations are not being used.

3 The student speaks clearly and uses academic language with minimal mispronunciations of words. His or her sentences are complete. The student's vocabulary is appropriate for the audience and content, and he or she demonstrates understanding of the content by answering questions. The student's voice is clear and loud enough to be heard by everyone most of the time, and he or she stands straight but makes limited eye contact. The student also uses little or no pictures or illustrations to make ideas clear.

4 The student speaks clearly and distinctly, using academic language and complete sentences. The student's vocabulary is appropriate for the grade level, audience, and content. The student also demonstrates understanding of the content by answering questions. The student's voice is clear and loud enough to be heard by everyone, and he or she stands straight and makes eye contact. The student also uses pictures or illustrations to help make ideas clear.

Listening Rubric

1 The student looks around or stares off into the distance and is obviously not listening. He or she does not take notes, ask questions, or make comments.

2 The student listens sporadically and does not look at the speaker. He or she does not take notes, ask questions, or make comments.

3 The student listens and makes some eye contact with the speaker. He or she takes limited notes (if appropriate), asks only *yes/no* questions, and makes no comments about the presentation.

4 The student listens attentively and makes eye contact with the speaker. He or she takes notes (if appropriate), ask relevant questions, and makes comments about the presentation.

Writing

Purpose

The writing program in *Open Court Reading* teaches students how to write skillfully. This is essential, as writing is a powerful tool that fosters learning, communication, creativity, and self-discovery. The writing in *Open Court Reading* teaches students how to use writing effectively for these purposes.

Writing is a complex process. It involves deftly juggling a variety of skills, strategies, and knowledge. Writers must make plans, consider the reader, draw ideas from memory, develop new ideas, organize thoughts, consider the conventions of the genre, translate ideas into words, craft sentences, evaluate decisions, make needed revisions, transcribe words into correctly spelled print, and monitor the writing process, among other things.

> *Children start school wanting to learn how to write and enjoying writing. The goal of writing in* Open Court Reading *is for children to become lifelong writers—people who enjoy writing and use writing effectively at work as well as in their personal lives.*

The writing in *Open Court Reading* is designed to ensure that students acquire the skills, knowledge, and strategies, and dispositions they need to become skilled writers. This includes the following:

- Knowledge about the qualities of good writing, characteristics of different genres, intended audience, and writing topics. Skilled writers know how to obtain information about their topics, are familiar with basic features of different genres, and possess basic schemas or frameworks for accomplishing common writing tasks.
- The writing strategies involved in basic composing processes such as prewriting, drafting, monitoring, evaluating, revising, editing/proofreading, and publishing. Skilled writers flexibly employ these strategies to create text.

- Command of basic writing skills and conventions such as handwriting, spelling, sentence construction, grammar, and usage. Skilled writers execute these basic writing skills with little conscious effort.
- Interest and motivation to write, as well as perceptions of competence as a writer. Skilled writers possess an "I can do" attitude.

Procedures

With *Open Court Reading,* evidence-based practices are used to teach students to write skillfully. These evidence-based practices are drawn from research on the effectiveness of specific writing interventions that show that the quality of students' writing can be improved by the following:

- explicitly teaching strategies for prewriting, drafting, revising, editing/proofreading, and publishing.
- modeling effective use of writing strategies.
- having students work together to prewrite, draft, revise, edit/proofread, and publish their compositions.
- using prewriting tools such as graphic organizers to gather information.
- involving students in inquiry activities designed to help them further develop their ideas for writing.
- making the goals for writing assignments clear and specific.
- teaching students how to construct more sophisticated sentences.
- providing students with the opportunity to read, evaluate, and emulate models of good writing.
- teaching students how to use word processing as a tool for composing.

The evidence-based practices in *Open Court Reading* are also based on the study of expert teachers who

- make sure their students are engaged, spending most of their writing time doing something that involves thoughtfulness, such as crafting a story or learning how to construct a complex sentence.
- teach basic writing skills, strategies, and knowledge balanced by ample opportunity to apply what is learned.
- involve students in writing for a variety of different purposes.
- create a writing classroom environment that is supportive, pleasant, and motivating.
- encourage students to accomplish as much as possible on their own (to act in a self-regulated fashion), but who are ready to offer support and instruction as needed.
- use reading to support writing development and vice versa.
- monitor students' growth in writing and encourage students to monitor their own growth.
- provide extra assistance to students who experience difficulty.
- are passionate about writing.

Knowledge about Writing

Purpose

Writing can be used to communicate, entertain, inform, reflect, persuade, and learn. To take full advantage of this flexible tool, students must acquire knowledge about the qualities of good writing and the various purposes and forms of writing. They must also carefully consider their audience and be knowledgeable about the topics they write about.

Procedures

Qualities of Good Writing

One way students learn about the qualities of good writing is by directly teaching them that good writing is characterized by the following seven traits:

- Clearly presented and fully developed ideas
- Writing that is easy to follow and logically organized
- Effective and precise word choice
- Varied use of sentence structure to promote fluency, rhythm, and natural speech patterns
- Writing that captures appropriate tone or mood to make the desired impact on the reader
- Correct spelling, usage, and grammar
- A written product that is legible, attractive, and accessible

For each writing assignment, teachers concentrate on one or more of these traits, teaching students strategies for enhancing the trait(s) in their writing. For example, students are taught to circle words that are vague in their writing and to replace them with more precise ones.

Another way that students learn about the qualities of good writing is through reading. The reading material in *Open Court Reading* provides concrete models that illustrate the characteristics of good writing, such as how authors

- present, develop, and organize ideas.
- use words to evoke specific images and feelings.
- manipulate sentences to speed up or slow down the flow of text.
- set and change the mood to match the action of the characters.
- use illustrations to reinforce and sharpen readers' understanding.

This knowledge is fostered in *Open Court Reading* through Writer's Craft. Teachers and students discuss what the author of a reading selection did to achieve certain purposes. For example, after reading a mystery, the class discusses how the author planted a false lead to make the story more interesting and complex. Students are then encouraged to use the same technique in a mystery they write.

Different Purposes and Genres of Writing

Students learn the purposes and forms of a wide range of genres they need to master for success both in and out of school. This includes using writing to do the following:

- Inform (writing lists, explaining how to do something, describing objects or places, describing events, news reports, reports, and biographies)
- Share their opinions
- Create personal narratives (journal writing, autobiography, writing about a personal event, and so on)
- Entertain (stories, plays, poems, and so on)
- Learn (reports, journal entries, summarizing, and biographies)
- Respond to literature (book evaluations, book reports, and book reviews)
- Persuade (advertisements, opinions about controversial topics)

In *Open Court Reading,* students learn to write opinion statements, informative/explanatory texts (informative reports, descriptions, explanations, summaries, book reviews), and narrative texts (personal narratives, autobiographies, biographies, realistic stories, fairy tales). They also use these various forms of writing to gather, think about, and report what they have learned when doing extended Inquiry projects.

One way they learn about the purposes and forms of these various genres is through the use of models of each type of writing. As students begin learning about a new genre, the teacher leads the class through an analysis of an exemplary model of the particular type of writing to determine its characteristics and functions. Then the teacher models the writing process to compose his or her own piece of writing. After seeing models of the new genre, students work together in groups to complete a writing assignment. Finally, students complete an individual writing assignment in which they focus on the characteristics and features of the genre. Providing several models and having students write in groups offers the necessary information and support students need before writing on their own

Students are also asked to carefully consider the purpose for each of their compositions and include this determination as part of the planning process. As they plan, the form and purpose of their compositions is further emphasized through the use of graphic organizers, in which students typically generate and organize ideas for each of the basic elements included in the type of composition they are composing.

Writer's Craft

Writer's Craft involves the elements and choices writers make to add interest to a written work. These elements may include text features such as headings, charts, and graphs; figurative language; dialogue; the use of description to set the mood or tone; and so on. In *Open Court Reading,* along with the different purposes and genres of writing, the writer's techniques within the selections are pointed out to students, discussed, and then taught and practiced within the context of students' own writing. Students learn to read selections "with a writer's eye."

Developing a Sense of Audience

While writing is often viewed as a solitary activity, it is typically meant to be read by others. Children and adults most often use writing to communicate, persuade, or inform others. Because the writer is usually not present when the composition is read, he or she must carefully consider the needs of the readers. *Open Court Reading* helps students develop a sense of audience by asking them to identify their audience when they write collaboratively or independently.

Tips

- Have students keep a log of new information they have learned about the attributes of good writing.
- Develop wall charts that specify the purpose and attributes of specific writing genres.

- Ask students to evaluate their writing and the writing of others based on the traits of good writing.
- Before students begin work on a writing assignment, hold a class discussion on the topic to share information, clarify misperceptions, and identify information students still need to locate.

Mastering the Writing Process

Purpose

To write skillfully, young writers must master the basic processes involved in writing. These processes include the strategic "know-how" involved in writing and include the following:

- **Prewriting:** Writers spend time thinking about and planning their topics. They consider their purposes, audience, and the focus of their topics. Writers make plans to guide the composing process, establishing goals for what to do and say. They gather possible ideas for their writing, drawing on memory and external sources such as books, interviews, articles, and the Internet. Writers make decisions about which information to include and how to organize it.
- **Drafting:** Writers draft or put their ideas into words, using the initial plans they developed as a guide. These plans are expanded, modified, and even reworked as writers create a first draft of their composition, often in a rough form.
- **Revising:** While some revising may occur during prewriting and drafting, writers revisit and revise their first drafts. They reread them to see whether the drafts say what the writers intended. Writers check to be sure the drafts make sense and that the meaning is clear for the audience. They consider whether their writing will have the desired impact on the audience. As they make changes in their text, they discover new things to say and new ways to present their ideas.
- **Editing/Proofreading:** Writers edit/proofread their work. They recognize that spelling, grammar, and usage errors make it harder for others to understand and enjoy their published work. Writers know that readers are more likely to value their message when they correct these mistakes.
- **Publishing:** Writers share their writing by reading their entire work, or part of their work, to others. They publish their work in books, newspapers, magazines, anthologies, and so on.

In Grades I-3 of *Open Court Reading,* the writing process is introduced in Getting Started, so that students start to become familiar with the steps of the writing process as well as the traits of good writing.

Procedures

Much of what happens during writing is not visible. It occurs inside the writer's head. *Open Court Reading* makes the processes involved in writing concrete and visible in the following four ways:

- Establishing a predictable writing routine during which students are expected to prewrite, draft, revise, edit/proofread, and publish.
- Using graphic organizers and revising, editing/proofreading, and publishing checklists that help developing writers carry out basic writing processes.
- Teaching strategies for prewriting, drafting, revising, editing/proofreading, and publishing.
- Providing feedback throughout the writing process through writing conferences and students' presentation of their works in progress and completed compositions.

Establishing a Predictable Writing Routine

One way to make the basic writing processes more concrete is to create a predictable classroom writing routine, during which students plan, draft, revise, edit, proofread, and publish their work. This establishes that these processes are important and ensures that time is provided for each process. It also allows students to work with minimum teacher direction and at their own pace.

Tips

- Guide students through the steps of the writing routine. Model each step of prewriting, drafting, revising, editing/proofreading, and publishing.
- Make sure students learn that the processes of writing do not always occur in the same order but are recursive. For example, revising may occur at any stage of the composing process. You should not only model this by showing how this is done, but the predictable routine should vary at times to reflect this flexibility.

Using Graphic Organizers and Revising, Editing/Proofreading, and Publishing Checklists

Graphic organizers and revising, editing/proofreading, and publishing checklists provide students with assistance in carrying out the thinking activities involved in a writing assignment.

Open Court Reading makes use of the **POW** and **TREE** mnemonic devices and graphic organizers to help students organize, plan, and draft their writing. In Grade I, students are taught to use **POW** to help them understand and remember the writing process. Students are taught to **P**ick an idea, **O**rganize their notes, and **W**rite. Using the **POW** mnemonic device and corresponding graphic organizer gives students the POWer to become good writers.

POW Graphic Organizer	
P	Pick an Idea
O	Organize my notes
W	Write and say more

In Grades 2–3, students are taught to use the **TREE** mnemonic device for opinion and informational writing. This strategy helps students specify what they believe, generate possible ideas for why they believe it, evaluate those ideas, and think about how to wrap it up. More specifically, **TREE** helps them to write a **T**opic sentence, generate **R**easons, **E**xplain the reasons, and write an appropriate **E**nding.

TREE Graphic Organizer	
T	Topic Sentence—Tell what you believe.
R	Reasons—3 or more.
E	Explain each reason further.
E	Ending—Wrap it up right.

Tips

It is important to be sure that students understand how to use graphic organizers and revising, editing/proofreading, and publishing checklists. Be sure to

- explain the purpose of the graphic organizer or revising, editing/proofreading, and publishing checklist.
- describe how students are to use the graphic organizer or revising, editing/proofreading, and publishing checklist.

- model aloud how to carry out the basic activities on the graphic organizer or revising, editing/proofreading, and publishing checklist.
- make sure students understand each part of the graphic organizer or revising, editing/proofreading, and publishing checklist.

Teaching Strategies for Carrying Out Basic Writing Processes

A strategy involves a series of actions a writer undertakes to achieve a desired goal. In *Open Court Reading* students are taught strategies to help them carry out each of the basic writing processes—prewriting, drafting, revising, editing/ proofreading, and publishing. Each strategy is also designed to enhance one or more of the seven traits of good writing. These include clearly presented and fully developed ideas; writing that is easy to follow and logically organized; effective and precise word choice; varied use of sentences to promote fluency, rhythm, and natural speech patterns; writing that captures appropriate tone or mood to make maximum impact on readers; correct spelling, usage, and grammar; and a written product that is legible, attractive, and accessible.

The goal is for students to be able to use the strategy independently and to make it part of their writing tool kit. The steps for teaching writing strategies are to

- describe the strategy.
- tell why the strategy is important.
- tell students when they should use the strategy.
- model how to use the strategy when writing, making your thoughts visible by saying aloud each thing you are doing and thinking.
- make sure students understand why the strategy is important, when to apply it, and how to use it.
- provide students with assistance in applying the strategy until they can do it on their own.
- remind students to use the strategy when they write.

Tips

- Ask students to evaluate their progress and how the strategy improved their writing.
- Be enthusiastic about learning the strategy.
- Establish the importance of effort in learning and using the strategy.
- Provide opportunities for students to see how the strategy improves their writing.
- Praise and reinforce students' use of the strategy.
- Foster students' ownership of the strategy.

Providing Feedback through Conferencing

Writers need feedback throughout the writing process. They need reactions to ideas, drafts, and revisions. Feedback is one of our most powerful tools for helping developing writers. Writers want to know how their works-in-progress sound to someone else, whether their compositions make sense, whether they contain any incorrect or misleading information, and where and how to make changes.

Regular feedback encourages developing writers to solve problems and make meaningful changes throughout the writing process.

> *Writers need feedback throughout the writing process. Feedback is one of our most powerful tools for helping developing writers.*

One way of providing feedback is through conferences. Teachers may initiate conferences, but students should also be encouraged to call conferences on an as-needed basis. Because conferences can be held at various times throughout the writing process, the focus will vary. Conferences held during the early stages of the writing process help students identify and refine a topic or identify research references. During the revision process, conferences help students learn to elaborate and reorganize their writing. During the final stages, students learn to edit and proofread stories before they are published. Conferences offer an excellent opportunity for the teacher and student to evaluate jointly the student's progress and set goals for future growth.

The basic procedures for writing conferences are as follows:

- Have the student read aloud his or her work.
- Review any feedback the student has received so far.
- Identify positive elements of the work.
- Use one or more of these strategies to help the student improve his or her work.
  - Have the student explain how he or she got his or her ideas.
  - Have the student think aloud about how he or she will address the feedback he or she has received.
  - Ask the student to help you understand any confusion you may have about his or her writing.
  - Have the student add, delete, or rearrange something in the work, and ask how it affects the entire piece.

- Think aloud while you do a part of what the student was asked to do. Then ask the student to compare what you did to what he or she did.
  - Have the student describe as if to a younger student how to revise the work.
- Ask two or three questions to guide the student through revising.
- Conclude the conference by having the student state his or her plan for continuing work on the piece of writing.

Tips

- Set aside a special area of the classroom for you to work with students or for students to work with each other.
- You don't have to meet with every student every day.
- Conferences should be brief; don't overwhelm students with too many comments or suggestions. Several short conferences are often more effective than one long one.
- If appropriate, suggest that students take notes to help them remember where changes are to be made.
- Don't take ownership of the students' work. Encourage students to identify what is good and what needs to be changed, and let the students make the changes.
- Focus on what is good about the students' work; discuss how to solve problems rather than telling students what to do.
- Peer conferencing should be encouraged during Workshop.
- As students engage in peer conferencing, note which students are participating, the types of questions they ask, and the comments they make. Use this information to help students become more effective in peer conferencing.
- You may need to structure peer conferences by asking students to first explain what they liked about the composition, and then teaching them how to give constructive feedback.

Providing Feedback through Presentation

Students are also encouraged to share what they write with their peers and others. The following are procedures for presenting and sharing:

- Before presenting, have the writer
  - decide what will be shared.
  - practice what will be shared.
- During presenting,
  - have the writer tell what is to be shared and why.
  - have the writer read aloud his or her work or idea.
  - remind students to listen carefully.
- After presenting,
  - have students tell what they like.
  - have students offer the writer helpful suggestions.
  - take notes of students' comments to share with the writer.

Having students present or share their work provides another opportunity for them to receive feedback about their writing. Student presentations can involve

- presenting an initial idea or plan for a writing assignment.
- sharing a first draft of a paper.
- presenting orally part or all of a final piece of writing.

Tips

- Everyone must listen carefully and provide constructive feedback. Focus on what is good about a piece and ways to make it better.
- The student author has ownership and can decide which suggestions to use. The author does not have to incorporate all suggestions from the audience.
- Have a chair designated as the "Author's Chair" from which the student author can read his or her work or share ideas. This lends importance to the activity.
- The student author should be encouraged to give a bit of background, including where he or she is in the process, why he or she chose a particular part, or what problem he or she is having. This helps orient the audience.
- Short pieces of writing can be read in their entirety. As students become more proficient and write longer papers, they should be encouraged to read just a part of their writing; for example, a part they need help with, a part that has been revised, or a part they particularly like.
- Take notes during the presentations, and encourage older students to do the same.
- Be sensitive to the attention span of the class and the feedback being given. Students have a tendency to repeat the same comments to each author.

Word Processing and Other Aspects of Electronic Composing

Using a word processor to compose a piece of writing makes many aspects of the writing process easier. Text can easily be changed, deleted, or moved during drafting or revising. Software such as spell-checkers or word prediction provides assistance with basic writing skills. Information for writing can be obtained on-line or through other electronic sources, such as encyclopedias. Students can use publishing software to develop a more polished and attractive final product by adding pictures to their composition, developing a cover, changing fonts, and so on. *Open Court Reading* supports the use of these technologies.

Teaching Basic Writing Skills

Purpose

Young writers need to learn many basic writing skills to the point that the skills can be executed with minimal effort so they do not interfere with other writing processes. Correct handwriting, spelling, and grammar should be mastered to the point that they require little attention on the part of the writer. While sentences cannot and should not be constructed without conscious attention and effort, developing writers need to become familiar with different sentence types, and they need to become proficient at building them.

Procedures

Sentence Construction

Open Court Reading teaches sentence construction skills through the use of sentence frames, sentence expansion, and sentence combining.

- **Sentence Frames** With sentence frames, students are given part of a sentence and asked to generate the rest of it. For example, students can be taught to write a simple sentence, with a single subject and predicate, by giving them a frame containing the subject (The dog _____ _____ .) and asking them to complete the sentence by telling what happened (The dog ran.). Sentence frames provide initial support for sentence writing.
- **Sentence Expansion** With sentence expansion, students are given a kernel sentence and asked to expand it by adding additional words. For example, students can be taught to make sentences more colorful and precise by adding descriptive words to a kernel sentence: Rewrite ***The cat and dog like the toy*** *so the sentence tells more about the cat and dog and the toy—The big dog and gray cat like the fuzzy little toy.*
- **Sentence combining** With sentence combining, students learn how to combine two or more kernel sentences into a more complex single sentence. For example, you can lead students to produce sentences with relative clauses by combining the following two sentences:

  John will win the race.
  John is very fast. (who)
  John, who is very fast, will win the race.

When teaching sentence construction skills, the following three steps should be followed:

- Describe the skill, establish why it is important, and model how to use it.

- Provide students with assistance until they can apply the skill correctly and independently.
- Ask students to apply the skill when they write.

Tips

- Use more than one method to teach a sentence construction skill.
- Ask students to monitor how often they use the sentence construction skill.
- Encourage students to set goals to use sentence construction skills in their writing.

Penmanship/Handwriting

Students need to develop both legible and fluent handwriting. An important aspect of meeting this goal is to teach them an efficient pattern for forming individual letters (both lowercase and uppercase letters). Effective teaching procedures include

- modeling how to form the letter.
- describing how the letter is similar to and different from other letters.
- using visual cues, such as numbered arrows, as a guide to letter formation.
- providing practice tracing, copying, and writing the letter from memory.
- keeping instructional sessions short, with frequent review and practice.
- asking students to identify or circle their best formed letter or letters.
- encouraging students to correct or rewrite poorly formed letters.
- monitoring students' practice to ensure that letters are formed correctly.
- reinforcing students' successful efforts and providing corrective feedback as needed.

In addition to learning how to write the letters of the alphabet correctly, students must be able to produce them quickly. Fluency generally develops as a consequence of writing frequently, but it can also be fostered by having students copy short passages several times, and trying to write them a little faster each time.

Tips

- Make sure that each student develops a comfortable and efficient pencil grip.
- Encourage students to sit in an upright position, leaning slightly forward, as they write.
- Show students how to place or position their papers when writing.

- Implement procedures for left-handed writers, such as how to properly position their papers when writing.
- Monitor students' handwriting, paying special attention to their instructional needs in letter formation, spacing, slant, alignment, size, and line quality.
- Encourage students to make all final drafts of their papers neat and legible.

Spelling

To become good spellers, students must learn to spell readily and correctly the words they are most likely to use when writing. They need to be able to generate and check plausible spellings for words whose spellings are uncertain. They also need to learn to use external sources such as dictionaries and spell-checkers to ensure correct spelling during writing. In *Open Court Reading* students are taught how to spell words they frequently use when writing as well as spelling patterns that help them spell untaught words.

Tips

- Teach students an effective strategy for studying spelling words.
- Reinforce the correct spelling of taught words in students' writing.
- Have students build words from letters or letters and phonograms, for example, c - at.
- Teach strategies for determining and checking the spelling of unknown words.
- Have students check the *Sound/Spelling Cards* for spelling unknown words.
- Model the use of correct spelling and how to correct spelling errors when you write in front of the class.
- Encourage students to correct misspelled words in all final drafts of their writing.
- Provide instruction and practice in proofreading.
- Encourage students to use spell-checkers, dictionaries, and so on to determine the correct spelling of unknown words.

Grammar and Usage

Traditional methods of teaching grammar and usage skills are often not effective. With such instruction, students are initially provided with an abstract definition, such as an adjective is a word that describes a noun or pronoun. This is often followed by asking students to practice applying the skill correctly without actually generating any textual material longer than a word or a phrase. For example, students might be asked to complete the following sentence: The _____ wagon rolled through the _____ town. It is not surprising that many students do not understand the rules they are taught or how to use them in their writing, because such instruction is abstract and decontextualized.

To make grammar instruction effective, *Open Court Reading* applies the following five principles. To make these principles concrete, the program illustrates each as it would apply to the rule for capitalizing the first letter in a person's name.

- *Grammar and usage skills need to be defined in a functional and concrete manner.* The rule of capitalizing the first letter in a person's name can be introduced by writing a sentence with two or three familiar names on the board. With the students' help, identify each name in the sentence, and ask them what they notice about the first letter in each name—They are capital letters. Repeat this process with a second sentence, and then establish the "capitalization rule" with students' help.
- *As soon as the skill is functionally described or defined, establish why it is important*—Capitalizing the first letter in a person's name makes the name stand out and shows respect for the person named. This is an important rule for writing.
- *Show students how to use the skill when writing.* Generate a sentence using the names of students in the class, or have your students help you generate such a sentence. Write it on the board, capitalizing the first letter while simultaneously telling the class what you are doing.
- *Provide students with guided practice in applying the skill when writing.* Generate with the class another sentence that includes three of your students' names. Tell the class you will write the sentence on the board, but they will need to tell you when to capitalize a word. Next, have students work together in pairs to generate two sentences using names of their friends, capitalizing the first letter in each name. Provide support as needed. Finally, have each student generate one sentence of his or her own containing two names. Monitor to ensure that students capitalize the first letter in each name. Have them share their sentences with a peer.
- *Ask students to apply the skill in their compositions.* Have students look at one of the papers in their writing portfolio and correct any capitalization mistakes involving people's names. Remind students to capitalize people's names when writing and revising subsequent writing assignments.

Tips

- Ask students to correct other students' papers, focusing on specific grammar and usage rules and mistakes.
- Encourage students to read their papers aloud when revising. This will help them spot grammar and usage mistakes.

Fostering Motivation

Purpose

Children start school wanting to learn how to write and enjoying writing. Too quickly, however, many begin to view writing as a chore or something to be avoided. The goal of the writing instruction in *Open Court Reading* is for children to become lifelong writers—people who enjoy writing and use writing effectively at work as well as in their personal lives.

Procedures

One way to foster an interest in writing is to have students write for real purposes and audiences. This includes having students identify why they are writing and what they hope to accomplish. Likewise, students need to share their writing with others. They are more likely to do their best writing when there is an audience. Students can share their plans, an initial draft, a portion of their composition, or the completed paper with you, their peers, or other children or adults.

Students are also likely to give their best effort when the writing environment is supportive and pleasant. This can be accomplished by the following:

- Establishing clear rules for student behavior during the writing period. Keep the rules simple and reasonable in number and consistently reinforce them. Students are not likely to enjoy writing, or learn well, if the classroom environment is chaotic.
- Creating a low-risk environment in which students feel comfortable taking risks with their writing. This means being accepting and encouraging of students' efforts and encouraging them to act in the same manner. For example, make it a rule in your class that when someone shares his or her writing, the first thing that you or other students do is say what you liked most about it.
- Supporting students as they begin to apply the knowledge, skills, or strategies you teach them. This can include providing strong models, teaching rubrics or scoring criteria in advance, reteaching, providing hints and reminders, giving useful feedback, and initially helping students apply what was taught.
- Having students help each other as they plan, draft, revise, edit/proofread, and publish their work. This is most effective when the process of working together is structured. For instance, students are more likely to give good advice for revising if they are asked to focus on specific aspects of the composition, such as identifying places where the writing is unclear or more detail is needed.

- Celebrating student success by displaying their work. This can be done by prominently displaying student work in the classroom or in other places in the school. Students can also be asked to publish their work in a class or school newspaper or to read their compositions aloud to younger children, in other classes, or at a special event.
- Fostering an "I can do" attitude among your students. Consistently emphasize that the key to good writing is effort and the use of what they have learned.
- Setting a positive mood during writing time. Be enthusiastic about writing and what your students write.

Tips

- Encourage students to make their own decisions and to accomplish as much on their own as possible.
- Increase students' ownership of a writing topic by allowing them to develop unique interpretations of the topic.
- Encourage students to take ownership of their writing. This includes allowing them to arrange a suitable writing environment, construct a personal plan for accomplishing the writing task, to work at their own pace when possible, and to decide what feedback from you and their peers is most pertinent for revising their writing.
- Look for opportunities to give students positive feedback about their work. Let them know when they have done something well in their writing.
- Encourage students to monitor their progress. For example, have students select their best writing to keep in a writing portfolio, identifying why they selected each piece.
- Show your students that you are a writer too. Share your writing with them. Talk about the various ways you use writing each day.
- Connect writing to students' lives and the world in general. Have them document the types of writing they do outside school. Develop a wall chart on which the class can identify how they use writing away from school.
- Provide incentives for writing at home. For example, have parents document that their child writes for twenty minutes at home a set number of nights for a month. Provide a special party for these children, allowing each one to select a book to keep from an array of books donated by parents or a sponsoring business partner.

Spelling Strategies

Spelling

Many people find English difficult, because English sound/spelling patterns seem to have hundreds of exceptions. The key to becoming a good speller, however, is not just memorization. The key is recognizing and internalizing English spelling patterns. Some people do this naturally as they read and develop large vocabularies. They intuitively recognize spelling patterns and apply them appropriately. Others need explicit and direct teaching of vocabulary and spelling strategies and spelling patterns before they develop spelling consciousness.

Purpose

Spelling is a fundamental skill in written communication. Although a writer may have wonderful ideas, he or she may find it difficult to communicate those ideas without spelling skills. Learning to spell requires much exposure to text and writing. For many it requires a methodical presentation of English spelling patterns.

Developmental Stages of Spelling

The most important finding in spelling research in the past thirty years is that students learn to spell in a predictable developmental sequence, much as they learn to read. It appears to take the average student three to six years to progress through the developmental stages and emerge as a fairly competent, mature speller.

Prephonemic The first stage is the prephonemic stage, characterized by random letters arranged either in continuous lines or in wordlike clusters. Only the writer can "read" it, and it may be "read" differently on different days.

Semiphonemic As emergent readers learn that letters stand for sounds, they use particular letters specifically to represent the initial consonant sound and sometimes a few other very salient sounds. This marks the discovery of phonemic awareness that letters represent speech sounds in writing.

Phonemic When students can represent most of the sounds they hear in words, they have entered the phonemic stage of spelling. They spell what they hear, using everything they know about letter sounds, letter names, and familiar words. Many remedial spellers never develop beyond this stage and spell a word the way it sounds whenever they encounter a word they cannot spell.

Transitional or Within-Word Pattern As they are exposed to more difficult words, students discover that not all words are spelled as they sound. They learn that they must include silent letters, spell past tenses with -ed, include a vowel even in unstressed syllables, and remember how words look. The transitional stage represents the transition from primarily phonemic strategies to rule-bound spelling.

Derivational The derivational stage occurs as transitional spellers accumulate a large spelling vocabulary and gain control over affixes, contractions, homophones, and other meaning patterns. They discover that related or derived forms of words share spelling features even if they do not sound the same. As spellers gain control over these subtle word features and spell most words correctly, they become conventional spellers.

English Spelling Patterns

A basic understanding of English spelling patterns will help provide efficient and effective spelling instruction. Just as the goal of phonics instruction is to enable students to read fluently, the goal of spelling instruction is to enable students to write fluently so they can concentrate on ideas rather than spelling.

Sound Patterns Many words are spelled the way they sound. Most consonants and short vowels are very regular. When a student learns the sound/spelling relationships, he or she has the key to spelling the majority of words in the English language.

Structural Patterns Structural patterns are employed when adding endings to words. Examples of structural patterns include doubling the final consonant, adding -s or -es to form plurals, and dropping the final e before adding -ing, -ed, -er, or -est. Often these structural patterns are very regular in their application. Many students have little trouble learning these patterns.

Meaning Patterns Many spelling patterns in English are morphological; in other words, the meaning relationship is maintained regardless of how a sound may change. Prefixes, suffixes, and root words that retain their spellings regardless of how they are pronounced are further examples of meaning patterns.

Foreign Language Patterns Many English words are derived from foreign words and retain those language patterns. For example, *kindergarten* (German), *boulevard* (French), and *ballet* (French from Italian) are foreign-language patterns at work in English.

Procedures

The spelling lessons are organized around different spelling patterns, beginning with phonetic spelling patterns and progressing to other types of spelling patterns in a logical sequence. Word lists focus on the particular patterns in each lesson. In general, the sound patterns occur in the first units at each grade, followed by structural patterns, and meaning patterns.

- As you begin each new spelling lesson, have students identify the spelling pattern and how it is like and different from other patterns.
- Give the pretest to help students focus on the lesson pattern.
- Have students proofread their own pretests immediately after the test, crossing out any misspellings and writing the correct spelling.
- Have them diagnose whether the errors they made were in the lesson pattern or in another part of the word. Help students determine where they made errors and what type of pattern they should work on to correct them.
- As students work through the spelling pages from *Skills Practice,* encourage them to practice the different spelling strategies in the exercises.

Sound Pattern Strategies

Pronunciation Strategy As students encounter an unknown word, have them say the word carefully to hear each sound. Encourage them to check the *Sound/Spelling Cards*. Then have them spell each sound. (/s/ + /i/ + /t/: *sit*). This strategy builds directly on the Dictation and Spelling introduced in kindergarten and taught in Grades 1–3.

Consonant Substitution Have students switch consonants. The vowel spelling usually remains the same. *(bat, hat, rat, flat, splat)* This is a natural extension of Phonemic Awareness activities begun in kindergarten.

Vowel Substitution Have students switch vowels. The consonant spellings usually remain the same. (CVC: *hit, hat, hut, hot;* CVCV: *mane, mine;* CVVC: *boat, beat, bait, beet)* This is another example of a natural extension of the Phonemic Awareness activities begun in kindergarten.

Rhyming Word Strategy Have students think of rhyming words and the rhymes that spell a particular sound. Often the sound will be spelled the same way in another word. *(cub, tub, rub)* Again, this is a natural extension of Phonemic Awareness activities begun in kindergarten.

Structural Pattern Strategies

Conventions Strategy Have students learn the rules and exceptions for adding endings to words (dropping the final *y,* dropping the final *e,* doubling the final consonant, and so on).

Proofreading Strategy Many spelling errors occur because of simple mistakes. Have students check their writing carefully and specifically for spelling.

Visualization Strategy Have students think about how a word looks. Sometimes words "look" wrong because a wrong spelling pattern has been written. Have them double-check the spelling of any word that looks wrong.

Meaning Pattern Strategies

Family Strategy When students are not sure of a spelling, have them think of how words from the same base word family are spelled. *(critic, criticize, critical; sign, signal, signature; nation, national, nationality)*

Meaning Strategy Have students determine a homophone's meaning to make sure they are using the right word. Knowing prefixes, suffixes, and base words will also help.

Compound Word Strategy Tell students to break apart a compound and to spell each word. Compounds may not follow convention rules for adding endings. *(homework, nonetheless)*

Dictionary Strategy Ask students to look up the word in a dictionary to make sure their spelling is correct. If they do not know how to spell a word, have them try a few different spellings and look them up to see which one is correct. *(fotograph, photograph)* Have students use the *Sound/Spelling Cards* to help them look up words. This develops a spelling consciousness.

Use the post test to determine understanding of the lesson spelling pattern and to identify any other spelling pattern problems. Encourage student understanding of spelling patterns and use of spelling strategies in all their writing to help transfer spelling skills to writing.

Grammar, Usage, and Mechanics

Purpose

The Study of English Conventions

Over the years the study of grammar, usage, and mechanics has gone in and out of favor. In the past century much research has been done to demonstrate the effectiveness of traditional types of instruction in the conventions of English. Experience and research have shown that learning grammatical terms and completing grammar exercises have little effect on the student's practical application of these skills in the context of speaking or writing. These skills, in and of themselves, do not play a significant role in the way students use language to generate and express their ideas—for example, during the prewriting and drafting phases of the writing process. In fact, emphasis on correct conventions has been shown to have a damaging effect when it is the sole focus of writing instruction. If students are evaluated only on the proper use of spelling, grammar, and punctuation, they tend to write fewer and less complex sentences.

Knowledge of English conventions is, however, vitally important in the editing and proofreading phases of the writing process. A paper riddled with mistakes in grammar, usage, or mechanics is quickly discounted. Many immature writers never revise or edit. They finish the last sentence and turn their papers in to the teacher. Mature writers employ their knowledge of English language conventions in the editing phase to refine and polish their ideas.

The study of grammar, usage, and mechanics is important for two reasons.

1. Educated people need to know and understand the structure of their language, which in large part defines their culture.
2. Knowledge of grammar gives teachers and students a common vocabulary for talking about language and makes discussions of writing tasks more efficient and clearer.

Procedure

The key issue in learning grammar, usage, and mechanics is how to do it and apply the knowledge to writing. On the one hand, teaching these skills in isolation from writing has been shown to be ineffective and even detrimental if too much emphasis is placed on them. On the other hand, not teaching these skills and having students write without concern for conventions is equally ineffective. The answer is to teach the skills in a context that allows students to directly apply them to a reading or writing activity. Students should be taught proper use of punctuation or subject/verb agreement at the same time they are taught to proofread for those conventions. As they learn to apply their knowledge of conventions during the final stages of the writing process, they will begin to see that correcting errors is an editorial rather than a composition skill.

> *A paper riddled with mistakes in grammar, usage, or mechanics is quickly discounted.*

History of English

A basic understanding of the history and structure of the English language helps students understand the rich but complex resource they have for writing.

Old English

The English language began about A.D. 450 when the Angles, Jutes, and Saxons—three tribes that lived in northern Europe—invaded the British Isles. Much of their language included words that had to do with farming (*sheep, dirt, tree, earth*). Many of their words are the most frequently used words in the English language today. Because of Latin influences, English became the first of the European languages to be written.

Middle English

In 1066 William the Conqueror invaded England and brought Norman French with him. Slowly Old English and Norman French came together, and Middle English began to appear. Today forty percent of Modern English comes from French. With the introduction of the printing press, English became more widespread.

Modern English

With the Renaissance and its rediscovery of classical Greek and Latin, many new words were created from Greek and Latin word elements. This continued intensively during the Early Modern English period. This rich language was used in the writings of Shakespeare and his contemporaries and profoundly influenced the nature and vocabulary of English. With dictionaries and spelling books, the English language became more standardized, although it continues to be influenced by other languages and new words and trends. These influences continue to make English a living, dynamic language.

Punctuation

Early writing had no punctuation or even spaces between words. English punctuation had its beginning in ancient Greece and Rome. Early punctuation reflected speaking rather than reading. By the end of the eighteenth century, after the invention of printing, most of the rules for punctuation were established, although they were not the same in all languages.

The Structure of English

Grammar is the sound, structure, and meaning system of language. People who speak the same language are able to communicate because they intuitively know the grammar system of that language, the rules to make meaning. All languages have grammar, and yet each language has its own unique structure—the way the words are organized into sentences.

Traditional grammar study usually involves two areas:

- **Parts of speech** (nouns, verbs, adjectives, adverbs, pronouns, prepositions, conjunctions) are typically considered the content of grammar.
- **Sentence structure** (subjects, predicates, objects, clauses, phrases) is also included in grammar study. Sentence structure involves the function of English.

Mechanics involves the conventions of punctuation and capitalization. Punctuation helps readers understand writers' messages. Proper punctuation involves marking off sentences according to grammatical structure. In speech students can produce sentences as easily and unconsciously as they can walk, but in writing they must think about what is and what is not a sentence.

In English there are about fourteen punctuation marks (period, comma, quotation mark, question mark, exclamation point, colon, semicolon, apostrophe, hyphen, ellipsis, parenthesis, bracket, dash, and underscore). Most immature writers use only three: period, comma, and question mark. The experienced writer or poet with the command of punctuation adds both flexibility and meaning to his or her sentences through his or her use of punctuation.

Usage is the way in which we speak in a given community. Language varies over time, across national and geographical boundaries, by gender, across age groups, and by socioeconomic status. When the variation occurs within a given language, the different versions of the same language are called dialects. The language used in American schools is called academic English and incorporates the skills of grammar, usage, and mechanics.

Usage involves the word choices people make when speaking certain dialects. Word choices that are perfectly acceptable in conversation among friends may be unacceptable in academic writing. Usage is often the most obvious indicator of the difference between conversation and composition. Usage depends on a student's cultural and linguistic heritage. If the dialect students have learned is not the formal language of school settings or if it is not English, students must be taught the rules of academic English.

The Grammar, Usage, and Mechanics lessons in ***Open Court Reading*** are structured to focus on skills presented in a logical sequence. A skill is introduced with appropriate models and then practiced in reading and writing on subsequent days to ensure that skills are not taught in isolation. Encourage students to use the focus of the English language convention presented in each lesson as they complete each Writing activity. Also encourage them to reread their writing, checking for proper use of the conventions taught. With practice, students should be able to apply their knowledge of conventions to any writing they do.

Tips

- Some of the errors students make in writing are the result simply of not carefully reading their final drafts. Many errors occur because the writer's train of thought was interrupted and a sentence is not complete or a word is skipped. These may look like huge errors that a simple rereading can remedy. Most often the writer can correct these types of errors on his or her own. A major emphasis of any English composition program should be to teach the editing and proofreading phases of the writing process so students can eliminate these types of errors themselves. This involves a shift in perception—from thinking of grammar as a set of discrete skills that involve mastery of individual rules to understanding grammar as it applies to the act of communicating in writing.
- As students learn academic English language conventions, they should be expected to incorporate them into their oral language and written work in school.

Assessment

Assessment can be your most effective teaching tool if it is used with the purpose of informing instruction and highlighting areas that need special attention.

Purpose

The assessment components of *Open Court Reading* are designed to help you make informed instructional decisions and help ensure you meet the needs of all your students. The variety of assessments is intended to be used continuously and formatively. That is, students should be assessed regularly as a follow-up to instructional activities, and the results of the assessment should be used to inform subsequent instruction.

You can use assessment as a tool to monitor students' progress, to diagnose students' strengths and weaknesses, to prescribe forms of intervention as necessary, and to measure student outcomes. Both formal and informal assessment can be used, though formal assessment will be your main assessment tool. Formal assessment of student learning consists of formative and summative evaluations relating to performance assessment (both reading and writing), objective tests (multiple choice, short answer, and essay), and assessment rubrics (used for writing, inquiry, and comprehension strategies). Informal assessment may consist of progress assessment (through students' everyday oral and written work), observing or listening to students as they work, and jotting down notes in a notebook.

The types of assessments within *Open Court Reading* are available not only in print but digitally as well. This system will allow you to develop your own test banks in addition to those provided, automatically score student responses, create reports, and note grouping for differentiated instruction.

Procedure

Formal Assessment

Formal assessment is addressed in *Open Court Reading* in the form of *Lesson and Unit Assessments* and *Benchmark Assessments.* Whether students take these assessments in paper-and-pencil format or online, these tests will help you measure students' understanding of the instructional content and use the results to inform and to differentiate instruction, especially for students needing some type of intervention to ensure they will not be at risk for reading failure.

Lesson and Unit Assessments

The *Lesson and Unit Assessments* cover the most important skills featured in the lessons of a given unit and the unit as a whole—skills that are closely related to reading success. These assessments will help you determine how well students are grasping the skills and concepts of the underlying standards as they are taught and will help inform you about any additional instruction they might need. In addition, a Diagnostic Assessment, located in Book I of *Lesson and Unit Assessment,* is given at the beginning of the year to help you gauge students' entry skills. The data from these assessments offers you a clear picture of student progress through the curriculum.

> *Observing students as they go about their regular classwork can be an effective way to learn your students' strengths and areas of need.*

The Diagnostic Assessment can be administered for the class, for small groups, or for individual students as an entry-level assessment to identify students at risk. The assessment covers the six technical skill areas of reading:

- Phonemic awareness
- Phonics and decoding
- Oral reading fluency
- Spelling
- Vocabulary
- Reading comprehension

After you have administered the Diagnostic Assessment, you will be able to use the results in a formative way to target instruction based on students' instructional needs and make key instructional placement decisions.

Instead of administering the entire Diagnostic Assessment, you might wish to administer specific technical skill sections of the assessment if your observation of a student's behavior and work (or the work and behavior of a group of students) leads you to a diagnosis you would like to verify.

The *Lesson and Unit Assessments* are easily administered and scored. They feature the same language used in the instructional components of *Open Court Reading* and correspond to its sequence of instruction. The format of these assessments ranges from multiple-choice questions to short answer to an extended writing response. Depending upon the grade level, skills assessed include the following:

- letter and number recognition
- phonological and phonemic awareness
- print and book awareness
- phonics
- high-frequency words
- vocabulary development
- spelling
- grammar, usage, and mechanics
- comprehension skills
- accessing complex text
- oral fluency
- writing

The *Lesson and Unit Assessments* are offered in several formats so that students can demonstrate their knowledge of content in a number of developmentally appropriate ways. Wherever possible, the assessments are designed to be administered to the whole class or small groups of students. In some cases, however, individually administered assessments are included, such as the oral fluency assessments, as well as critical pre-literacy skills such as phoneme blending or segmentation as well as letter and number recognition.

The *Lesson and Unit Assessments* will allow you to monitor students' progress as they are assessed on the standards-based instruction in lessons and units. The results will provide instructionally relevant information that you can use to differentiate instruction for students who may need additional learning opportunities.

Benchmark Assessments

The *Benchmark Assessments* are a form of general outcome measurement that offer an overall framework for assessment and serve as a predictor of how well students will perform at the end of the school. Each *Benchmark Assessment* has material that students will learn over the course of the school year, and each *Benchmark Assessment* is of equivalent difficulty. Students are not expected to score high on the initial screening benchmark; instead, students are expected to show growth as they move on to each subsequent benchmark. Only at the end of the year are students expected to have mastered the materials on these assessments.

The *Benchmark Assessment* will be administered at the beginning of the year for screening. This can serve as the baseline score against which you can measure students' progress throughout the year. Subsequent benchmarks will also be given at midyear and at the end of the year. Since the tests are of equivalent difficulty and contain the same types of items, students' higher scores will reflect their increasing mastery of the curriculum over the course of the year. Use the data from the *Benchmark Assessments* to identify students who are at risk for reading failure, to identify strengths and weaknesses of students, and to gauge student progress toward high-stakes tests.

Depending upon the grade level, tested benchmark skills include the following:

- letter recognition
- phonological and phonemic awareness
- phonics
- high-frequency word recognition
- vocabulary
- spelling
- grammar, usage, and mechanics
- comprehension
- oral fluency
- writing

Note that it is not necessary to administer both the *Lesson and Unit Assessments* and the *Benchmark Assessments*. However, you may find these tools helpful in different ways— one to assess students' understanding of the skills taught in a particular lesson or unit, and the other to assess how well students are progressing toward end-of-year goals.

Informal Assessment

Monitoring Progress

Students work on several different skills throughout the day. Each of these assignments can provide you with valuable information about your students' progress. One very helpful resource that students will work in daily is the *Skills Practice Book.* These books include lessons that act as practice and reinforcement for the skills taught before and during the reading of the lesson as well as in conjunction with the Language Arts lesson. These skills pages give you a clear picture of students' understanding of the skills taught. Use them as a daily informal assessment of student progress in the particular skills taught throughout the program.

Portfolios

Portfolios are more than just a collection bin or gathering place for student projects and records. They add balance to an assessment program by providing unique benefits to teachers, students, and families.

- Portfolios help build self-confidence and increase self-esteem as students come to appreciate the value of their work. More importantly, portfolios allow students to reflect on what they know and what they need to learn. At the end of the school year, each student will be able to go through their portfolios and write about their progress.
- Portfolios reinforce the notion that a piece of writing can be revisited and revised at a later date to add new techniques that students have recently learned.
- Portfolios provide you with an authentic record of what students can do. Just as important, portfolios give students a concrete example of their own progress and development. Thus, portfolios become a valuable source of information for making instructional decisions.
- Portfolios allow families to judge student performance directly. Portfolios are an ideal starting point for discussions about a student's achievements and future goals during teacher/family conferences.

You will find that there are many opportunities to add to students' portfolios.

> *Assessment can be your most effective teaching tool if it is used with the purpose of informing instruction and highlighting areas that need special attention.*

Fluency

- During partner reading, during Workshop, or at other times of the day, invite students, one at a time, to sit with you and read a story from an appropriate *Decodable* or the *Student Anthology.*
- As each student reads to you, follow along and make note of any recurring problems the student has while reading. Note students' ability to decode unknown words as well as any attempt—successful or not—to use strategies to clarify or otherwise make sense of what they are reading. From time to time, check students' fluency by timing their reading and noting how well they are able to sustain the oral reading without faltering.
- If a student has trouble reading a particular *Decodable,* encourage the student to read the story a few times on her or his own before reading it aloud to you. If the *Decodable* has two stories, use the alternate story to reassess the student a day or two later.
- If after practicing with a particular *Decodable* and reading it on his or her own a few times, a student is still experiencing difficulty, try the following:
  - Drop back two *Decodables.* (Continue to drop back until the student is able to read a story with no trouble.) If the student can read that book without problems, move up one book.
  - Continue the process until the student is able to read the current *Decodable.*

Observation

Informal assessment is a part of the everyday classroom routine. Observing students as they go about their regular classwork can be an effective way to learn your students' strengths and areas of need. The more students become accustomed to you jotting down informal notes about their work, the more it will become just another part of classroom life that they accept and take little note of. This gives you the opportunity to assess their progress constantly without the interference and possible drawback of formal testing situations.

- During each lesson, observe a particular aspect in the performances of several students.
- When observing students, do not pull them aside; rather, observe students as part of the regular lesson, either with the whole class or in small groups.
- Record your observations.
- It may take four to five days to make sure you have observed and recorded the performance of each student.
- If you need more information about performan ce in a particular area for some of your students, you may want to observe them more than once.

Dictation

In grades 1–3, students use dictation to practice the sound/spelling associations they are learning and/or reviewing. Collect the dictation papers and look through them to see how the students are doing with writing and with proofreading their words. Record notes on the papers and keep them in the student portfolios.

Writing Rubrics

Writing Rubrics

Rubrics are particularly effective for writing assignments, which do not have simple right or wrong answers. Different sets of rubrics cover various elements of the writing, including genre, writing process, and writing traits. They are intended to help teachers provide criteria and feedback to students.

SRA Open Court Reading provides four-point rubrics for writing in each of four areas. This enables teachers to clearly distinguish among different levels of performance.

I Point score indicates that a student is performing below basic level.

2 Point score indicates that a student's abilities are emerging.

3 Point score indicates that a student's work is adequate and achieving expectations.

4 Point score indicates that a student is exceeding expectations.

Writing Genres

Genre	I Point	2 Points	3 Points	4 Points
Descriptive Writing	The writing includes little or no description of setting, character, or motivations.	The writing includes minimal description.	The writing includes adequate detail description.	The writing includes sensory details, motivations, and scenery details that add depth of understanding.
Narrative Writing	The narrative does not establish a situation or introduce a narrator or characters. A logical event order is not apparent in the plot. The use of dialogue or descriptions of characters' thoughts and feelings are not included. The narrative has no real ending.	The narrative includes a plot outline but does not elaborate on the details of character, plot, or setting. The use of dialogue or descriptions of characters' thoughts and feelings are minimally touched on. The narrative does not have an ending.	The narrative includes some development of plot, character, and setting. Some use of temporal words and phrases to signal event order is included. The narrative does not have a sense of closure or an ending.	The narrative fully develops and elaborates on plot, character, and setting. A situation is clearly established, and the event sequence logically unfolds. The narrative includes the use of temporal words and phrases to signal order event, and characters' thoughts are feeling are clearly evident. A strong ending is included.
Personal Writing	Personal writing is seen as an assignment rather than as an aid to the writer. Minimal effort is made, and the writing does not reflect the writer's ideas.	Some elements of personal writing reflect the writer's thoughts and ideas.	The writer uses personal writing to record or develop his or her thoughts.	The writer relies on personal writing to record, remember, develop, or express his or her thoughts.
Poetry	Little effort is made to select and arrange words to express a particular thought or idea. The main idea of the poem is not evident.	Some effort is made to work with word choice and arrangement to develop a thought in poetry form.	The writer has a clear idea and has attempted to use poetic form to express it. Poetry form may reflect established forms.	The writer has expressed an idea in an original or established poetic form. The writer has carefully selected words and arranged them for poetic effect.
Opinion Writing	The topic is unclear or confusing. The writer's opinion is not stated clearly. No reasons are given for the writer's preference, and no linking words such as *because* or *since* are used. A closure is not included.	The topic may be stated but the writer's opinion is unclear. Some reasons are given but are unrelated to the topic. Use of linking words such as *because* or *since* are not included. A closure may not be clearly stated.	The topic is stated, but the writer's opinion or the reasons for the opinion are not included or are not relevant to the topic. Use of linking words such as *because* or *since* are included. The closure is stated but may not clearly relate to the opinion.	The topic is clearly stated, as is the writer's opinion. Reasons are also clearly stated and support the writer's opinion. The use of linking words such as *because* or *since* are appropriately used, and the closure supports the opinion.
Informative Writing	The topic of the writing is not stated. The writing is not clearly organized. Linking words such as *also, another,* or *but* are not used. The main points and supportive details can be identified, but they are not clearly marked. No conclusion is included.	The topic of the writing is stated, and there is some organization of apparent. Linking words such as *also, another,* or *but* are not used. The main ideas are stated but are not supported by facts or accompanying details. A conclusion may be stated but may not clearly support the topic.	The writer presents adequate, appropriate evidence to make a point or support a position. Linking words such as *also, another,* or *but* are used. The main points and supportive details can be identified, but they are not clearly marked. A conclusion is stated.	The writer clearly introduces a topic. Main ideas are supported by facts related to the topic. Linking words such as *also, another,* or *but* are used appropriately. A conclusion is clearly stated and supports the topic.
Letter Writing/ Thank-You Note	The greeting is included, but the body of the letter is incoherent, so the intent is unclear. The date of the letter is missing. Neither a closing nor a signature is included.	The greeting is evident, but the topic of the letter is not clearly evident, so the intent is unclear. A closing or a signature may be included, but the date is missing.	The greeting is included, as is the topic and intent of the letter. The letter may include a signature but not a closing or a date.	All the elements of a letter are clearly stated, including the date, greeting, topic, closing, and signature. The intent of the letter is clear.

Assessment Rubrics

In addition to the formal assessment opportunities available in the *Lesson and Unit Assessments, Benchmark Assessments,* and progress assessment, *Open Court Reading* provides rubrics to evaluate students' performance in comprehension, Inquiry, speaking and listening, and writing. Rubrics provide criteria for different levels of performance. Rubrics established before an assignment is given are extremely helpful in evaluating the assignment. When students know what the rubrics for a particular assignment are, they can focus their energies on the key issues. You can find the Rubrics in the Level Appendix of the *Teacher's Edition.*

Responding to Assessment Results

The point of assessment is to monitor progress in order to inform instruction, diagnose students' strengths and weaknesses, and differentiate instruction for students who need extra practice in certain skills or an extra challenge.

Open Court Reading offers you opportunities to diagnose areas that may cause problems for students, differentiate instruction according to their abilities, monitor their progress on an ongoing basis, and measure student outcomes through the *Lesson and Unit Assessment* books, in addition to high-stakes state assessments. *Open Court Reading* also provides several ways to differentiate instruction based on the results of the various assessments. These include the following:

- Reteach lessons for students who are approaching level and appear to grasp a given concept but need more instruction and practice to solidify their learning.
- *Intervention* lessons provide options for you to use with students who need more intensive support and who are struggling to understand the on-level material. In addition to the support for the weekly lesson, controlled vocabulary lessons and specific skills lessons can help bring students up to grade level.
- *English Learner* lessons are available for students who are having difficulty with the concepts because they lack the necessary English language background. These resources will provide English Learners with the vocabulary, phonics, comprehension, grammar, and writing support they need to access the *Open Court Reading* lessons.

These materials, along with formal and informal assessments, help ensure that assessment and instruction work together to meet every student's needs.

Workshop and Differentiating Instruction

Purpose

Workshop is the time each day when students work independently, alone, or in small groups to review and apply skills and strategies taught in the lesson, practice fluency, work on inquiry, complete writing assignments, hold peer conferences, and make personal choices. Workshop is also the time for teachers to work with individuals or small groups of students to differentiate instruction, to preteach and reteach, to extend the lesson, to hold writing conferences, and to conduct fluency checks.

An additional purpose for Workshop is to build student independence. With support and scaffolding, students learn to make decisions about their use of time and materials, to collaborate with their peers, and to become productive, engaged learners.

Procedure

Initially for many students you will need to structure Workshop carefully. Eventually students will automatically go to the appropriate areas and get the necessary materials. Workshop will evolve slowly from a very structured period to a time when students make choices and move freely from one activity to the next.

Setting up Workshop guidelines is key. By the time students have completed the first few weeks of school, they should feel confident during Workshop. If not, continue to structure the time and limit options. For young students, early periods of Workshop may run no more than five to eight minutes. The time can gradually increase to fifteen minutes or longer as students gain independence. Older students may be able to work longer and independently from the very beginning of the school year.

Introducing Workshop

Introduce Workshop to students by explaining that every day there will be a time when they are expected to work on activities on their own or in small groups. For younger students, in the beginning there may be just a couple of activities but gradually new ones will be introduced and students can choose what they want to do. With older students and for those who have experienced Workshop in early grades, you may want to introduce the concept of Workshop and discuss the range of Workshop options from working on fluency to completing their writing.

Establish and discuss rules for Workshop with students. Keep them simple and straightforward. You may want to write the finalized rules on the board or on a poster. You may want to review these rules each day at the beginning of Workshop for the first few lessons or so. You may also wish to revisit and revise the rules from time to time. Suggested rules include the following:

- Share.
- Use a quiet voice.
- Take only the materials you need.
- Return materials.
- Always be working.
- When the teacher is working with a student or small group, do not interrupt.

Early in the process, review rules routinely, and discuss how Workshop is going. Is the class quiet enough for everyone to work on his or her own? Are there any rules that need to be changed? What problems are students having with materials?

For young students in the beginning you will assign the Workshop activities to help them learn to work on their own. Point out the shelf or area of the classroom where Workshop materials are stored. Tell students that when they finish working with the materials for one activity, they will choose something else from the Workshop shelf. New activity materials will be added to the shelf from time to time. Make sure students know that they may always look at books during Workshop.

Tell older students that they will have an opportunity each day to work on their unit inquiry activities, their writing, and other projects. Students will be working independently and collaboratively during this time.

Guidelines

- Make sure each student knows what he or she needs to do during Workshop.
- Demonstrate for the entire group any activity or game assigned for Workshop, for example, teaching students a new game, introducing new materials or projects, or explaining different areas.
- For young students, it is essential to introduce and demonstrate different activities and games before students do them on their own. With games, you may want to have several students play while the others watch. Make sure that all students know exactly what is expected of them.

- In the beginning, plan to circulate among students, providing encouragement and help as necessary.
- When students are engaged in appropriate activities and can work independently, meet with those students who need your particular attention. This may include individual students or small groups.
- Let students know that they need to ask questions and to clarify assignments during Workshop introduction so that you are free to work with small groups.
- Make sure when using the digital *eGames* during Workshop that students have the log-in information readily available.
- Be sure that students know what they are to do when they have finished an activity and where to put their finished work.

Setting Up Your Classroom for Workshop

Carefully setting up your classroom to accommodate various Workshop activities will help assure that the Workshop period progresses smoothly and effectively. While setting up your classroom, keep the primary Workshop activities in mind. During Workshop, students will be doing independent and collaborative activities. In kindergarten and first grade, these activities may include letter recognition and phonemic awareness activities and writing or illustrating stories or projects. In addition, they will be working on individual or small-group projects.

Many classrooms have areas that students visit on a regular or rotating basis. Unlike traditional centers, all students do not rotate through all the areas each day.

The following are suggestions for space and materials for use during Workshop:

1. Reading Area supplied with books and magazines. The materials in the Reading Area should be dynamic—changing with students' abilities and reflecting unit themes they are reading. You may wish to add books to your classroom library.

2. Writing Area stocked with various types and sizes of lined and unlined paper, pencils, erasers, markers, crayons, small slates, and chalk. The area should also have various *Letter Cards* and other handwriting models for those students who want to practice letter formation or handwriting. Students should know that this is where they come for writing supplies. In addition to the supplies described above, the Writing Area can also have supplies to encourage students to create and write on their own:

- Magazines and catalogs to cut up for pictures; stickers, paint, glue, glitter, and so on to decorate books and book covers; precut and stapled blank books for students to write in (Some can be plain and some cut in special shapes.)
- Cardboard, tag board, construction paper, and so on for making book covers (Provide some samples.)
- Tape, scissors, yarn, hole punches for binding books
- Picture dictionaries, dictionaries, thesauruses, word lists, and other materials that may encourage independence

3. Listening Area supplied with computers, tablets, and headphones, so that students can listen and react to the stories, poems, and songs from *Open Court Reading.* Students can take the time to listen to and follow along with the selections in their *Big Books, First Reader,* or *Student Anthologies* as well as in the *Pre-Decodables* and *Decodables* for their grade level. This will give students a chance to listen to fluent readings of those selections.

4. Phonics Activities supplied with *Letter Cards,* individual *Alphabet Sound Card* sets (Kindergarten), individual *Sound/Spelling Cards* (Grades 1–3) and *High-Frequency Flash Cards* (Grades K–3), and other materials that enhance what students are learning. Other classroom materials that enhance reading can be included, such as magnetic write-on/wipe-off boards, magnetic letters, puzzles, and the phonics section of *eGames.*

5. Fluency Area supplied with *Pre-Decodables* and *Decodables* and other resources for practicing fluency. Some teachers have folders for each student with materials to practice during the week. In addition, some Fluency areas have timers and microphones on computers so that you can record students' fluency measures.

Because students will be working on their inquiry investigations during Workshop, make sure there are adequate supplies to help them with their research. These might include dictionaries, encyclopedias, magazines, newspapers, and computers with Internet capability.

How these areas are set up depends upon the teacher and the size of the classroom. Some teachers who have the physical space have tables with different Workshop activities, and students may work at those tables during Workshop or during free time during the day. In other classrooms where space is an issue, teachers keep Workshop materials on labeled bookshelves. During Workshop, students go to the bookshelves, take out the Workshop materials, and use them at their seats or in small groups on the floor. There is no one way to organize materials. The important points to keep in mind are that the materials should be connected to what students are learning in the Foundational Skills, Reading and Responding, and Language Arts lessons and that these materials should change over time as the instruction in the lessons change and as students' skills develop.

Students thrive in an environment that provides structure, repetition, and routine. Within a sound structure, students will gain confidence and independence. This setting allows you to differentiate instruction to provide opportunities for flexibility and individual choice. This will allow students to develop their strengths, abilities, and talents to the fullest.

Suggestions for English Learners

Workshop affords students who are English Learners a wealth of opportunities for gaining proficiency in English. It also encourages them to share their backgrounds with peers. Since you will be working with all students individually and in small groups regardless of their reading ability and language level, students who need special help with language will not feel self-conscious about working with you. In addition, working in small groups made of students with the same interests rather than the same abilities will provide the opportunity to learn about language from peers during the regular course of Workshop activities.

Some suggestions for meeting the special needs of students with diverse backgrounds are as follows:

- Preread a selection with English Learners to help them identify words and ideas they wish to talk about. This will prepare them for discussions with the whole group.
- Preteach vocabulary and develop selection concepts that may be a challenge for students.
- Preteach key linguistic structures to support selection comprehension.
- Review the meaning of selection vocabulary words or even the selection itself by asking questions, checking for comprehension, and allowing English Learners the opportunity to speak as much as possible. This will not only give you a chance to assess their comprehenision, but it will also give them the opportunity to develop their oral language skills.
- Draw English Learners into small-group discussions to let them know their ideas are valid and worth attention.
- Pair English Learners with native English speakers to share their experiences and provide new knowledge to others.
- Have English Learners draw or dictate to you or another student a description of a new idea they may have during Workshop activities.

Suggestions for Approaching-Level Learners

Workshop is an excellent vehicle for spending time with students who need additional support. Whether working with individual students or small groups of students, a range of activities can give them the scaffolding necessary to practice and master skills.

Some suggestions for students at the Approaching Level include the following:

- Review sounds and spellings with students, using *Individual Sound/Spelling Cards.*
- Have students practice blending in small groups using the *Letter Cards.*
- Preteach vocabulary and develop selection concepts that may be a challenge for students.
- Have students practice a skill using *eGames.*
- Give students extra background information regarding the selection.
- Review the meaning of selection vocabulary words or even the selection itself by asking questions, checking for comprehension, and allowing struggling students the opportunity to speak as much as possible. This will not only give you a chance to assess their comprehenision, but it will also give them the opportunity to develop their oral language skill.
- Draw students into small-group discussions to let them know their ideas are valid and worth attention.
- Direct students to use the extension activities on the Website.
- Have students use the *Pre-Decodables* and *Decodables* to practice their decoding and fluency skills. They can read to you before or after listening to a fluent model of reading on the digital version of the books.
- Use the suggestions in the Intervention portion of the program to break down the information into smaller, more manageable chunks for students who are struggling.

Suggestions for Beyond-Level Learners

During Workshop, allow students who are excelling to work individually or in small groups on a variety of activities, incuding the following:

- Have students note interesting words within the selections and keep a personal dictionary of the words, either to use in their own writing or to look for in other reading.
- Allow students to work in pairs to quiz one another on the week's spelling words.
- Have students write a story using the words from the word lines.

- Encourage students to create a crossword puzzle with the selection vocabulary words.
- Pair students with struggling learners for partner reading of a *Decodable* or *Student Anthology* selection.
- Tell students to keep a running list of base words or roots that can take multiple prefixes or suffixes to create new words. For example, the root *nat* can be combined with a variety of prefixes or suffixes to create words such as *nation, national, international, nationality,* and so on.
- Have students practice a skill using *eGames.*
- Allow students to participate in a Book Club, in which they read the same book outside of class. They can use the following Book Review guidelines when discussing the book.

Book Review

Sessions can be small or large. Students can share the reading they do on their own. They can discuss a book they have all read, or one person can review a book and answer the group's questions.

During Workshop, students can discuss and review a variety of books:

- Full-length versions of *Student Anthology* selections
- Books that students learn about when discussing authors and illustrators
- Books related to the investigations of unit concepts that can be shared with others who might want to read them
- Interesting articles from magazines, newspapers, and other sources

When a student reviews a book others have not read, he or she can use some of the sentence starters to tell about the book. These may include "This book is about . . . ," "I chose this book because . . . ," "What I really like/don't like about this book is . . . , " and so on.

- When several students read the same book and discuss it during Workshop, they can use discussion starters.

Developing Workshop

Use the following Workshop suggestions to develop Workshop and to ensure that it runs smoothly.

Note that these suggestions for a weekly unit/lesson may not exactly correspond to a particular unit/lesson in a given grade level but will give you a sense of how Workshop should develop. All suggestions depend upon the needs of the class and their readiness to work independently.

Kindergarten through Grade I

Unit I, Week I Introduce Workshop as whole-class Workshop. Explain Workshop and its rules. Give the class an activity to do, for example, putting letters in alphabetical order (Grade I) or copying their names (kindergarten). Tell the class that they will be doing Workshop today. As they do their activity, you will walk around, observing students and noting how well Workshop is going. The class is working quietly and independently. Workshop may last only a few minutes in kindergarten and about ten minutes in first grade.

Unit I, Weeks 2 and 3 Depending upon your class, you can move to whole-group Workshop with two activities. Give half the class one activity and the other half the other. Explain to the class that for the next few Workshop sessions, there will be two different activities but that the class is supposed to work quietly and independently. Switch activities for the next day, and repeat this format for the next few days or so. Introduce the concept of "debriefing." Take a few minutes at the end to have several students share what they did or learned during Workshop. Have students tell what they like about Workshop and if any changes need to be made.

Unit 2, Week I Begin introducing Workshop Areas, explaining the materials and how they can be used. Explain to students that the materials in these areas will be changing regularly so students will be able to practice and use their new reading and writing skills. Workshop activities should change routinely and reflect the changing nature of the curriculum. Often, during the early weeks of Workshop, teachers assign students to different activities and, as students become ready, turn over to students the responsibility for choosing activities.

Unit 3 Add new activities for students. Encourage them to do a couple of Workshop activities each day, perhaps working on their writing in progress and fluency practice (reading a Pre-Decodable or Decodable). Other options might include on-line phonemic awareness and phonics activities, phonics activities such as word sorts, using blended words in written sentences, practicing high-frequency sight words, and so on.

Unit 4 By this time, students should be making choices and working independently. Each Workshop session may be fifteen minutes long with the teacher working with small groups. Take time to review Workshop activities to be sure they are being used and that students are learning from the activities. If activities become stale, vary them, or change them altogether.

Grades 2–3

Unit 1, Lesson 1 Introduce Workshop to students. Make sure they know where materials are located. Post the rules on the board or other prominent place in the classroom. Keep Workshop time short (less than thirty minutes) and very directed during the first few weeks until students can work independently.

Unit 1, Lesson 2 Discuss using small groups for preteaching or reteaching purposes and how you will indicate who will be in the groups. Start by forming one small group randomly and having other students do something specific such as a writing assignment. When you have finished with the small group, send them to do independent work. Call another small group of students to work with you. Continue this each day until students are accustomed to forming groups and working independently.

Unit 1, Lesson 3 Encourage a student-formed and student-run book discussion. Encourage participating students to choose a book that they all will read and discuss. Several different groups may form on the basis of the books students choose.

Unit 1, Lessons 4–5 For the first few weeks of the school year, make sure each student has a plan for using Workshop time.

Unit 1, Lesson 6 Allow time for presentation and discussion of research activities. Use an entire Workshop day, and have all groups present their findings, or split the presentations over several days, depending on the needs of your class.

Review how students have used Workshop during this unit. Have they used their time well? Do they have the materials they need? Discuss suggestions for improving their use of this time. Take a few minutes at the beginning of each Workshop ensure students know what they will be doing.

Unit 2, Lesson 1 Form small extra-practice groups with the more advanced students from time to time, as they also need special attention.

Unit 2, Lesson 2 To keep the entire class informed about the independent research being done, every other day or so invite a research group to explain what it is doing, how the research is going, and any problems they are encountering.

Unit 2, Lesson 3 Discuss the use of Workshop time for doing Inquiry and research projects, and share *eInquiry* with different research activities.

Unit 2, Lesson 4 Make sure small extra-practice groups are formed based on your observations of students' work on the different daily lessons. Small groups should be fluid and based on demonstrated need rather than become static and unchanging.

Unit 2, Lesson 5 One purpose of Workshop is to help students learn independence and responsibility. Assign students to monitor Workshop materials. They should alert you whenever materials are running low or missing, and they can be responsible for checking on return dates of library books and making sure the books are either returned or renewed.

Unit 2, Lesson 6 Students sometimes have difficulty starting discussions in Reading Roundtable. Try some of these discussion starters with students, and print them on a poster for student use.

> *I didn't know that . . .*
> *I liked the part where . . .*
> *Does anyone know . . .*
> *I'm still confused by . . .*
> *I figured out that . . .*
> *This made me think . . .*
> *I agree/disagree with because . . .*

Unit 3, Lesson 1 By this time students should be accustomed to the routines, rules, expectations, and usage of Workshop time and be moving smoothly from small teacher-led groups to independent work. Monitor small groups occasionally to see that they are on task and making progress on their activities.

Unit 3, Lesson 2 Make a practice of reading aloud to students. All students enjoy being read to, no matter their age or grade. Encourage them to discuss the shared reading in groups and to bring books and read them aloud to their classmates.

Unit 3, Lesson 3 Encourage cooperation and collaboration by providing students with opportunities to engage in small groups.

Unit 3, Lesson 4 Spend a few minutes each day circulating around the room and monitoring what students are doing independently or in small groups. Students can then share with you on a timely basis any questions or problems they are having.

Unit 3, Lesson 5 Take note of various small groups. Make sure that quieter students are able to participate in the discussions. Often the stronger, more confident students dominate such discussions. Encourage them to give all participants an opportunity to share their ideas.

Unit 3, Lesson 6 If students are not productive during Workshop, keep them in the small group you are working with until they can successfully benefit from independent work. Discuss strategies they could use to become more independent.

Unit 4, Lesson 1 Individual students can monitor Workshop materials and alert you when materials or supplies are running low or missing and can check that library books are either returned or renewed.

Unit 4, Lesson 2 From time to time, join a Reading Roundtable group, and take part in their discussion. Make sure students lead the discussion.

Unit 4, Lesson 3 Encourage responsibility and independence by reminding students to show respect for each other and the materials provided.

Unit 4, Lesson 4 Be sure students discuss during Reading Roundtable what they like or dislike about a book, why they wanted to read it, and how the book either lived up to their expectations or disappointed them. Discussions should not be about basic comprehension but should help students think more deeply about the ideas presented in the book.

Unit 4, Lesson 5 Make sure students continue to use the activities provided for use with this unit at **www.Connected.com.**

Unit 4, Lesson 6 If students are not productive in Workshop, keep them in the small group you are working with until they can successfully benefit from independent work. Discuss strategies they could use to become more independent.

Unit 5, Lesson 1 Students often make great tutors for other students. They are uniquely qualified to understand problems that others might be having. Encourage students to pair up during Workshop to help each other with their daily lessons.

Unit 5, Lesson 2 Form small extra-practice groups with the more advanced students from time to time, as they also need special attention.

Unit 5, Lesson 3 To keep the entire class informed about the independent research being done, every other day or so, invite a research/investigation group to explain what it is doing, how the research is going, and any problems they are encountering.

Unit 5, Lesson 4 Many of the *Student Anthology* selections are well known, and the authors have written many pieces of fine literature. Encourage students who enjoy the selections to find other books by the same author, or to find other versions of the same story. Have them think about and discuss what about that particular author's work attracts them, or compare and contrast the different versions of the same selection.

Unit 5, Lesson 5 Share your impressions of books from your classroom library or other readings during Reading Roundtable. Note which students initiate sharing and which are reluctant to share.

Unit 5, Lesson 6 Review with students the time they have used in Workshop. Have they used their time well? Do they have the materials they need? Discuss suggestions for improving the use of this time.

Unit 6, Lesson 1 Spend a few minutes each day circulating and monitoring what students are doing independently or in small groups. Students can share with you on a timely basis any questions or problems they are having.

Unit 6, Lesson 2 Students should be accustomed to the routines, rules, expectations, and usage of Workshop time and be moving smoothly from small teacher-led groups to independent work. Make sure to monitor small groups occasionally to see that they are on task and making progress with their activities.

Unit 6, Lesson 3 Make sure students continue to use the activities provided for use with this unit at **www.Connected.com.**

Unit 6, Lesson 4 If the reading selection is an excerpt from a longer piece, encourage students to read the book from which the excerpt is taken and to discuss how the excerpt fits into the larger work.

Unit 6, Lesson 5 Students often make great tutors for other students. The fact that they, too, are just learning the materials makes them uniquely qualified to understand problems that others might be having. Encourage students to pair up during Workshop to help each other on their daily lessons.

Unit 6, Lesson 6 Allot time for presentation and discussion of research activities. You may want to use a whole Workshop day and have all groups present their findings or split the presentations over several days, depending on the urgency of the small-group instruction your class needs.

Scope and Sequence

Foundational Skills

	K	1	2	3
Phonemic Awareness (Recognize Discrete Sounds in Words)				
Long and Short Vowels Differentiation	●	●		
Phoneme Addition: Final Sounds	●	●		
Phoneme Addition: Initial Sounds	●	●		
Phoneme Addition: Medial Sounds	●			
Phoneme Blending: All Sounds in a Word	●	●		
Phoneme Blending: Final Sounds	●	●		
Phoneme Blending: Initial Sounds	●	●		
Phoneme Blending: Medial Sounds	●	●		
Phoneme Blending: Onset and Rime	●	●		
Phoneme Blending: Syllables	●	●		
Phoneme Blending: Vowel Substitution	●	●		
Phoneme Blending: Words/Word Parts	●	●		
Phoneme Isolation: Final Sounds	●	●		
Phoneme Isolation: Initial Sounds	●	●		
Phoneme Isolation: Medial Sounds	●	●		
Phoneme Substitution: Final Sounds	●	●		
Phoneme Substitution: Initial Sounds	●	●		
Phoneme Substitution: Medial Sounds	●	●		
Phoneme Matching: Final Sounds	●	●		
Phoneme Matching: Initial Sounds	●	●		
Phoneme Matching: Medial Sounds	●	●		
Phoneme Pronunciation: Final Sounds	●	●		
Phoneme Pronunciation: Initial Sounds	●	●		
Phoneme Pronunciation: Medial Sounds	●	●		
Produce Rhyming Words	●	●		
Recognize Rhyming Words	●	●		
Segmentation: Final Consonants	●	●		
Segmentation: Identifying All Sounds in a Word in Sequence	●	●		
Segmentation: Identifying the Number of Sounds in Words	●	●		
Segmentation: Initial Consonants/Blends		●		
Segmentation: Medial Consonants	●	●		
Segmentation: Onset and Rime	●	●		
Segmentation: Syllables	●	●		
Segmentation: Words/Word Parts	●	●		
Print and Book Awareness (Recognize and Understand the Concepts of Print and Books)				
Capitalization	●	●		
Differentiate Between Letters and Words	●			
Differentiate Between Words and Sentences	●			
End Punctuation	●	●		
Follow Words Left-to-Right	●	●		
Follow Words Page by Page	●	●		
Follow Words Top-to-Bottom	●	●		
Follow Letter Formation	●	●		

Foundational Skills

	K	1	2	3
Print and Book Awareness (continued)				
Page Numbering	●			
Parts of a Book	●	●		
Picture/Text Relationship	●	●		
Punctuation	●	●		
Quotation Marks	●	●		
Recognize First Word in Sentence	●	●		
Relationship Between Spoken and Printed Language	●	●		
Sentence Recognition	●	●		
Spacing Between Sentences	●	●		
Spacing Between Words	●	●		
Word Length	●	●		
Write Left-to-Right	●	●		
Write Top-to-Bottom	●	●		
Alphabetic Knowledge				
Letter Order (Alphabetic Order)	●	●		
Letter Sounds	●	●		
Lowercase Letters	●	●		
Sounds in Words	●	●		
Uppercase Letters	●	●		
Phonics and Word Analysis				
Antonyms		●	●	●
Base Words or Roots			●	●
Blending Sounds into Words	●	●	●	●
Comparatives/Superlatives			●	●
Compound Words		●	●	●
Consonant Blends	●	●	●	●
Consonant Digraphs		●	●	●
Contractions		●	●	●
Distinguish Between Long and Short Vowels	●	●	●	●
Distinguish Between Similarly Spelled Words	●			
Greek and Latin Roots				●
High-Frequency Words	●	●	●	●
Homographs		●		●
Homophones		●	●	●
Inflectional Endings	●	●	●	●
Irregular Plurals			●	●
Irregularly Spelled Words		●	●	●
Letter-Sound Correspondence	●	●	●	●
Multiple-Meaning Words			●	●
Plurals	●	●	●	●
Position Words	●			
Prefixes	●	●	●	●
Shades of Meaning/Levels of Specificity				●

Foundational Skills

	K	1	2	3
Phonics and Word Analysis (continued)				
Silent Letters		●	●	●
Suffixes	●	●	●	●
Syllables: Vowels in Words		●	●	●
Syllables: Multisyllabic Words		●	●	●
Synonyms		●	●	●
Vowel Diphthongs		●	●	●
Vowels: l-controlled		●	●	●
Vowels: Long Sounds and Spellings	●	●	●	●
Vowels: r-controlled		●	●	●
Vowels: Short Sounds and Spellings	●	●	●	●
Word Families/Words with the Same Base	●	●	●	●
Fluency				
Purpose	●	●	●	●
Rate	●	●	●	●
Self-Correct	●	●	●	●
Successive Readings	●	●	●	●
Understanding	●	●	●	●
Word Recognition	●	●	●	●
Dictation				
Antonyms				●
Root Words				●
Comparatives/Superlatives				●
Compound Words				●
Contractions				●
Greek and Latin Roots				●
Homographs				●
Homophones				●
Inflectional Endings	●	●	●	●
Irregular Plurals			●	●
Irregular Verbs				●
Letter/Sound Relationships	●	●	●	●
Long-Vowel Spellings	●	●	●	●
Multiple-Meaning Words				●
Multisyllabic Words		●	●	●
Phonograms			●	●
Prefixes		●	●	●
r-Controlled Vowel Spellings		●	●	●
Shades of Meaning				●
Short-Vowel Spellings	●	●	●	●
Silent Letters			●	●
Special Spelling Patterns/Rules			●	●
Special-Vowel Spellings		●	●	●
Suffixes		●		●
Synonyms				●

Foundational Skills

	K	1	2	3
Penmanship				
Print Letters	●	●		
Print Numbers	●	●		
Oral Language Development				
Answer Questions	●	●	●	●
Ask Questions		●	●	●
Listen and Respond	●	●	●	●
Participate in Group Discussion	●	●	●	●
Read Orally	●	●	●	●
Share Information		●	●	●
Speak Clearly at Appropriate Volume	●	●	●	●
Using Complete Sentences	●	●	●	●

Reading

	K	1	2	3
Accessing Complex Text Skills				
Cause and Effect	●	●	●	●
Classify and Categorize	●	●	●	●
Compare and Contrast	●	●	●	●
Fact and Opinion		●	●	●
Main Idea and Details	●	●	●	●
Making Inferences		●	●	●
Sequence	●	●	●	●
Comprehension Strategies				
Asking Questions/Answering Questions	●	●	●	●
Clarifying	●	●	●	●
Making Connections	●	●	●	●
Predicting/Confirming Predictions	●	●	●	●
Summarizing	●	●	●	●
Visualizing	●	●	●	●
Writer's Craft				
Author's Purpose		●	●	●
Captions and Headings	●	●	●	●
Figurative Language			●	●
Genre Knowledge	●	●	●	●
Idiom				●
Language Use: Alliteration	●	●	●	●
Language Use: Content Words		●	●	●
Language Use: Descriptive Words	●	●	●	●
Language Use: Dialogue	●	●	●	●
Language Use: Onomatopoeia	●	●	●	●
Language Use: Repetition	●	●	●	●
Language Use: Rhyme	●	●	●	●
Language Use: Rhythm		●	●	●
Language Use: Sensory Details	●	●	●	●
Mood and Tone			●	●
Personification	●	●	●	●
Point of View: Informational or Persuasive Text		●	●	●
Point of View: Narrative		●	●	●
Punctuation	●	●	●	
Sentence Variety		●	●	
Similes and Metaphors			●	●
Stage Directions		●		●
Story Elements: Character	●	●	●	●
Story Elements: Plot	●	●	●	●
Story Elements: Setting	●	●	●	●
Story Elements: Style			●	●
Text Features	●	●	●	●
Text Structure		●	●	●

Reading

	K	1	2	3
Writer's Craft (continued)				
Theme		•	•	•
Transitions		•	•	
Using Comparisons		•	•	
Word Choice		•	•	•
Vocabulary				
Apposition		•	•	•
Concept Words	•	•	•	•
Context Clues		•	•	•
Expanding Vocabulary		•	•	•
High-Frequency Words	•	•		
Idioms				•
Multiple-Meaning Words	•	•	•	•
Selection Vocabulary	•	•	•	•
Time and Order Words (Creating Sequence)	•	•	•	•
Utility Words (Colors, Classroom Objects, etc.)	•	•		
Fluency				
Accuracy		•	•	•
Automaticity		•	•	•
Expression		•	•	•
Prosody		•	•	•
Purpose		•	•	•
Rate		•	•	•
Self-Correct		•	•	•
Successive Readings		•	•	•
Understanding		•	•	•
Word Recognition		•	•	•
Research/Inquiry				
Comparing Information across Sources	•	•	•	•
Charts, Graphs, and Diagrams/Visual Aids	•	•	•	•
Collaborative Inquiry	•	•	•	•
Communicating Research Progress Results	•	•	•	•
Compile Notes		•	•	•
Conducting an Interview	•	•	•	•
Finding Needed Information	•	•	•	•
Follow Directions	•	•	•	•
Formulating Conjectures	•	•	•	•
Formulate Questions for Inquiry and Research	•	•	•	•
Give Reports	•	•	•	•
Make Outlines			•	•
Maps				•
Note Taking		•	•	•
Parts of a Book	•	•	•	•

Reading

	K	1	2	3
Research/Inquiry (continued)				
Planning Inquiry	●	●	●	●
Recognizing Information Needs	●	●	●	●
Revising Questions and Conjectures	●	●	●	●
Summarize and Organize Information	●	●	●	●
Time Lines				●
Use Appropriate Resources (Media Sources, Reference Books, Experts, Internet)	●	●	●	●
Using a Dictionary/Glossary	●	●	●	●
Using a Media Center/Library	●	●	●	●
Using a Thesaurus		●	●	●
Using an Encyclopedia	●	●	●	●
Using Newspapers and Magazines	●	●	●	●
Using Technology	●	●	●	●
Print and Book Awareness				
Capitalization	●	●		
Differentiate Between Letters and Words	●	●		
Differentiate Between Words and Sentences	●	●		
End Punctuation	●	●		
Follow Words Left-to-Right	●	●		
Follow Words Page by Page	●	●		
Follow Words Top-to-Bottom	●	●		
Follow Letter Formation	●			
Page Numbering	●	●		
Parts of a Book	●	●		
Picture/Text Relationship	●	●		
Punctuation	●	●		
Quotation Marks	●	●		
Recognize First Word in Sentence	●	●		
Relationship Between Spoken and Printed Language	●	●		
Sentence Length	●			
Sentence Recognition	●	●		
Spacing Between Sentences	●	●		
Spacing Between Words	●	●		
Word Length	●	●		

Language Arts Writing/Composition

	K	1	2	3
Approaches				
Collaborative Writing	●	●	●	●
Individual Writing	●	●	●	●
Writing Process				
Brainstorming/Prewriting	●	●	●	●
Drafting	●	●	●	●
Revising	●	●	●	●
Editing	●	●	●	●
Proofreading	●	●	●	●
Publishing	●	●	●	●
Writing Genres				
Action Tale			●	
Autobiography/Biography	●	●	●	●
Business Letter			●	●
Descriptive Writing	●	●	●	●
Expository/Informational Text	●	●	●	●
Fantasy	●	●	●	●
Folklore (Folktales, Fairy Tales, Tall Tales, Legends, Myths)				●
Friendly Letter			●	
Instructions		●		
Making a List		●	●	
Narrative	●	●	●	●
News Story	●	●		
Opinion Statement	●	●	●	●
Personal Writing			●	
Persuasive Writing	●	●	●	●
Poetry	●		●	●
Realistic Fiction	●	●	●	●
Report	●	●	●	●
Responding to Literature	●	●	●	●
Summary	●	●	●	●
Writing Strategies				
Action and Describing Words	●	●	●	●
Adding Details	●	●	●	●
Audience and Purpose	●	●	●	●
Brainstorming	●	●	●	●
Cause and Effect			●	●
Choosing a Topic	●	●	●	●
Compare and Contrast			●	●
Creating Vivid Images		●	●	●
Dialogue	●	●	●	●
Effective Beginnings/Endings		●	●	●
Elements of a Letter			●	●
Elements of Persuasion	●	●	●	●

Language Arts Writing/Composition

Writing Strategies (continued)	K	1	2	3
Eliminating Irrelevant Information	●	●	●	●
Evaluate Personal Growth as a Writer			●	
Formality of Language			●	●
Generate Additional Ideas	●	●	●	●
Highlight a Memorable Event			●	
Identifying Best Feature of Something Written			●	
Illustrations and Drawings	●	●	●	●
Information from Multiple Sources	●	●	●	●
Main Idea and Details	●	●	●	●
Organizing a Multi-Paragraph Composition			●	●
Planning	●	●	●	●
Plot Structure—Beginning, Middle, Climax, and End	●	●	●	●
Point of View			●	●
Presenting Facts and Examples Objectively			●	●
Proofreading	●	●	●	●
Purpose	●	●	●	●
Realism				●
Referencing a Source				●
Revising	●	●	●	●
Rhythm and Rhyme	●		●	●
Sensory Details	●	●	●	●
Sentence Combining		●	●	●
Sequence	●	●	●	●
Setting	●	●	●	●
Story Elements	●	●	●	●
Summary		●	●	●
Taking Notes		●	●	●
Transition Words/Devices		●	●	●
Using a Checklist	●	●	●	●
Using a Graphic Organizer	●	●	●	●
Using a Model as a Guide to Writing	●	●	●	●
Using Outlines to Organize Information				●
Using Multimedia Sources	●	●	●	●
Vary Sentence Beginnings	●	●	●	●
Vary Sentence Length		●	●	●
Vary Sentence Types	●	●	●	●
Voice				●
Voicing an Opinion	●	●	●	●
Word Choice	●	●	●	●
Writing Coherent Paragraphs		●	●	●

Language Arts Writing/Composition

Writing Traits	K	1	2	3
Audience	•	•	•	•
Conventions	•	•	•	•
Elaboration			•	•
Focus	•	•	•	•
Ideas/Content	•	•	•	•
Organization	•	•	•	•
Presentation	•	•	•	•
Purpose		•	•	•
Sentence Fluency	•	•	•	•
Sentence Variety	•	•	•	•
Vocabulary	•	•	•	•
Voice				•
Word Choice		•	•	•

Language Arts Grammar, Usage, and Mechanics

Parts of Speech	K	1	2	3
Adjectives (Describing Words)	•	•	•	•
Adverbs		•	•	•
Articles	•	•	•	
Conjunctions		•	•	•
Nouns	•	•	•	•
Prepositions	•	•	•	•
Pronouns	•	•	•	•
Verbs	•	•	•	•

Sentences	K	1	2	3
Complete and Incomplete Sentences	•	•	•	•
Complex Sentences				•
Compound Sentences		•	•	•
Declarative Sentences	•	•	•	•
Exclamatory Sentences	•	•	•	•
Fragments			•	
Imperative Sentences		•	•	•
Independent and Dependent Clauses				•
Interrogative Sentences (Questions)	•	•	•	•
Parts (Subjects and Predicates)		•	•	
Pronoun/Antecedent Agreement				•
Run-on Sentences			•	
Sentence Combining		•	•	•
Simple Sentences	•	•	•	•
Subject/Verb Agreement		•	•	•

Language Arts Grammar, Usage, and Mechanics

	K	1	2	3
Capitalization				
Pronoun "I"	•	•		
Proper Nouns	•	•	•	•
Sentence Beginning	•	•	•	•
Title		•	•	•
Punctuation				
Apostrophe		•	•	•
Colon			•	
Commas in Compound Sentences		•	•	•
Commas in Dialogue			•	•
Commas in Greetings or Closings			•	•
Commas in a Series		•	•	•
End Punctuation	•	•	•	•
Exclamation Mark	•	•	•	•
Parentheses				•
Period	•	•	•	•
Question Mark	•	•	•	•
Quotation Marks		•	•	•
Usage				
Antonyms		•		•
Contractions		•	•	•
Determiners		•		
Regular and Irregular Plurals		•	•	•
Synonyms		•	•	•
Verb Tenses	•	•	•	•
Verbs (Action, Helping, Linking, Regular/Irregular)	•	•	•	•

Language Arts Penmanship

	K	1	2	3
Penmanship				
Cursive Letters				•
Print Letters		•	•	

Language Arts Spelling

Spelling	K	1	2	3
Antonyms				•
Base or Root Words		•	•	•
Comparatives/Superlatives			•	•
Compound Words			•	•
Consonant Digraphs		•		
Contractions				•
Diphthongs		•	•	•
Greek and Latin Roots				•
Homographs				•
Homophones			•	•
Inflectional Endings		•	•	•
Irregular Plurals			•	•
Long-Vowel Spellings		•	•	•
Multiple-Meaning Words				•
Multisyllabic Words		•	•	•
Prefixes		•	•	•
r-Controlled Vowel Spellings		•		
Shades of Meaning				•
Short-Vowel Spellings		•		
Silent Letters		•	•	•
Sound/Letter Relationships		•	•	•
Special Spelling Patterns/Rules		•	•	•
Special-Vowel Spellings		•	•	•
Suffixes			•	•
Synonyms				•
Words with the Same Base			•	•

Glossary of Reading Terms

This glossary includes linguistic, grammatical, comprehension, and literary terms that may be helpful in understanding reading instruction.

accessing complex text skill a skill that aids in understanding text, including comprehending **cause-and-effect** relationships, **classifying and categorizing** information, **comparing and contrasting** items and events, distinguishing **fact from opinion,** identifying **main ideas and details, making inferences,** and understanding **sequence.**

acronym a word formed from the initial letter of words in a phrase, **scuba (self-contained underwater breathing apparatus).**

acrostic a kind of puzzle in which lines of a poem are arranged so that words or phrases are formed when certain letters from each line are used in a sequence.

adjective a word or group of words that modifies or describes a noun.

adventure story a narrative that features the unknown or unexpected with elements of excitement, danger, and risk.

adverb a word or group of words that modifies a verb, adjective, or other adverb. An adverb answers questions such as **how, when, where,** and **how much.**

affix a word part, either a prefix or a suffix, that changes the meaning or function of a word root or stem.

affricate a speech sound that starts as a stop but ends as a fricative, the /ch/ in **catch.**

agreement the correspondence of syntactically related words; subjects and predicates are in agreement when both are singular or plural.

alliteration the repetition of the initial sounds in neighboring words or stressed syllables.

alphabet the complete set of letters representing speech sounds used in writing a language. In English there are twenty-six letters.

alphabet book a book for helping young children learn the alphabet by pairing letters with pictures whose sounds they represent.

alphabetic principle the association between sounds and the letters that represent them in alphabetic writing systems.

alveolar a consonant speech sound made when the tongue and the ridge of the upper and lower jaw stop to constrict the air flow, as /t/.

anagram a word or phrase whose letters form other words or phrases when rearranged, for example, **add** and **dad.**

analogy a likeness or similarity.

analytic phonics also deductive phonics, a whole-to-part approach to phonics in which student are taught a number of sight words and then phonetic generalizations that can be applied to other words.

antonym a word that is opposite in meaning to another word.

appositive a word that restates or modifies a preceding noun, for example, **my daughter, Charlotte.** Appositives are also definitions of words usually set off by commas.

aspirate an unvoiced speech sound produced by a puff of air, as /h/ in **heart.**

aspirated stop a stop consonant sound released with a puff of air, as /k/, /p/, and /t/.

auditory discrimination the ability to hear phonetic likenesses and differences in phonemes and words.

author's purpose the motive or reason for which an author writes; includes to entertain, inform, persuade, and explain how.

automaticity fluent processing of information, requiring little effort or attention.

auxiliary verb a verb that precedes another verb to express time, mood, or voice; includes verbs such as **has, is,** and **will.**

base word a word to which affixes may be added to create related words.

blank verse unrhymed verse, especially unrhymed iambic pentameter.

blend the joining of the sounds of two or more letters with little change in those sounds, for example, /spr/ in **spring;** also **consonant blend** or **consonant cluster.**

blending combining the sounds represented by letters or spellings to sound out or pronounce a word; contrast with **oral blending.**

breve the symbol placed above a vowel to indicate that it is a short vowel.

browse to skim through or look over in search of something of interest.

canon in literature, the body of major works that a culture considers important at a given time.

categorizing an accessing complex text skill in which the reader recognizes that related facts and details in a text can be put together into different groups, or categories.

cause-effect relationship a stated or implied association between an outcome and the conditions that brought it about; also the accessing complex text skill associated with recognizing this type of relationship as an organizing principle in text.

chapter book a book long enough to be divided into chapters, but not long or complex enough to be considered a novel.

characterization the way in which an author presents a character in a story, including describing words, actions, thoughts, and impressions of that character.

choral reading oral group reading to develop oral fluency by modeling.

clarifying a comprehension strategy in which the reader rereads text, uses a dictionary, uses decoding skills, or uses context clues to comprehend something that is unclear.

classifying a skill in which the reader recognizes that related facts and details in a text can be grouped together.

clause a group of words with a subject and a predicate used to form a part of or a whole sentence, a dependent clause modifies an independent clause, which can stand alone as a complete sentence.

close reading the act of rereading a passage or a page to find specific information for a specific purpose.

collaborative learning learning by working together in small groups.

command a sentence that asks for action and usually ends with a period.

common noun in contrast to **proper noun,** a noun that denotes a class rather than a unique or specific thing such as **girl** versus **Susan.**

comprehension the understanding of what is written or said.

comprehension strategy a sequence of steps for monitoring and understanding text, includes asking and answering questions, clarifying, making connections, predicting and confirming predictions, summarizing, and visualizing.

conjugation the complete set of all possible inflected forms of a verb.

conjunction a part of speech used to connect words, phrases, clauses, or sentences, including the words **and, but,** and **or.**

consonant a speech sound, and the alphabet letter that represents that sound, made by partial or complete closure of part of the vocal tract, which obstructs air flow and causes audible friction.

context clue information from the immediate and surrounding text that helps identify a word.

contraction a short version of a written or spoken expression in which letters are omitted, for example, **can't.**

convention an accepted practice in spoken or written language, usually referring to spelling, mechanics, or grammar rules.

cooperative learning a classroom organization that allows students to work together to achieve their individual goals. Related term is **collaboration.**

creative writing prose and poetic forms of writing that express the writer's thoughts and feelings imaginatively.

cueing system any of the various sources of information that help identify an unrecognizable word in reading, including phonetic, semantic, and syntactical information.

cumulative tale a story, such as "The Green Grass Grew All Around," in which details are repeated until the climax.

dangling modifier usually a participle that because of its placement in a sentence modifies the wrong object.

decodable text text materials controlled to include a majority of words whose sound/spelling relationships are known by the reader.

decode to analyze spoken or graphic symbols for meaning.

diacritical mark a mark, such as a breve or macron, added to a letter or graphic character to indicate a specific pronunciation.

dialect a regional variety of a particular language with phonological, grammatical, and lexical patterns that distinguishes it from other varieties.

dialogue a piece of writing written as conversation, usually punctuated by quotation marks.

digraph two letters that represent one speech sound, for example, /sh/ or /ch/.

diphthong a vowel sound produced when the tongue glides from one vowel sound toward another in the same syllable, for example, /oi/ or /ou/.

direct object the person or thing that receives the action of a verb in a sentence, for example, the word **cake** in this sentence: **Madeline baked a cake.**

drafting the process of writing ideas in rough form to record them.

drama a story in the form of a play, written to be performed.

edit in the writing process, to revise or correct a manuscript. Often this is part of the final step in the process with a focus on correcting grammar, spelling, and mechanics rather than content, structure, and organization.

emergent literacy the development of the association of meaning and print that continues until a child reaches the stage of conventional reading and writing.

emergent reading a child's early interaction with books and print before the ability to decode text.

encode to change a message into symbols, for example, to change speech into writing.

epic a long narrative poem, usually about a hero.

exclamatory sentence a sentence that shows strong emotion and ends with an exclamation point.

expository writing or **exposition** a composition in writing that explains an event or process.

fable a short tale that teaches a moral.

fantasy a highly imaginative story about characters, places, and events that cannot exist.

fiction imaginative narrative designed to entertain rather than to explain, persuade, or describe.

figure of speech the expressive, nonliteral use of language usually through metaphor, simile, or personification.

fluency freedom from word-identification problems that hinder comprehension in reading. Fluency involves rate, accuracy, and expression.

folktale a narrative form of genre such as an epic, myth, or fable that is well-known through repeated storytellings.

foreshadowing giving clues to upcoming events in a story.

free verse verse with irregular metrical pattern.

freewriting writing that is not limited in form, style, content, or purpose; designed to encourage students to write.

genre a classification of literary works, including tragedy, comedy, novel, essay, short story, mystery, realistic fiction, and poetry.

grammar the study of the classes of words, their inflections, and their functions and relations in sentences; includes phonological, morphological, syntactic, and semantic descriptions of a language.

grapheme a written or printed representation of a phoneme, such as **c** for /k/.

guided reading reading instruction in which the teacher provides the structure and purpose for reading and responding to the material read.

handing off a method of turning over to students the primary responsibility for controlling discussion.

indirect object in a sentence, the person or thing to or for whom an action is done, for example, the word **dog** in this sentence: **Madeline gave the dog a treat.**

inference a conclusion based on facts, data, or evidence.

infinitive the base form of a verb, usually with the infinitive marker, for example, **to go.**

inflectional ending an ending that expresses a plural or possessive form of a noun, the tense of a verb, or the comparative or superlative form of an adjective or adverb.

informative writing a composition in writing that explains how to do something or gives information about something.

interrogative word a word that marks a clause or sentence as a question, including **interrogative pronouns who, what, which, where.**

intervention a strategy or program designed to supplement or substitute instruction, especially for those students who fall behind.

invented spelling the result of an attempt to spell a word based on using the sounds in the letter names to determine the sound the letter names. Gradually sounds are connected to letters, which leads to conventional spelling.

irony a figure of speech in which the literal meanings of the words is the opposite of their intended meanings.

journal a written record of daily events or responses.

legend a traditional tale handed down from generation to generation.

letter one of a set of graphic symbols that forms an alphabet and is used alone or in combination to represent a phoneme, also **grapheme.**

linguistics the study of the nature and structure of language and communication.

literary elements the elements of a story such as **setting, plot,** and **characterization** that create the structure of a narrative.

macron a diacritical mark placed above a vowel to indicate a long vowel sound.

main idea the central thought or chief topic of a passage.

making connections a reading strategy used to connect information being read to one's own experiences, to other reading materials, or to one's knowledge of the world. Making connections fosters engagement, while reading helps the reader make sense of the text and connect information.

mechanics the conventions of capitalization and punctuation.

metacognition awareness and knowledge of one's mental processes or thinking about what one is thinking about.

metaphor a figure of speech in which a comparison is implied but not stated; for example, **She is a jewel.**

miscue a deviation from text during oral reading in an attempt to make sense of the text.

modeling an instructional technique in which the teacher makes public the thinking needed to use critical reading and writing behaviors.

mood literary element that conveys the emotional atmosphere of a story.

morpheme a meaningful linguistic unit that cannot be divided into smaller units, for example, **word; a bound morpheme** is a morpheme that cannot stand alone as an independent word, for example, the prefix **re-;** a **free morpheme** can stand alone, for example, **dog.**

myth a story designed to explain the mysteries of life.

narrative writing or **narration** a composition in writing that tells a story or gives an account of an event.

nonfiction prose designed to explain, argue, or describe rather than to entertain with a factual emphasis; includes biography and autobiography.

noun a part of speech that denotes persons, places, things, qualities, or acts.

novel an extended fictional prose narration.

onomatopoeia the use of a word whose sound suggests its meaning, for example, **purr.**

onset the beginning of a syllable, which usually consists of an initial consonant or a consonant blend; almost always done in conjunction with **rime;** see also **rime.**

opinion writing a composition intended to let the reader know what the writer thinks about something.

oral blending the ability to fuse discrete phonemes into recognizable words; oral blending puts sounds together to make a word, see also **segmentation.**

orthography correct or standardized spelling according to established usage in a language.

oxymoron a figure of speech in which contrasting or contradictory words are brought together for emphasis.

paragraph a subdivision of a written composition that consists of one or more sentences, deals with one point, or gives the words of one speaker, usually beginning with an indented line.

participle a verb form used as an adjective, for example, **the skating party.**

personification a figure of speech in which animals, ideas, or things take on human characteristics.

persuasive writing a composition intended to persuade the reader to adopt the writer's point of view.

phoneme the smallest sound unit of speech, for example, the /k/ in **book.**

phonemic awareness the ability to recognize that spoken words are made of discrete sounds and that those sounds can be manipulated.

phonetic spelling the respelling of entry words in a dictionary according to a pronunciation key.

phonetics the study of speech sounds.

phonics a way of teaching reading that addresses sound/symbol relationships, especially in beginning instruction.

phonogram a letter or symbol that represents a phonetic sound.

phonological awareness the ability to attend to the sound structure of language; includes sentence, word, syllable rhyme and phonological awareness.

plot the literary element that provides the structure of the action of a story, which may include rising action, climax, and falling action leading to a resolution or denouement.

plural a grammatical form of a word that refers to more than one in number; an irregular plural is one that does not follow normal patterns for inflectional endings.

poetic license the liberty taken by writers to ignore conventions.

poetry a metrical form of composition in which language is chosen and arranged to create a powerful response through meaning, sound, or rhythm.

point of view (informational or persuasive text) the position or perspective the author takes on a subject.

point of view (narrative text) the position or perspective of the narrator of a story; a story could be told from the **first-person point of view,** in which the narrator is actually a character in the story and tells the story as he or she perceives what is happening, or it could be told from the **third-person point of view,** in which the narrator does not take part in the story but is able to relate everything that all the characters are thinking and feeling.

possessive showing ownership either through the use of an adjective, an adjectival pronoun, or the possessive form of a noun.

POW a pneumonic device that helps students understand and remember the writing process. The initials **POW** stand for **P**ick my idea, **O**rganize my notes, and **W**rite and say more.

predicate the part of the sentence that expresses something about the subject and includes the verb phrase; a **complete predicate** includes the principal verb in a sentence and all its modifiers or subordinate parts.

predicting a comprehension strategy in which the reader attempts to anticipate what will happen, using clues from the text and prior knowledge, and then confirms predictions as the text is read.

prefix an affix attached before a base word that changes the meaning of the word.

preposition a part of speech in the class of function words such as **of, on,** and **at** that precede noun phrases to create prepositional phrases.

prewriting the planning stage of the writing process in which the writer formulates ideas, gathers information, and considers ways to organize them.

print awareness in emergent literacy, a child's growing recognition of conventions and characteristics of written language, including reading from left to right and from top to bottom in English and that words are separated by spaces.

pronoun a part of speech used as a substitute for a noun or noun phrase.

proofreading the act of reading with the intent to correct, clarify, or improve text.

pseudonym an assumed name used by an author; a pen name or nom de plume.

publishing the process of preparing written material for presentation.

punctuation graphic marks such as commas, periods, quotation marks, and brackets used to clarify meaning and to give speech characteristics to written language.

question an interrogative sentence that asks a question and ends with a question mark.

realistic fiction a story that attempts to portray characters and events as they actually are.

rebus a picture or symbol that suggests a word or syllable.

revise in the writing process, to change or correct a manuscript to make its message more clear.

rhyme identical or very similar recurring final sounds in words, often at the ends of lines of poetry.

rime a vowel and any following consonants of a syllable; almost always done in conjunction with **onset**. See also **onset.**

segmentation the ability to break words into individual sounds; see also **oral blending.**

semantic mapping a graphic display of a group of words that are meaningfully related to support vocabulary instruction.

semantics the study of meaning in language, including the meanings of words, phrases, sentences, and texts.

sentence a grammatical unit that expresses a statement, question, or command; a **simple sentence** is a sentence with one subject and one predicate; a **compound sentence** is a sentence with two or more independent clauses usually separated by a comma and conjunction, but no dependent clause; a **complex sentence** is a sentence with one independent and one or more dependent clauses.

sentence combining a teaching technique in which complex sentence chunks and paragraphs are built from basic sentences.

sentence lifting the process of using sentences from children's writing to illustrate what is wrong or right to develop children's editing and proofreading skills.

sequence the order of elements or events.

setting the literary element that includes the time, place, and physical and psychological background in which a story takes place.

sight word a word that is taught to be read as a whole word, usually words that are phonetically irregular.

simile a figure of speech in which a comparison of two things that are unlike is directly stated, usually with the words **like** or **as;** for example, **She is like a jewel.**

spelling the process of representing language by means of a writing system.

statement a sentence that tells something and ends with a period.

study skills a general term for the techniques and strategies that help readers comprehend text with the intent to remember; includes following directions, organizing, locating, and using graphic aids.

style the characteristics of a work that reflect the author's particular way of writing.

subject the main topic of a sentence to which a predicate refers, including the principal noun; a **complete subject** includes the principal noun in a sentence and all its modifiers.

suffix an affix attached at the end of a base word that changes the meaning and the function of the word.

summarizing a comprehension strategy in which the reader constructs a brief statement that contains the essential ideas of a passage.

syllable a minimal unit of sequential speech sounds comprised of a vowel sound or a vowel-sound combination.

symbolism the use of one thing to represent something else in order to represent an idea in a concrete way.

synonym a word that means the same as another word.

syntax the grammatical pattern or structure of word order in sentences, clauses, and phrases.

synthetic phonics also called inductive phonics, this is a part-to-whole approach to phonics in which students are first taught the letter and sound correspondences before being asked to blend the sounds and spellings into words.

tense the way in which verbs indicate past, present, and future time of action.

text complexity a measure of how difficult a text is to read and comprehend.

text evidence information found in a particular text to prove a point.

text structure the various patterns of ideas that are built into the organization of a written work.

theme a major idea or proposition that provides an organizing concept through which, by study, students gain depth of understanding.

topic sentence a sentence intended to express the main idea of a paragraph or passage.

TREE a pneunomic device used in opinion and informational writing that stands for **T**opic sentence, **R**easons, **E**xplain, and **E**nding.

verb a word that expresses an action or state that occurs in a predicate of a sentence; an irregular verb is a verb that does not follow normal patterns of inflectional endings that reflect past, present, or future verb tense.

visualizing a comprehension strategy in which the reader constructs a mental picture of a character, setting, or process.

vowel a voiced speech sound and the alphabet letter that represents that sound, made without stoppage or friction of the air flow as it passes through the vocal tract.

vowel digraph a spelling pattern in which two or more letters represent a single vowel sound.

word calling proficiency in decoding with little or no attention to word meaning.

writing also **composition** the process or result of organizing ideas in writing to form a clear message; includes persuasive, expository, narrative, and descriptive forms.

writing process the many aspects of the complex act of producing a piece of writing, including prewriting, drafting, revising, editing/proofreading, and publishing.